VIKSIT BHARAT

CHALLENGES AND SOLUTIONS

DR. KESHAB CHANDRA MANDAL

To

The People of India

Contents

FOREWORD

For the last 25 years, Dr. Keshab Chandra Mandal has deeply engaged in research and publications. He has published 18 research-oriented books, four monographs, and more than one hundred scholarly articles. He has presented papers and delivered lectures in more than 9 dozen national and international seminars, conferences, and symposiums, and was invited to attend conferences from various universities in Europe. He has extensively contributed to gender studies, local governments, state politics, national development, and Sustainable Development Goals. His four works are in six publications in the English language, and he has 46 world library holdings. He is an academic genius, and all his research works are top-notch. The present work, ***Viksit Bharat: Challenges and Solutions***, demonstrates how India can overcome the existing challenges and become a Superpower by 2047.

The book has been written in 6 interesting chapters. Each Chapter title speaks volumes of knowledge that the present generation needs to fulfill the dream of a Viksit Bharat. Chapter One: *The Power of India*; Chapter Two: *India's Take from Others*; Chapter Three: *Public Policies of India*; Chapter Four: India's *Foreign Policy*; Chapter Five: *Keys for Turning India Into a Superpower*, and Chapter Six: *Challenges and Solutions* are immensely useful in this endeavor. This volume provides a formula to turn India into a Viksit Bharat by 2047.

This book does not only discuss the vision of the Hon'ble Prime Minister; it also informs readers how to achieve it. In this endeavor, Dr. Mandal has cited many examples from some economically and technologically developed countries such as the USA, China, Japan, Germany, and Israel which might guide the Indian policymakers and other stakeholders to emulate. There are a total of 57 keys provided by Dr. Mandal in the last two chapters which are sure to bring about the vision of Viksit Bharat i.e. a developed country by 2047, if followed by all the concerned people. There is no other book so far written in India or anywhere in the world that delineates such an elaborate and extraordinary roadmap for India's transformation from a developing country to a developed country. Moreover, reading this work has been a source of immense pleasure and satisfaction. The narrative conception and the construction of sequential events are magnificent and enriching. Great credit goes to the knowledgeable author, Dr. Keshab Chandra Mandal, for presenting the narrative in eloquent, impressive, and clear language, making it an unputdownable and compelling study. This book, I am sure, will influence people of all ages, including young minds and especially students. Policymakers and development researchers will also benefit equally from this book. It is essential for everyone to own a copy and use it for daily reference.

I sincerely hope he will publish more valuable books, like this one, that benefit all.

Kishen SSR, Hyderabad

15/12/2024

PREFACE

The root of Indian culture and tradition is based on the broad concept of 'work with skill' for the welfare of mankind on this planet. Indian people are traditionally simple and hard-working, entrepreneurial, and explorers of the truth. At present, India is a young country. The majority of the youths are educated. These English-speaking, energetic, and skilled youths are full of dynamism and optimism and are ready to accept any challenge – whether local, national, or global. India's science, technology, and research & development have reached an all-time new height. India's defense research, space research, technology, trade & commerce, industry, and agriculture have excelled in many of their global counterparts. Despite having all the strengths, potentialities, and innovative ideas of our youths, entrepreneurs, scientists, researchers, industrialists, and farmers; the quality of life, growth of GDP, GDP per capita income, Human Development Index, and others are much lesser than the developed countries. Climate change and the level of pollution are a matter of grave concern to environmentalists. Peace, equality, and justice are also costly to the people in India.

Despite having indispensable infrastructure and exigent facilities, every year a lot of valuable brains drain in India. By stopping such brain drain with our indigenous talented researchers, scientists, doctors, and technocrats, we can build our country so strongly from all aspects that within a quarter-century, India shall be recognized as a *Viksit Bharat* with a vibrant economy and 10-fold growth of GDP Per Capita Income. With this single aim and objective in mind, the book begins its journey and ends its journey with the same goal. The chapters focus on India's strengths in the contemporary world; what India can learn from the USA, China, Germany, Japan, and Israel; public policies from Nehru to Modi; foreign policy of India right from India's Independence to Modi era; the mantras for the turning India into a Viksit Bharat by 2047; Constraints standing in the way of achieving the goal; and finally a roadmap has given for removing all the shortcomings and how India can emerge as a Superpower in the global arena during the *Amrit Kal* (from 2022 to 2047).

In the end, I must concede that I am completely aware of my own flashpoints and the difficulty of the task before me, and I humbly confess the shortness of my knowledge and learning; still, I shall consider my back-breaking and knee-paining labor of the last several years will be amply rewarded by you with your unbiased judgment, proper attention, and treatment of this volume. It is expected that the book will come into use for the readers, particularly children, students, and youths, to get inspiration for serving the motherland through personal skill development, income generation, and a change of attitude. This book also shows a clear path to the readers for the achievement of their goals. It is our duty to show our youths and students the right path, and I have merely endeavored to perform my duty. I shall be happy if this book can help the youth to learn some new ideas and transform the lives of people. Lastly, I must warrant that all the views and opinions expressed in the book are completely mine, and I take the responsibility for those.

Dr. Keshab Chandra Mandal
M.A. (Triple), Ph. D., B.Ed., PGDBM
Kolkata, India
1st January, 2025 (revised on 2nd May, 2025)
ORCiD iD:https://orcid.org/0000-0003-3863-7739
Website: www.wisdomgrowth.org

ACKNOWLEDGEMENTS

In writing this book my ideas and thoughts have been shaped by several hundred people across the world – some among them are very renowned teachers of universities. My interaction with them and with some of my colleagues, friends, and students working in various fields in different states of India helped me to understand the aspirations, hardships, and requirements of people. Also, the informal conversations with my students, their guardians, neighbors; news reporters, bureaucrats, and researchers have helped me to realize the lapses in contemporary India that require government intervention. Further, regular interaction with my daughter, who is preparing for the Indian Civil Services Examination, on various subjects enriched and widened my knowledge base. The study of the Indian Constitution, Indian Art and Culture, Geography, History, Politics, Economics, International Relations, Sustainable Development Goals, ecology, biodiversity, climate change, science, and technology, etc. have helped me to perceive the richness of India more accurately and exclusively. Hundreds of books studied from the archive of Kolkata National Library were immensely helpful for this study. I express my thankfulness to all the staff of the Library for their kind behaviour and cooperation. Also, I extend my heartfelt gratitude to the American Library of Kolkata for supporting me in my research works for several years. This time also all the staff of the library particularly Mr. Debasish Ghosh extended his helping hand in writing this book. I am especially indebted to him.

Like the National Library and American Library of Kolkata I am indebted to a lot of other institutions, organizations, and persons. It is difficult to mention the names of all the people who directly or indirectly helped me in making this invaluable and matchless document simply because of the vastness of the list. However, it would be an injustice if I did not acknowledge those who were at the forefront of my most significant creation. I must take the name of my mother first because it was she who built the foundation of my knowledge. My late father was a living legend and idol of righteousness before all of our siblings. His subtle and exquisite teachings through the stories and fables have strengthened my belief of the society and its people, religion, caste system, etc. The regular conversations my father had with his music students, local followers, and friends were also very helpful in learning about discipline, sincerity, and punctuality. I learned the Eightfold Path of Buddhism, i.e. *Astangik Marg* in my childhood days from my father. My love and affection for others even for distant relatives and neighbors have grown from the close association of my mother, and elder sisters. Their love and affection for me have inspired me to work for the development and empowerment of people, especially youths, women, and children. I express my gratitude and love to my parents and sisters. My teachers, right from primary school to the University level, are oceans of love and affection. I convey my reverence to them all for their support, encouragement, and love for me. Their teaching and interaction with various ecosystems have enriched my base of knowledge and belief system. My university teachers are my all-time favorite and most inspiring guide in my academic activities. The first name that appears in my mind is Professor Amartya Mukhopadhyaya, who was a very strict and disciplined but affectionate teacher in the Department of Political Science, University of Kalyani, who taught me in the nineties, is now my navigator and mentor. This amazing and illustrious teacher is so erudite that I consider him as the polestar amongst the stars. His blessings and sagacious words continue to inspire and boost me to work harder for the welfare of society and its people. I express my reverence to my AM Sir. Another teacher Professor Dipankar Sinha, now teaching at Calcutta University, is one of the greatest Political Scientists in contemporary India. He is an exceptional teacher, compassionate person, and brilliant author. Every conversation with him always brings some fresh ideas to me. I owe a lot to him. His advice and teachings have helped me to write this book.

My other teacher Professor Partha Pratim Basu, presently teaching at Jadavpur University, is an icon of sobriety, calmness, and patronage to his students. I express my humble gratitude to PB Sir. I bow down my head to acknowledge my thankfulness to my other teachers at the University of Kalyani - Professor Malyashree Mukherjee, Professor Aneek Chatterjee, Professor Shibaji Pratim Basu, late Professor Prasanta Sengupta, and late Professor Tarun Chandra Bose, who were some of the great luminaries in the Department of Political Science, during the academic years 1989 and 1991. Prof. Pratip Chattopadhyaya, Prof. Nibedita Saha and other current faculty members of the Department are also very supportive and cooperative in my research works. I pay my healtfelt regards to them. Further, Professor Anil Kumar Jana, my Ph. D. Supervisor at Vidyasagar University, was a great luminary in the Department of Political Science with Rural Development. He taught me how to prepare a questionnaire, and hypotheses, select respondents and a field of study, take interviews with the respondents, analyze data, and finally, write a thesis. Without him, I could never stand in my life. He is the main instrument behind my higher academic excellence. Prof. Shibnath Banerjee, Prof. Kishalaya Majumder, and Prof. Swarup Roy were my most respected teachers at Chakdaha College. Dr. Dipankar Debnath, the Head Master of Birnagar High School is still my boyhood hero who inspired me to learn the English language. I express my humble respect to him. Professor Parimal Kanti Sarkar of Ranaghat College, who taught me English in Classes XI and XII, is a great source of my inspiration and hard work. I express my gratitude to him too. However, I bow down my head and touch the rose-petal-like feet of all my teachers who taught me somewhere and sometime during my entire life.

Further, I wish to express my gratitude to my school friends - Gurudas Biswas, Biswanath Pramanik, Goutam Saha, Debasish Santra, Nirmal Ghosal, Subol Mondal, Sital Ghosh, Uttam Majumder, Dinabandhu Pramanik, Soumen Sarkar, Late Sailen Das, and others. My University friends - Pinaki Sukul, Naran Sarkar, Tiya Biswas, Susmit Das, late Arindam Sinha, Susnata Dhar, Ratna Bhowmik, Chaiti Ghosh, Bithi Brahma, are some of the excellent people, who continuously inspire me to write. I owe a lot to them. I also express my heartfelt gratitude to all the members and office bearers of the West Bengal Political Science Association (WBPSA) and Bengal Institute of Political Studies (BIPS). Prof. Bimal Shankar Nanda, the President of WBPSA and Prof. Rajkumar Kothari, the President of BIPS are two wonderful persons who always encourage me in my research works. Dr. Debasish Nandi (Asso. Prof. of Kazi Nazrul University), Prof. Arindam Roy, and Prof. Anil Biswas (both from Burdwan University), Dr. Abhishek Karmakar, and Dr. Pradipta Mukherjee are some friends of mine and great teachers of our State, whom I extend my gratitude and love for extending their academic support in my research studies. I must convey my gratitude to all my colleagues from previous School, especially Prabhas Babu, Jafar Babu, Tushar Babu, and Absar Babu. I also like to bring out my gratitude to all my colleagues and the members of the Managing Committee for extending their support and good wishes.

Finally, I express my love and gratitude to my charming wife - Reba. Without her love, cooperation, and inspiration, I could never finish this book. She, as one of my most prominent critics, helped me correct my mistakes. My graceful daughter Roshni and well-disposed son Arkaprabha are my grand source of motivation. My waist-breaking and time-consuming research work throughout their entire student life hampered their studies a lot. Despite their inconveniences in the preparation of lessons, they have extended their cooperation and helped in the completion of my research including the present work. I am greatly indebted to all of them. Also, I like to convey my thanks and gratitude to the publisher for his encouragement and whole-hearted support. I admit with gratitude that the book might not have seen the light of the day in such a wonderful way without his cooperation and guidance. Once again I convey my heartfelt thanks to all the friends, well-wishers, and even the critics for putting their valuable inputs in shaping my thoughts for this volume.

PROLOGUE

"Where the mind is without fear and the head is held high ...
Into that heaven of freedom, my Father, let my country awake."
- Rabindranath Thakur

From the very name of the book, anyone can presume what might be the contents of it. The name itself is self-explanatory. Notwithstanding it is necessary to explain the readers in the prologue about the aims & objectives and the contents of the book. It is the moral duty of an author. A few years back one of my childhood friends Nital urged me to write a simple book, which should help the general people in our country. Since then he kept on nagging whenever and wherever we met. My young son also requested that I should write a book about students of his age. I could not honor their appeals due to some professional obligations and time constraints. However, I kept in mind their requests and tried to finish all my academic works in hand quickly so that I could concentrate on a book that would be easy to read and realize by the common Indian readers. Then I thought that India was celebrating *Azadi Ki Amrit Mahotsab* and I must participate in the grand celebration by writing a book with noble and innovative ideas that might strengthen India's global position, make aware of my fellow citizens about the strengths of India and give a blueprint to the readers how to achieve a \$30 trillion economy by the time when India celebrates its 100th year of Independence. In addition to this, I intended to infuse authentic information of rich and glorious culture and heritage of India, and the existing strengths of contemporary India to the students and youths to influence their thought process in an affirmative way; to sensitize them to patriotism, fellow-feeling, self-dignity, respect for elders and hard-working mentality with a purpose of national development through personal skill development. I started thinking for several days on how India can achieve a \$30 trillion economy by 2047. It is a very big goal indeed. My researcher mind determined to contribute to the national development through this treatise.

These considerations prompted me to pick up a pen and paper to prepare a blueprint of this book and finally it confined me in my study room to bend over my laptop for the next several months. My thoughts urged me to rush to my bookshelves, where I found lacking study materials necessary for writing a genuinely inspiring book for the people of my country especially the youths. So, I decided to explore the availability of books as per my requirements. Without wasting a moment, I wrote a message on WhatsApp to one of my friends working in the American Library, Kolkata, but he said it was closed for the members due to COVID-19. Further, I personally visited the National Library, Kolkata, to inquire about the situation. Showing my double dose vaccination certificate at three gates of the entrance from outside to the reading room, I managed to enter the Bhasa Bhawan to search, borrow and read relevant books. I registered myself on their website, renewed my membership card online, and continued visiting after booking a seat almost regularly. The reading atmosphere at the library is superb. The officers and librarians are excellent with their behavior and reader-friendly attitude. I know a few of them personally. In the last 24 years, many of my known officers have been retired, while the directors have also been retired. My familiarity with some present staff turned into friendship when they came to know that I am a veteran researcher and author, and already my 11 books are available in the library with call numbers.

I always kept in mind the words of my childhood friend Nital who asked me to write a book in a very simple language so that an average Indian reader could understand it easily. He also said, "We do not understand the cumbersome words of your books; tell simply the simple things for the simple people of India." Also, he warned me against writing only for a particular section of society, as I have been writing for almost a quarter century on issues of gender empowerment; rather, he put up a proposal to write on the issues that must help readers to turn India into a developed country i.e. *Viksit Bharat*. I said to him, there is lack of literatue on this subject. But he was persistent like my college-going son. It is he and my young son, who have encouraged me mostly and showed their full faith in my capability to transform young minds into 'agents of change' through this literature. So, I humbly accepted the demands of my friend and son Arkaprabha (Ari) and took up the opportunity to embark on this noble mission. Against this backdrop, the journey of my present book started. Emperor Asoka once said, "Doing good work is difficult. He who does it first, does a difficult thing" (Sharma, 1947, p. vii). However, this present volume is divided into six chapters, which are briefly delineated hereunder.

The First Chapter – *The Power of India* - draws a picture of different indicators of power in India. The components of power include a powerful Union government with a two-thirds majority; world-class defense with supersonic missiles, a strong navy, and a large military; a sound economy; robust agriculture, and sturdy health system indicate India's grand position in the global arena. India's science, technology, and epistemology have been described in this chapter to attract the attention of fellow Indian citizens as well as foreign investors. Finally, the contribution of millions of common but great Indian citizens has been discussed to encourage their further performance in the days to come.

Chapter Two - *India's Take From Others* - is a learning chapter for the students, researchers, and policymakers, where the growth stories of various developed countries such as China, the USA, Germany, Japan, and Israel have been investigated. This chapter tells the readers how China overcame India in the last 70 years, though both countries became independent simultaneously. This chapter highlithts that Chinese philosophy is competition, they emphasize savings and building big manufacturing industries, and underlined infrastructure development. How the USA became unbeatable was further discussed. Based on their science, technology, engineering, investment, and hard work they became the most powerful country in the world. In the USA there is no trade unionism like India. Their financial system supports entrepreneurship, they have world-class universities, and their work culture is also very high. Further, India has many things to learn from Japan. They stressed on electronics, manufacturing, consumer goods, and manufacturing. The Japanese people take competitive and national interests seriously. In Japan, the people respect seniors, family members, and above all their work. At present, they love peace and follow mutual interests. Japan's robust industrial policy helped Japan to grow miraculously. Germany also emphasized manufacturing and skill development. But the most interesting country is Israel. It is a very small country and its population is smaller than Kolkata. Despite that, Israel has now become so powerful. How and why Israel became technologically developed is not a mystery. It is their hard work, love for work, government policy, the mentality of people, etc. that have helped them to grow so stupendously in the international market.

The role of public policy in transforming the socio-economic condition of a country is, no doubt, enormous. Therefore, Chapter Three titled *Public Policies of India* had been incorporated. In this chapter, an endeavor has been taken to highlight the policies taken by various governments right from Jawaharlal Nehru to Narendra Modi. Every government seeks to achieve certain goals through policy formulation and implementation of the same.

However, in this chapter at first endeavor has been taken to differentiate between a public policy and a private policy. Unlike a private policy, a public policy is formulated by a government. It is a set of laws, regulations, directives, and budget allocations that governments or their representatives put in place to achieve public good goals. The components of public policy have been drawn. The public policies have been divided into two parts – one from 1947 to 2014, and the other from 2014 to 2024. Being a vast matter, only a few important policies have been dealt with. In the first part, a few significant public policies taken by India's first Prime Minister Pundit Jawaharlal Nehru, Indira Gandhi, P.V. Narasimha Rao, and Dr. Manmohan Singh have been highlighted. In the latter part, some important policies taken by Narendra Modi-led NDA Government have been examined. The main objectives behind the examination of these policies are to show how the policies have been able to transform the standard of life of Indian people, how the Indian economy was growing, and what restrictive measures were taken by the respective government to control corruption and other malpractices. However, emphasis has been given to the major policies of the NDA Government because this government under Narendra Modi has devised the Scheme of *Viksit Bharat*.

Chapter Four - *India's Foreign Policy* - examines the foreign policy of India right from India's Independence. The overview of India's foreign policy discusses its salient features. The core philosophy of India's foreign policy is the protection of the national interest of ours. India's foreign policy is guided by Non-Alignment and Panchsheel policy initiated by our first Prime Minister Pundit Jawaharlal Nehru. The Post-World War II period witnessed unprecedented antagonism between two superpowers - the USA and Russia. India decided not to join any bloc. Along with some newly independent countries such as Indonesia and Yugoslavia, India adopted a non-partisan policy of Non-Alignment. Since then India has followed the principles of Panchsheel in International Relations. The objectives of India's foreign policy have been enumerated in this chapter. Pundit Jawaharlal Nehru shaped the direction of Indian foreign policy through his statements and speeches. To understand India's foreign policy one of his statements can be highlighted here. He said, "We are permanently neutral; it has no means except permanent retirement from public affairs in the national sense, 'sanyas.' His policies were followed by his daughter Indira Gandhi. The policies adopted by Smt. Gandhi was elaborately discussed in this chapter. Further, foreign policy of P.V. Narasimha has been analyzed. He developed relations with the Middle East, and Germany, and invited Yasser Arafat, the Chairman of the Palestine Liberation Organization to visit India. He initiated the Look East Policy. Dr. Manmohan Singh also undertook drastic steps such as signing the Civil Nuclear Agreement with the USA. He succeeded in improving relations with Japan and signed a treaty in 2006. He also developed a good relationship with former US President Barack Obama.

Chapter Four is divided into two parts: the first part deals with the foreign policies of the earlier Governments since the time of Pundit Jawaharlal Nehru while the second part discusses the foreign policy of the Modi Government. Emphasis has been given to the policies adopted by Narendra Modi. It is Narendra Modi who has created a sensation in the Western world through his policies as well as his role in establishing global peace and harmony. Some of his foreign policies regarding SAARC, Look East Policy, and BIMSTEC have been examined. How Modi shifted the erstwhile foreign policy of Non-Alignment to Multi Alignment has been highlighted. His role in the QUAD, UNO, G20, and other global agencies and organizations has been explored. However, this chapter discusses at length the emerging role of India in global politics such as solving Russia-Ukraine conflict; Israel-Palestine war, and mitigating international crises in Afghanistan, Sri Lanka, Bangladesh, Canada, etc. Along with these, India's relations with the major global powers such as the USA, UK, Russia, China, Japan, Germany, and the European Union leaders have been explored. His role in G-20 and the inclusion of the African Union as a member of this organization is praiseworthy. This chapter makes an in-depth study of India's foreign policy under the Modi Government. How India is growing its position as a 'problem solver', and a 'protector and promoter of peace' in the world have been perused in this chapter. This chapter argues for India as a global power for its active role in the world affairs.

Chapter Five - *Keys for Turning India into a Superpower* - is the most significant chapter of this book, as it shows the paths of how to fulfill the national goal through the achievements of personal skill development, income growth, and mutual respect. At first, the concept of *Viksit Bharat* has been elaborately delineated. This chapter nicely alludes to a projection of people that would be around 1.62 billion in 2047, and if sixty percent of those people can earn Rs. 2.5 lakh in a month, it would be a $30 trillion economy. But the question is how this big amount could be earned by poor and disadvantaged people of India.

This is a trillion dollar question before India. For solving this problem, a clear roadmap has been presented for all the stakeholders. These include the number of new micro small and medium scale enterprises to be set up at least 100 in every district in a year for the coming 23 years. Some 30 points have been mentioned here for the achievement of Viksit Bharat's goal. These include arousing respect of the people for the country, setting a big goal, working hard to develop skills, taking lessons from the USA, Japan, Germany, and Israel, etc. Along with these, more gazelles and startups are to be set up, manufacturing industries to be increased, foreign direct investments are to be attracted, India's exports to be increased, corruption must be dealt with an iron hand, communal harmony to be strengthened, participation of women and backward communities to be ensured on an equal basis. More doctors and nurses, technocrats, scientists, and fundamental researches are to be encouraged, and for that purpose, more funds should allocated to the health and education sectors. Population control and infiltration from neighboring countries require government attention. Government policy requires to be more full proof and implementing agencies should be accountable to the people not in merely black and white; but rather in a practical sense. The CBI and Enforcement Directorate staff should be more professional and their success rates must have to be hiked to bring acceptability and respect in the eyes of common citizens. Political reforms such as one-party rule or strong coalition to be formed for running a government; sabotaging by opposition parties and bad naming the existing government in foreign lands should be strictly dealt with by the Judiciary. Instead of the distribution of doles, the skill development of people especially students is to be ensured at the earliest.

Moreover, the National Education Policy 2020 has to be implemented in every state of India. Skill development training must be imparted to the students from Class VI. There should not be any political interference in educational institutions and academic decisions of the Universities. Science & technology, information and communication technology, and STEM (Science Technology Engineering and Mathematics) should be popularized among the existing students, and proper staff and infrastructure have to be provided to all the institutions. At least 6 percent of the GDP has to be allocated in the annual budget for education and research purposes to turn India a *Viksit Bharat* within the next two and a half decades. This chapter shows how and by whom all these policies would be adopted and implemented. This is the most significant part of the book. It does not merely tell the readers about the policies, but it says how to implement the same within our limited resources and existing infrastructure.

The Final Chapter - *Challenges and Solutions* - points out some constraints standing in the way of India's achievement of a $30 trillion economy. Some issues and challenges such as the absence of a good, uniform, and value-based education system; shortness of government tenure; lack of encouragement of the students and scholars; people's belief in fate, and finding faults of others have posed major constraints for progress and development. The majority of our people do not or cannot call a spade a spade due to a lack of courage or fear of oppression by fellow citizens or state machinery. Personal happiness and comfort can never make our development as well as national development. Many of us do not have patriotism as it should have been for every citizen in our country. National interest should always get priority above all personal interests. The majority of people are unaware of the Constitutional rights and duties, and other provisions; hence, often they behave, speak, and write unconstitutionally. There are scanty numbers of honest and quality politicians in our Parliament. Besides, too much politicking trammels our development. Unbridled corruption pervades Indian politics. Moreover, criminal politicians overshadow the Indian Parliament. Mere indicating the problems are not all; people demand solutions. Hence, a bunch of concrete prescriptions have been provided for the policymakers and general citizens, particularly the youths, who are the key persons for the achievement of India's very ambitious development target. However, some most important and specific duties for all stakeholders particularly the youths and students have been highlighted in the concluding part.

References:

1. Sharma, S.R. (1947). *Ancient Indian History and Culture*. Hind Kitabs Limited.

I

The Power of India

"We owe a lot to the Indians, who taught us how to count without which no worthwhile scientific discovery could have been made."
- Albert Einstein

India was a very powerful and affluent country in the pre-Christian era, and now also India is a very strong country in all aspects such as economy, polity, military, agriculture, manufacturing, science and technology, infrastructure, and trade and commerce. To understand the strength of India well we may quote our former Prime Minister Smt. Indira Gandhi. She once remarked:

"If you wish to know something about India, you must empty your mind of all preconceived notions, of what you have heard or read. Why be imprisoned by the limited vision of the prejudiced? Also, don't try to compare - India is different and would like to remain so. You will not find any of your familiar labels useful. India is many and in a unity that stretches way back into unwritten history" (Pakistan Horizon, 1983, pp. 18–25).

Now we will examine how powerful the present India is. Let me begin with polity. The strength of a country depends upon the robustness of the Government. In the case of India, it is the Union Government. It depends on the number of State governments being ruled by the same political party ruling in the Centre. At present, there are 28 State Governments and 8 Union Territories in India. The BJP is ruling in 14 States. On the other hand, the main Opposition party - the Indian National Congress - has only 3 State Governments under its control. The 18th general elections (2024) brought back the BJP-led National Democratic Alliance to the center of power with 293 seats out of 543. Indian Parliament is bicameral. In the upper chamber

– Rajya Sabha – the NDA has a total of 121 seats out of 245. In the state legislatures at present, the ruling NDA has a total strength of 2170 seats out of 4036 seats.

Thus it is seen that the ruling BJP-led NDA has a clear majority in Parliament, and it can make any law for the welfare and socio-economic development of the people. When there is a two-thirds majority of a single political party or an alliance in Parliament, the Union Government becomes competent and very powerful. Now, the Indian government is strong enough and stable.

The world is now complex and tightly linked. It is very competitive and volatile too. Every country now is trying to showcase its powers and strengths to the world. Marc Fetscherin in one of his articles cited the works of Jaffe and Nebenzahl (2021): "Governments are turning to branding techniques to differentiate their country on the global stage in order to establish a competitive edge over rival countries in the belief that a strong country brand can contribute to the country's sustainable development" (Fetscherin, 2001, p. 466). Countries are now in the fray of branding themselves. "Switzerland, for example, established the Presence Switzerland organization in order to coordinate and establish priorities among different entities such as Pro Helvetia, location Switzerland, OSEC Business Networks, and Swiss Tourism" (Fetscherin, 2001, p. 467). Country branding is a new concept in the public domain. Hence, it is necessary to clarify the term 'branding' and the objectives of it. Marc Fetscherin (2001, pp. 467-68) further indicated that "a country brand belongs to the public domain; it is complex and includes multiple levels, components, and disciplines. It entails the collective involvement of the many new stakeholders it must appeal to. It concerns a country's whole image, covering political, economic, social, environmental, historical, and cultural aspects. The main objectives of a country branding are to stimulate exports, attract tourism, investments, immigration, and create positive international perceptions and attitudes." Globalization has made the world a big village, and a supermarket, where everyone is trying to show its products and best commodities in the form of strengths to attract the attention of buyers and admirers. Hence, the aim of the chapter is to brand India to the global village.

The power of a country is determined by a bunch of indicators such as the strength of the ruling party in parliament, its military/defense system, economy, trade & commerce, exports, foreign direct investment, health of people, educational attainment, infrastructure, agricultural production, research and innovation, science and technology, natural resources, and above all its human resource. Let us highlight some of these indicators precisely in the following part.

Indian Parliament is Very Strong

Indian parliament is one of the best political institutions in the world. Devesh Kapur and Pratap Bhanu Mehta (2006) consider, "Over the past half-century, India has been a complex experiment in institutionalizing democratic accountability through parliamentary institutions. During this period, the country has sustained, against great odds, a lively, stable, multicultural, and functioning democracy with regular and free elections, an independent judiciary, and a vibrant civil society. While Indian politics has been contentious and has intermittently lapsed into violence, India's democratic institutions have shown remarkable endurance. India's democratic experience has been a prodigious act of faith" (Kapur and Mehta, 2006, p. 1). The strength of a government is measured by the laws it enacts and the policies and decisions taken by the Cabinet headed by the Prime Minister. Indian Parliament is modeled on the 'Mother of all Parliaments' i.e. the British Parliament. The present government since coming into power took several epoch-making decisions and enacted laws that no other Prime Minister has ever thought of or even dared to table in the Parliament. It seems to me that, the Government of India has introduced some long-awaiting reforms in the country. But it does not mean that the government did not face any challenges from the Opposition parties, intellectuals, and media from within and outside of India. Even foreign media and others have criticized some of the policies initiated by the present government. To name a few major decisions, I must say that the demonization of banknotes was the most adventurous act of the present government. The last demonetizations were held in 1946 and 1978, and in both cases, the goal was to combat tax evasion via "Black money" held outside the formal economic system. An article was published in the Front Line (2017) that reads: "On the evening of November 8, 2016, Prime Minister Narendra Modi went on all media channels to announce that his government had decided to demonetize 500-rupee and 1,000-rupee currency notes "to break the grip of corruption and blank money", and announced that the "five-hundred and thousand-rupee notes hoarded by anti-national and anti-social elements will become just worthless pieces of paper" (Reddy, The Frontline, 8 Nov. 2017). Demonetization was the need of the hour; it was just a step of the Union Government to combat corruption and tax evasion because many

Indian businessmen, politicians, smugglers, criminals, hoarders, and others evade Income Tax and stash away wealth in offshore banks. Hence, the Union Government's decision to demonetization was very appropriate and timely.

Also, the present Government has initiated a war against corruption and black money, which no previous Government dared to think of. "The Government of India, in pursuance of its commitment to "Zero Tolerance Against Corruption" has taken several measures to combat corruption which, inter alia, include: (i) Systemic improvements and reforms to provide transparent citizen-friendly services and reduce corruption. These, inter alia, include a. Disbursement of welfare benefits directly to the citizens under various schemes of the Government in a transparent manner through the Direct Benefit Transfer initiative. b. Implementation of E-tendering in public procurements. C. Introduction of e-Governance and simplification of procedure and systems. d. Introduction of Government Procurement through the Government-Marketplace (EeM).....The Prevention of Corruption Act, 1988 has been amended on 26.07.2018. It clearly criminalized the act of giving bribes and will help check big-ticket corruption by creating a vicarious liability in respect of senior management of commercial organizations....Central Vigilance Commission (CVC), through various orders and circulars recommended the adoption of Integrity Pact to all the organizations in major procurement activities and to ensure effective and expeditious investigation wherever any irregularity/ misconduct is noticed" (Ministry of Personnel, Public Grievances and Pensions, 10 Feb, 2021). Further, the Central Bureau of Investigation and the Enforcement Directorate are independently working to root out corruption from the soil of India. Many opposition party leaders complain that the probe agencies are working at the behest of the Union Government. However, it is a fact that there is corruption prevailing in society in different forms such as question leaking, bribe taking before competitive examinations, and selling out jobs to unskilled and inefficient people in exchange for money. Some Government officers and leaders are engaged in abnormal corrupt practices, and whenever the Central agencies are active in examining the cases, a section of political leaders are united to support the corrupt practices in the name of 'political vendetta', harassment, etc. I strongly support the actions of the Union Government and the independent agencies regarding controlling corruption in society. But the lingering process of the probe and their rate of conviction and success have put their performance-critical and reputation at stake. The general people of India demand quick completion of all probes and bring the culprits into books without any further delay.

Abolition of the Articles 370 and 35A

Further, in our student life, we have read about the unity and integrity of India in an English Essay. I felt it was partial unity and incomplete national integration, because Jammu & Kashmir, a part of India, was exempted from the rules made by the Indian Parliament. It pained me since my boyhood days for several reasons. If you are a man from Kolkata, Delhi, Kerala, or elsewhere, you cannot marry a Kashmiri girl, though Pundit Nehru's wife Kamala Nehru was a Kashmiri woman. Moreover, there were many other restrictions such as nobody from outside could purchase land and property or settle there. Moreover, the state made its own rules about permanent residency, ownership of property, and fundamental rights. The Narendra Modi government took a very bold decision to abolish Articles 370 and 35A which gave special powers and status to the state of Jammu and Kashmir. "Article 370 exempts J&K from the Indian Constitution (except Article 1 and Article 370 itself) and permits the state to draft its own Constitution. It restricts Parliament's legislative powers in respect of J&K. For extending a central law on subjects included in Instrument of Accession (IoA), mere "consultation" with the state government is needed. But for extending it to other matters, "concurrence" of the state government is mandatory. The IoA came into play when the India Independence Act of 1947 divided British India into India and Pakistan" (Mustafa, The Indian Express, 6 Aug. 2019). On the other hand, "Article 35A, which provides special rights and privileges to the citizens of Jammu & Kashmir, was incorporated in the Constitution of India in 1954 by an order of then President Rajendra Prasad, on the advice of the Jawaharlal Nehru Cabinet. It gives the J&K legislature full discretionary powers to decide who 'permanent residents' of the state are. It also gives them special rights and privileges in employment with the state government, acquisition of property in the state, settling in the state, and the right to scholarships and other forms of aid the state government provides. It also allows the state legislature to impose any restrictions upon persons other than the permanent residents regarding the above" (Business Standard, 8 October, 2023). This was completely unacceptable and derogatory to the sovereignty of a country like India. As a result, the Government of India on August 5, 2019, bifurcated Jammu & Kashmir into two Union territories of Jammu & Kashmir and Ladakh, and nullified J&K's

earlier powers, which gave the erstwhile state its special status and the mandate to define its domicile rules. This has paved the way for the 'one country one law, and one Constitution' policy of the present Modi Government. The Chief Justice of India in his observation said, "Article 35A gave special rights and privileges to permanent residents and virtually took away the rights for non-residents. These rights included the right to equal opportunity of State employment, right to acquire property and the right to settle in Jammu and Kashmir" (Rajagopal, The Hindu, 28 August, 2023).

Jammu and Kashmir is a very beautiful Himalayan region that both India and Pakistan said is fully theirs. But it was once a princely state, and it joined India in 1947 after the sub-continent was divided up at the end of the British Raj. India and Pakistan subsequently went to war over its occupancy, and each came to control different parts of the territory with a ceasefire line agreed upon. In the border area, there has been continuous violence and separatist insurgency against the Indian government for the last several decades. Any adult Indian citizen knows that the Kashmir border is always a matter of tension of war between Pakistan and India, the persons working in Kashmir border areas were always in tensions of mines and bomb blasts or cross firings, their family members and relatives and friends remain also in tension when their men went to guard the border as Border Security Force of Indian Army. Schools and colleges were closed and frequent class suspension was a daily incident.

After the abolition of Articles 370 and 35A Kashmir is no longer having a separate constitution but will have to abide by the Indian Constitution much like any other state. All Indian laws will be automatically applied to Kashmiris, and people from outside the state will be able to buy property and live there. After 2019 "The rules were changed into July to allow domicile certificates to be granted to the husbands of local women married to people from outside Jammu & Kashmir. The move will allow them to buy land and property in the Union Territory, or apply for government jobs...After the abrogation of Article 370, the civil secretariat in Srinagar hoisted the Indian Tricolor, while the state's own flag was missing" (Chaturvedi, The Hindustan Times, 5 August, 2021). As a consequence, the regions will automatically be developed in the days to come under the rule of a strong Union Government, and subsequently further elections will hand over power of administration and governance to the local people. Recently, there was an Assembly election and the National Conference Party won the majority seats to rule the Union Territory. Now, the Territory is ruled by an elected government.

Construction of Ram Temple

The construction of the Ram Temple was another major success of the Government under Narendra Modi, which was a hot issue of debate in Indian politics for hundreds of years. Since our college days in the eighties of the last century, we have been concerned with the issue of the Babri Masjid-Ram Temple in Ayodhya, Uttar Pradesh. But when I started studying the matter in depth before the *Bhoomi Pujan* (worship of foundation stone by Prime Minister Shri Narendra Modi) of the Temple recently, I found that it was an issue more than one and a half centuries old. Babri Masjid was constructed in Ayodhya about 230 years ago, but the first religious violence over the site took place in 1853. It was during the rule of Nawab Wajid Shah of Awadh that a Hindu sect Nirmohis claimed that a Hindu temple had been destroyed during Babur's times to build the mosque. Seeing the communal violence and religious tension, the British administration erected a fence to divide the site into two parts – while the Muslims were allowed to pray inside the mosque, the outer court was reserved for the Hindus. Queen Victoria was assisted by Abdul Karim in matters related to happenings in India and others. When there was communal tension for worshipping at Babri mosque, it was reported to the Queen, and subsequently, an order was issued by her representative in India that hardly went in favor of the Hindus. Thus Ayodhya became a political as well as religious issue for the Hindus and Muslims in the nineteenth century.

Deepak Mehta writes, "From at least the middle of the 19th century, Ayodhya has witnessed longstanding and bitter violence between Hindus and Muslims regarding the exact status of this spot. This is because Hindus hold that the Babri Masjid, constructed in 1528 by the Mughal emperor Babur, took the place of the razed temple the *Janamsthan*. Beginning in 1980, several Hindu organizations, collectively known as the Sangh Parivar, advocated the destruction of the mosque and its replacement with a grand temple dedicated to Rama. Even before Hindu activism, we find a long history of litigation - since 1885, civil courts at various levels of the judicial hierarchy (Sessions Courts, District Courts, High Courts, and the Supreme Court of India) have debated the status of the temple-mosque complex" (Mehta, 2015, pp. 1-2). The dispute within and outside of the courts reached its climax in 1992, when on 6 December 1992 (according to the Liberhan Commission of Enquiry) "...about 150,000 people had gathered around the temple-mosque complex on that day and that 150 *karsevaks* (religious workers) actually participated in its destruction" as per (Mehta, 2015, p. 2).

I still remember the day when the *Karsevaks* in the presence of Lal Krishna Advani, Murli Manohar Joshi, Uma Bharati, Binay Katiyar, and others tried to demolish the disputed Babri mosque, which provoked widespread communal riots across the country. About two thousand people died in the violence.

Though the violence and riot quelled after some time, the contention relating to the Mandir and Masjid issue remained alive in the minds of both Hindus and Muslims. The legal battle was going on in the courts, while the verbal and written war was continuing in both print and electronic media. In 2010, the Allahabad High Court pronounced its judgment on the four title suits on the dispute and divided the land into three parts – one-third to Ram Lalla, represented by Hindu Mahasabha; one-third to the Islamic Waqf Board; and the remaining third to the Nirmohi Akhara. In December of the same year, the Akhil Bhartiya Hindu Mahasabha and the Sunni Waqf Board moved to the Supreme Court, challenging the High Court ruling. In the following year, all three claimant parties of the land approached the Supreme Court and appealed against the Allahabad High Court verdict. The Supreme Court upheld the HC order of splitting the disputed site into 3 parts. Finally, in 2016 Subramanian Swamy, a reputed lawyer, filed a plea in the Supreme Court seeking the construction of Ram Temple. Ultimately in 2019, a five-member bench of the Supreme Court headed by then Chief Justice Ranjan Gogoi passed a revolutionary judgment. The order said that the disputed land of 2.77 acres was to be handed over to a trust (to be created by the Government of India) to build the Ram Janambhoomi temple. The court also ordered the government to give an alternative five acres of land in another place to the Sunni Waqf Board to build a mosque.

The decade-long dispute in Ayodhya was over after the verdict of the Supreme Court. The long-drawn legal battle and communal tension on the Ayodhya temple-Babri mosque issue was over, and the demand of lakhs of sadhus, saints, and the average Hindu population in the country was fulfilled. Prime Minister Narendra Modi hit the last nail in the dispute by laying the foundation stone for the construction of Ram Temple on August 5, 2020, amid the Coronavirus pandemic. The Prime Minister also unveiled a plaque and released a commemorative postal stamp on the occasion. It is reported in *The Hindustan Times* that, the construction of the Ram Temple in Ayodhya is in full swing and the ground floor of the three-storey structure is set to be open to devotees in January (2024) and the entire temple will be completed by 2025. This is going to a huge Hindu temple in India. "The temple is 380 feet in length, 250 feet in width, and 161 feet high from the courtyard. The sanctum sanctorum is spread over 20 feet" (Dixit, The Hindustan Times, 9 July, 2023).

Introduction of Uniform Goods and Services Tax

Indian Government brought the Goods and Services Tax (GST) which is considered the major tax reform. It was a much-needed reform. India was seen as a non-friendly country for doing business owing to its complicated tax laws. The GST subsumed 17 existing indirect taxes to make compliance with taxation laws in the business world simple. It was a major decision of the Government to ease trade and business. Through the Insolvency and Bankruptcy Code (IBC) Law enacted in 2016, the government of India has solved the problems of banking ailment which was considered a long-term problem for economic growth and policymaking. Now it is described by many as a silver bullet to tackle India's chronic problem of non-performing assets. After the enactment of the law, banks have started to recover debts that were earlier thought to be irretrievable. Sengupta, Munjal, and others in a conference paper (May, 2020) highlighted that "Before the implementation of GST, there were many indirect taxes which the business had to pay. Then came GST which is one of the biggest and significant economic reforms. Basically, the aim is to provide a simplified tax framework that is imposed on economic activities and will help in increasing the efficiency of the business. It is a comprehensive nature tax that is levied on manufacturing, selling, and consuming goods and services. GST has replaced almost all the indirect taxes except a few on which states and central levy taxes. Almost 160 countries across the globe have implemented GST in place of indirect taxes. GST is collected by the state, where the goods and services are consumed. This implies that it is a destination-based tax. India has implemented a dual GST model i.e., both the states and central will levy taxes on goods and services. GST was finally implemented with effect from 1st July 2017. The state GST which is collected by the state is called SGST. The central GST which is collected by the Centre is called CGST. The tax applicable on interstate and import transactions is called IGST, collected by Centre, and the tax applicable on transactions within the union territories without legislature like Daman & Diu, Chandigarh, Lakshadweep islands is called UTGST, collected by the Union territory" (Sengupta, Munjal et al., 2020, p. 3). After the introduction of a uniform tax policy, there arose a political uproar in India. The following part discusses the necessity and importance of a Uniform Tax Policy.

Necessity of a Uniform Tax Policy

It was one of the major tax reforms since independence. "GST helps in reduction of double taxation, cascading effect, issue of classifying taxes, multiplicity of taxes, etc. GST created a wider tax base, rationalization of tax structure, and harmonization of state and center administration. Before GST there were different VAT rates across the country which differ from state to state but with the introduction of GST, there is a uniform tax system across the country and the taxes are divided between the state and the central government" (Sengupta, Munjal et al., 2020, p. 3). Further, Sengupta et. al. indicate that "GST will help reduction of tax theft and corruption in our economy" (Nayar & Singh, 2018, p. 2). However, there were confrontations and protests from different quarters before the introduction of GST. It is shocking that, before the introduction of any new concept and good concept, people started protests and movements. Like before the introduction of GST, thousands of small traders nationwide staged protests against the new Union government. Nikkei Asia reported, "Bhartiya Udyog Vyapar Mandal, an organization that claims to represent 17,000 trade associations across the country, said its members had shut up shop in a last-ditch attempt to force changes" (Sharma, Nikkei Asia, 30 June, 2017).

Empowerment of Muslim Women by Abolition of Triple Talaq

To ensure the empowerment of women and give our women sisters their due dignity in society, the Modi Government has taken many steps and the latest one was the implementation of the Muslim Women (Protection of Rights on Marriage) Act, 2019 which ended the woes of Muslim women through the termination of the Triple Talaq system which allowed a husband to divorce his wife by repeating the word *"talaq"* (divorce) three times in any form including writing a letter, an email, a WhatsApp message, Skype, or a text message, maybe in good mental condition or intoxication. What a horrible situation our Muslim sisters had in India! The Supreme Court declared the practice unconstitutional in 2017. The new measure protects Muslim women and arranges for punishment for men found in breach of the law or jail for up to three years. The law allows the Muslim woman to seek custody of her minor children as well as maintenance from her husband by approaching a magistrate after she has registered a complaint with the police station. This was a heinous crime against Muslim women, which was stopped by the Indian parliament in 2019. The Economic Times reported that "There has been about 82 percent decline in triple talaq cases since the law against the "social evil" was put in place" (The Economic

Times, 22 July, 2020). The Minority Affairs Minister Mukhtar Abbas Naqvi criticized the protests by so-called 'champions of secularism' including the Congress, Communist Party, Samajwadi Party, Bahujan Samaj Party, and Trinamool Congress Party. It is to be remembered that when the late Rajiv Gandhi was the Prime Minister he had more than 400 MPs in Lok Sabha out of 545. On the other hand, out of 245 Rajya Sabha members, the ruling Congress party had 159 MPs. Despite that, the Congress Government did not take the initiative to serve the mothers and sisters of the Muslim community. While India's neighboring Muslim-dominated countries such as Pakistan, Bangladesh, and Sri Lanka had banned triple talaq, why India should be left behind? With the implementation of the 2019 Law, India joined with the other 22 countries that have banned the practice. You will not find this injustice and inhuman act in Turkey, Cyprus, Tunisia, Algeria, Malaysia, Jordan, Egypt, Iran, Iraq, Brunei, the UAE, Indonesia, Libya, Sudan, Lebanon, Saudi Arabia, Morocco and Kuwait. On 15th August, Prime Minister Narendra Modi in his Independence Day speech said, "The sword of Triple Talaq was hanging over the heads of our Muslim sisters. This fear was affecting their lives. Even Islamic nations had abolished it earlier. But we were hesitant in empowering our Muslim sisters" (Prime Minister of Independence Day Speech, 15th August, 2019).

Political Empowerment of All Women Ensured

Through the 73rd and 74th Constitution (Amendment) Acts, 1991, the Government of India showed its courage and goodwill towards the empowerment of women. This author in one of his books wrote in 2010 that "The 73rd Amendment Act is a landmark in the history of empowerment of women in rural India" (Mandal, 2010, p. 64). Similarly, the 74th Constitutional Amendment Act (1992) can be called "the harbinger of a new era of empowerment and vigorous system of urban local self-government" (Jha, Urban India, July-December, 1993, p. 68). Though women's 33% participation in three-tier *Panchayati Raj* Institutions and Urban Local Bodies was ensured, there has been a long-time demand from different women's organizations and social thinkers for similar reservation of seats in parliament and state legislatures. Finally, the Women's Reservation Bill 2023 (The Constitution (One Hundred Twenty-Eight Amendment) Bill, 2023 was first introduced in the new Parliament's Lok Sabha on 19th September, and it was passed on the following day i.e., on 20th; and, it was passed by the Rajya Sabha on 21 September, 2023. Since 1996, when Mr. Deve Gowda first tabled the bill in the form of the 81st Constitution Amendment Bill in Lok Sabha during the United Front government, 27 years have passed since the passing of the women's reservation bill in 2023. The consecutive governments in New Delhi were either unwilling to pass the bill, or they faced tremendous opposition from different political parties such as Samajwadi Party (SP), Rashtriya Janata Dal (RJD), Janata Dal and some other parties who were demanding quota within quota. The happenings in the last decade of the previous century are still vivid in my mind. Nitish Kumar, the present chief minister of Bihar in 1997 vehemently advocated for OBC women and facilitated in obstructing the bill. He, then pointed out that, "The Bill provides for a reservation to women belonging to SCs and STs. I think that women belonging to OBCs should also get a fair deal. Therefore, I want one-third reservations should include women belonging to OBCs...The reservation should be in proportion to the population of OBCs" (Manoj, Indian Express, 19 Sept., 2023). Similarly, on another occasion, the late Sharad Yadav of Rashtriya Janata Dak (RJD) remarked "*Kaun mahila hai, nahin hai, keval bal kati mahila bhar nahin rahne denge* (Who is a woman, who is not, only short-haired women won't be allowed)" (Manoj, Indian Express, 19 Sept., 2023). Lok Sabha also saw many unruly behaviors and betrays of different political leaders of various political parties. In 2023 also, Sri Rahul Gandhi raised the question regarding the lower representation of the Other Backward Communities in the governance in the Lok Sabha. However, the firmness, goodwill, and two-thirds majority of the present NDA government successfully placed the bill and got it passed in both Houses of Parliament and the Bill now awaits the President's nod. Further, it will require the approval of the half of the states. About the historic event, the UN Women said "At the time of the bill's passage, about 14 percent of Lok Sabha legislators were women. While that represents India's highest proportion since its independence, it was far below the global average of 26.6 percent, or the Central and Southern Asia average of 19 percent" (UN Women, 4 October, 2023). The bill once implemented will usher in a new era in the history of gender empowerment and women's decision-making power in the highest political bodies of the Union and State Legislatures.

Key Features of the Bill

It is necessary to highlight some important features of the Bill. According to the Women's Reservation Bill, 2023, "The Bill reserves, as nearly as may be, one-third of all seats for women in Lok Sabha, state legislative assemblies, and the Legislative Assemblies of the National Capital Territory of Delhi. This will also apply to the seats reserved for SCs and STs in Lok Sabha and state legislature...The reservation will be effective after the census conducted after the commencement of this Bill has been published. Based on the census, delimitation will be undertaken to reserve seats for women. The reservation will be provided for 15 years. However, it shall continue till such date as determined by a law made by Parliament...Seats reserved for women will be rotated after each delimitation, as determined by a law made by Parliament" (Ministry of Law and Justice, Government of India).

Citizenship Amendment Act and National Register of Citizens

The other two most powerful decisions of the Modi Government are the introduction of the Citizenship Amendment Act (CAA) and the National Register of Citizens (NRC) for which India witnessed widespread violence and protest. "It is perhaps a first in independent India's political history. The protest against the Citizenship (Amendment) Act (CAA) 2019 has spread to almost every corner of the country, yet the reasons for the protest vary with the geography. Some are protesting because the CAA allegedly violates the secular identity of the country while others fear that it will endanger their linguistic and cultural identity" (Deka, India Today, 23 December, 2019). The NRC exercise was brought mainly to identify illegal immigrants from Indian citizens. Indian borders are vulnerable, and infiltration is a regular incident. India is already a country with 1.43 billion population, and it has already overtaken China to become the world's most populous country. Besides, the illegal infiltrators often engage in anti-national and anti-government activities, because they have no responsibility and patriotism for our motherland. Moreover, the infiltration reduces our per capita income and gross domestic product. Hence, the CAA and NRC were the most desired steps taken by the Government of India. When the two amendments were passed by the Parliament on 11 December 2019 there were much confusion and tension among a section of people. This section does not only belong to the Muslim community and mostly uneducated people, but in my private conversation with friends and teachers, I found confusion and distrust among a large section of Hindu families including servicemen, professors, school teachers, and the general public. Hence, we should focus more light on the CAA and NRC.

The Citizenship (Amendment) Act of 1955 has been amended several times in the past; the latest amendment was passed in Parliament in December 2019. "According to the CAA, Hindu, Buddhist, Jain, Sikh, and Parsi migrants who have entered India illegally - that is, without a visa- on or before December 31, 2014, from the Muslim-majority countries of

Pakistan, Afghanistan, and Bangladesh and have stayed in the country for five years, are eligible to apply for Indian citizenship" (Deka, India Today, 23 December, 2019). The CAA enables migrants/foreigners of six minority communities from these three specified countries who have come to India because of persecution on grounds of their religion to apply for Indian citizenship. Such a foreigner has to become eligible to apply for citizenship after fulfilling the minimum legal requirements. The Union government clarifies that, as the people of these six faiths have faced persecution in these three Islamic countries, Muslims haven't. It is, therefore, India's moral obligation to provide them shelter" (Deka, India Today, 23 December, 2019). On the other hand, the National Register of Citizens (NRC) is a record of the citizens of India. The Citizenship Act, of 1955 provides for compulsory registration of every citizen of India and issuance of a National Identity Card to the person. The difference between the CAA and NRC is that the CAA is applicable for illegal migrants residing in India and does not apply to any Indian citizen at all, while the NRC consists of a record of citizens of India only excluding others.

After the passing of the Citizenship (Amendment) Act (CAA) in 2019, there was an unprecedented protest against it across the country, which took away almost one hundred lives and burnt and destroyed government property worth crores of rupees. As a result, this Act has not yet been implemented. However, the National Register of Citizens (NRC) has also not been implemented yet in India. This indicates that India is a tolerant country, and it is a vibrant democracy, where people's opinions and public views are respected. At the same time, we find how strong the Indian parliament is! When there is a two-thirds majority in both houses of Parliament, it can make any law except making a woman a man. The construction of Ram Mandir, the introduction of GST, the abolition of 370 and 35A, the empowerment of Muslim women through the abolition of triple talaq, the passing of the women's reservation bill after more than two decades, etc. are some of the extraordinary achievements of the National Democratic Government led by Narendra Modi. Now let us discuss India's defence.

India has World Class Defense and Security System

Another main pillar of strength in a country is its defense. The Indian government has a full Ministry of Defence which is responsible for national security. The Ministry of Defence provides policy framework and resources to the armed forces to discharge their responsibility in the context of the defense of the country. The Indian Armed Forces consist of the Indian Army, Indian Air Force, Indian Navy, and Indian Coast Guard. These forces are primarily responsible for ensuring the territorial security and integrity of India. Our country is now having a very strong Army. How strong is the Indian military, can you guess? Let me refer to the latest report of the Global Firepower (GFP) that assessed over 60 individual factors for the '2023 Military Strength Ranking'. The said report listed 145 countries, and it indicated that "The United States has the strongest military force in the world, with Russia and China in second and third and India in fourth place" (The Hindustan Times, 10 July, 2023). India's defense system in the 21st century is stronger than ever. India's defense training institutions impart quality training to our defense personnel to equip them to fight any challenges. "In India, collective training is similar to that provided in the United States...Indian commanders are responsible for preparing their staffs and subordinate units for wartime missions, which are specific to a geographic assignment. Units train collectively by designing and executing exercises, including field training and command-post training, using their own resources" (Johnson, Moroney, Cliff et. al., 2009, p. 179).

Further analysis of India's military strength can be found in the latest report of Global Firepower (2023). India ranked 4 out of 145 countries in the world in 2023 with a score of 0.1025 (a score of 0.0000 is considered 'perfect'). Here, a comparison among the top four countries can be made. It is learned that, in terms of land area, China is the largest country with a total area of 17,098,242 sq. km., and India's rank is fourth with 9,596,961 sq. km land area, while the USA holds the third position and Russia occupies the 7th position. In terms of age of the top four countries, it is observed that the USA is the oldest at almost two hundred and forty-seven (in 2023) years old, Russia was born in 1922, which means it was born one hundred one years ago, India took birth in 1947 and the country just completed Diamond Jubilee anniversary, and China is two years junior to India in terms of age. As per Worldometer, India's total population is 1,432,547,865 (Rank 1, now at 10.39 p.m, on 18.10.2023 as per Worldometer), while China trails behind India with 1,425,523,367 population. The USA occupies the third position, and Russia's population (9th position) is much lower than India's (less than one-tenth). America's defense budget is the highest in the world with $761,681,000,000, and the second position is held by China with $230,000,000,000; while Russia holds the third position with $82,600,000,000, and the fourth rank is held by India, which is almost one-fifth of China. While analyzing the Air Power of the four top countries in the world, one can easily find that, the world's maximum number (13,300) of aircraft is available with the USA; followed by Russia (4,182), China (3116) and India (2,210). In all sectors of Fighter Aircraft, Dedicated Attack, Transports, Trainers, Special Missions, Aerial Tankers, Helicopters, and Attack Helicopters, the U.S. holds the first position, while in six fields Russia occupies the second position, and China holds the third position and India remains in fourth position, except attack helicopters, where India ranks 17th position (The Global Firepower 2023, https://www.globalfire power.com/).

One of the most significant indicators of power is the Defence system of a country. The U.S.A. is the most powerful country in the world in terms of defense system as a whole. However, the defense consists of various sub-sections. Now we will analyze the land power of the top four countries in the world. Russia holds the first position with 12,566 tanks in its possession, while the USA has less than half of the former with 5,500 tanks. China occupies the fourth rank with 4,950 tanks and India holds the fourth position with 4,614 numbers of tanks. However, "The Indian Army has already placed an order for 118 indigenously-built Main Battle Tank (MBT) Arjun with the Ordnance Factory Board (OFB), and it will probably be its last order for the heavyweight tank. The order is scheduled to be completed by 2025-26...The Indian Army already has 124 Arjun MBTs, among the world's heaviest tanks at 65.25 tons...In terms of weight, MBT Arjun is at par with Challenger 2 of the UK, weighs 62.5 tons (combat-ready weight of 75 tonnes), Leopard 2A6M of Canada weighs 62.5 tons, and Abrams M1A1 of the US weighs 67.5 tons" (Sharma, The Eurasian Times, 5 August, 2023). Further, during a Defence Expo in 2020 Indian Defence Minister Rajnath Singh revealed that "in the next five years, India was considering exports of military hardware worth US$5 billion, and African countries will form a big chunk of it" (Sharma, The Eurasian Times, 5 August, 2023). Despite all the words of hope, India must increase its budgetary allocation and add more armored vehicles, self-propelled artillery, towed artillery, and mobile rocket launchers, because India's global ranking is at present between 4 to 7; but we need to reach the top position (The Global Firepower 2023, https://www.globalfirepow er.com).

The Indian Navy traces its origin back to the East India Company's Marine which was founded in 1612. During colonial rule, the navy was titled His Majesty's Indian Navy. When India became a Republic on 26th January 2050, the prefix 'Royal' was dropped, and it was renamed as Indian

Navy. Also, the Crown of the Royal Indian Navy's Crest was replaced by the Ashoka Lion Motif for the Indian Navy's Crest was replaced by Ashoka Lion Motif for Indian Navy's Emblem. The Navy works in conjunction with other Armed Forces of the country and acts to deter or defeat any threat or aggression against the Indian Territory, people, or maritime interests of India, both in war and peacetime.

The sea is an important mode of communication, a means for doing business and commerce and carrying men, materials, and machines. Dominance overseas indicates a country's power. India's biggest challenge in the maritime domain in the 21st century is undoubtedly China. "Alfred Thayer Mahan, the acclaimed naval historian, saw the sea as a "great highway" and a "wide common" over which commerce and military force flowed freely. The renowned American theorist described "sea power" as an indispensable instrument of state power, and "maritime access" - commercial, diplomatic, and military - as the critical element of maritime strategy. Comprehensive access to vital sea spaces, he averred, had the potential to propel a nation to great power status" (Singh, Observer Research Foundation, 14 August, 2023).

At present, the fleet strength of the Indian Navy is merely 295 and its global rank is 7, while China's (Rank 1) strength is 730, Russia holds the second position with 598 fleet and the USA ranks 3rd. Secondly, the USA has 11 aircraft carriers; but both China and India have one each, while Russia has only one aircraft carrier. In terms of submarines, China tops the list with 78 submarines, while Russia ranks second with 70 numbers of submarines, the USA occupies the third position with 68, and India holds the eighth position with only 18 submarines. Helo carriers are primarily responsible for carrying helicopters. India and Russia do not have a single such carrier, while the USA has 9, and China has only 3. Further, in terms of destroyers, frigates, corvettes, patrol vessels, and others, India's rank is between 4 and 5. In the sphere of mine warfare, India's rank is 145, while China holds 2nd position. India has only 11 destroyers (Rank 6); but the USA has 92 (Rank 1), China has 50 (Rank 2), and Russia has only 4 (Rank 15) (he Global Firepower 2023, and https://pib.gov.in/PressRelease Page.aspx?PRID=1888480).

Logistic support is another big component of power. According to the Global Firepower Report (2023), out of 145 countries, India holds 20th rank with 346 airports, while the U.S.A. ranks first with 13,513 airports. Russia ranks 5 with 1,218 airports, but China ranks 12 with 507 airports. Secondly, China, the second largest country, has 6,662 merchant marines (Rank 2), and the USA ranks 6th with almost half the number (3,627) of the marines of China, and Russia ranks 8th with 2,873 merchant marines; but India holds the 12th position globally with only 1,801 merchant marine comprising both commercial and civilian vessels engaged in the carriage of goods. Indian ports and terminals are also only 13 (Rank 8); while the USA (Rank 2) has 35 ports and terminals. This rate for Russia and China is 8 (Rank 13) and 22 (Rank 22) respectively. China's labor force participation rate is the highest, while the second position is occupied by India, the USA holds the third position, and Russia holds the 6th position. According to the report of Global Fire Power India ranks third with 4,699,024 km of road, but it seems that the latest data from the Ministry of Road Transport & Highways is not available with the Global Fire Power. The latest report of the Ministry of Road Transport & Highways, Press Information Bureau of the Government of India indicates that India's total road size is 63.73 lakh km as of 4.01.2023. Hence, it is the 2nd largest roadway network in the world. Further, in terms of railways, India holds the fifth position with its track length of 68,525 km, while the USA has 293,564 kilometer (Rank 1) railway track. China's rank (131,000 km) is second and Russia with an 87,157-kilometer railway track holds the third position in the world.

India is Well-Prepared to Fight Back any Foreign Aggression

What would happen, if India is attacked? Many of my friends are asking this question. For my friends, I want to say that, India is a very strong country as I have told you earlier too. Indian soldiers, the bravest and most disciplined in the world, are performing their duty at the borders to protect the country's dignity and territorial integrity. India takes pride in having such a wonderful defense staff. The Indian government is making all efforts to create a more conducive operational environment for the Indian Air Force during war-like situations. So that fighter planes can land on any national highway in times of crisis, all the national highways are being strengthened with solid metal cover. The highways have been widening too. The work is in progress in some states like Gujarat, Uttar Pradesh, and West Bengal.

To combat the current situation, the army required a limited number of close-quarter battle rifles on an immediate basis. Hence, it has ordered over 350,000 close-quarter battle carbines. Recently five Rafale fighter jets landed in Ambala. It has taken the Indian Air Force's squadron strength to 31. When all the 36 Rafale jets are delivered by 2020, it will take it to 32 squadrons. The state-of-the-art 4.5 Generation Rafale jet can reach almost double the speed of sound, with a top speed of 1.8 Mach. With its multi-role capabilities, including electronic warfare, air defense, ground support, and in-depth strikes, the Rafale lends air superiority to the Indian Air Force. While China's J20 Chengdu jets are called five-generation combat jets, compared to the 4.5 generation Rafale of India; the J20 has no actual combat experience, whereas the Rafale is combat-proven, having been used by the French Air Force for its missions in Afghanistan, Libya, and Mali. It has also been used for missions in the Central African Republic, Iraq, and Syria. Rafale can also carry more fuel and weapons than the J20. Recently the Indian Defence Research and Development Organization (DRDO) successfully testified its Laser-Guided Anti Tank Guided Missile (ATGM) from MBT Arjun Tank at KK Ranges, Armored Corps Centre and School in Ahmednagar. According to DRDO, in these tests, ATGM successfully defeated a target at 3 km.

It is learned from the Indian Defence Research Wing that, The Ministry of Defence (MoD) is preparing to acquire 30 General Atomics MQ-9B Guardian drones from the United States, in a deal valued at approximately $3 billion (Rs 22,000 crore). A recent series of meetings within the Ministry of Defence has cleared the way for the procurement of an initial lot of six Reaper Medium Altitude Long Endurance drones. These six drones—two each for the army, navy, and air force—are to be procured immediately from the US, indicating the urgency of the acquisition. India will acquire 30 drones which are considered an 'acceptance of necessity' (AON). The contract is being broken up into two parts—six MQ-9s worth approximately $600 million (Rs 4,400 crore) are to be purchased outright and delivered in no time.

India's Supersonic Missiles

India has developed its defense system. It has either made the missiles and weapons indigenously or in collaboration with other countries or imported from our friendly countries. Let's have a look at those powerful supersonic weapons and missiles.

BrahMos

India has developed some very powerful missiles indigenously and in collaboration with its international partners. The BrahMos is one such missile. It is a short-range ramjet supersonic cruise missile. It can be launched from aircraft, land, submarines, or ships and has been developed at a low budget of $300 million. BrahMos is a two-stage missile with a solid propellant booster engine as its first stage brings it to supersonic speed and then gets separated. The liquid ramjet or the second stage then takes the missile closer to 3 Mach speed in the cruise phase. The missile has a flight range of up to 290 kilometers with supersonic speed all through the flight leading to shorter flight time, consequently ensuring lower dispersion of targets, quicker engagement time, and non-interception by any known weapon system in the world. It operates on the "Fire and Forget Principle" adopting a variety of flights on its way to the targets. Its destructive power is enhanced due to the large kinetic energy on impact. Its cruising altitude could be up to 15 kilometers and its terminal altitude is as low as 10 meters. It carries a conventional warhead weighing 200 to 300 kg. Compared to the existing state-of-the-art subsonic cruise missiles, BrahMos has (1) three times more velocity, (2) 2.5 to 3 times more flight range, (3) 3 to 4 times more seeker range, and (4) 9 times more kinetic energy (BrahMos Aerospace, https://www.brahmos.com/content.php?id=10&sid=10). The missile has an identical configuration of the land, sea, and sub-sea platforms and uses a Transport Launch Canister (TLC) for transportation, storage, and launch.

Agni Missiles

Next, we can name the Agni series which has five missiles with varying strike capabilities and ranges. Agni 1 is a single-stage solid-fuel missile with a range of 1250 km while Agni 2, an improved version of Agni 1, is a two-stage missile capable of striking targets 2000 km away. Agni 2, if launched from a strategic location, can target western, central, and southern China. Agni 4 has a range of close to 4,000 kilometers. It, however, can strike targets in nearly all of China, including Beijing, provided they are launched from the northeast. All the missiles in the Agni series are capable of carrying nuclear warheads. On 19 April 2012, India made its entry into the Intercontinental Ballistic Missile (ICBM) club after the successful test launch of its indigenous Agni V missile. Continuous development of the missile has increased its capability to reach even 5,000 kilometers. However, the Chinese defense experts often complained that the Agni V missile has the potential to hit about 8000 kilometers away. The missile features multiple independently targetable reentry vehicles (MIRVs) with each missile being capable of carrying 2-10 separate nuclear warheads. Each warhead can be assigned to a different target. One of the main advantages of Agni missiles is that they all use solid fuel which greatly reduces their launch time. If the missile is fitted to a mobile launcher, it can be launched within minutes. Some of the Chinese missiles use liquid propellants, which take time to launch compared to solid-fuelled missiles because of the time needed to fuel the missile.

But China has a Dongfeng missile. Their lethal missiles can reach even the United States. Dongfeng is a family of missiles developed by China that consists of short, medium, intermediate-range, and intercontinental ballistic missiles (ICBM). The development of Dongfeng missiles started in the 1950s with Soviet assistance after the signing of the Sino-Soviet Treaty of Friendship, Alliance, and Mutual Assistance. Dongfeng 1 and Dongfeng 2 were the first two developed in this missile family with ranges of 500 kilometers and 1,250 kilometers respectively. Both were in use in the 1960s but are not in operation anymore. Dongfeng 3 is considered to be a copy of the Soviet R-14 Chusovaya missile, which had a range of 2,500 km, but even this has been retired from the service and replaced by DF 21. Dongfeng 4 and 5 were also developed, while the former will be replaced by DF-31 and the latter has an improved version DF-5A that can carry nuclear warheads over 12,000 km. Several other missiles in the series also exist but our concerns are DF-21, DF-26, and DF-31.

India's Agni-V is comparable to DF-26. ICBM is also nicknamed Guam Killer. The ICBM, with a reported range of 3,500 km, can reach a major US base in Guam in the western Pacific. DF-26, a two-stage solid-fuel rocket ICBM, measures 14 meters long with a diameter of 1.4 meters and a launch weight of 20 tonnes. It can carry a nuclear or conventional warhead that weighs 1,200-1,800 kilograms and has an estimated maximum range of more than 5,000 km.

India has other three heavy powerful missiles such as Akash, Trishul, and Prithvi. Akash is India's first indigenously produced medium Surface to Air missile that can hit multiple targets from multiple directions. The all-weather missile can engage targets at a speed 2.5 times more than the speed of sound (nearly 860 meters per second) and can detect and destroy targets flying at low, medium, and high altitudes. Nuclear-capable missiles can fly at a height of 18 kilometers. It can strike enemy aerial targets like fighter jets, drones, cruise missiles, air-to-surface missiles as well as ballistic missiles from a distance of 30 km. The missile has a launch weight of 720 kg, a wingspan of 1,105 mm, a length of 5.8 m, and a diameter of 350 mm. It can carry a warhead of 50-60kg. The missile can be launched from mobile platforms like battle tanks or wheeled trucks.

Prithvi-II and Akash Missiles

Recently India conducted a successful night test-fire of its indigenously developed nuclear-capable surface-to-surface Prithvi-II missile as part of a user trial by the Army from a base in Odisha. Prithvi-II is capable of carrying 500 to 1,000 kg of warheads and is powered by liquid propulsion twin engines. The state-of-the-art missile uses an advanced inertial guidance system with a maneuvering trajectory to hit its target. Already inducted into the armory of the defense forces in 2003, the nine-meter-long 'Prithvi' was the first missile to have been developed by DRDO under the Integrated Guided Missile Development Program (IGMDP). AKASH is a medium-range, surface-to-air; low-reaction, all-weather missile. Its range is 25 km with a capacity to a payload of 60 kg and its speed is 2.5 Mach. Under the Make in India project, the Defence Ministry is projected to produce at least 2,610 future infantry combat vehicles (FICVs) for the Army at an estimated cost of about Rs 60,000 crore. Another major Make in India project is the manufacture of 200 Kamov-226T helicopters, worth Rs 6,680 crore. The first 60 choppers will be made in Russia and the rest in India.

Nag: an Anti-Tank Missile

India's Defence Research and Development Organization (DRDO) has developed indigenously Nag which is a third-generation, fire-and-forget, anti-tank guided missile to support both mechanized infantry and airborne forces of the Indian Army. The missile incorporates an advanced passive homing guidance system and possesses a high single-shot kill probability. It is designed to destroy modern main battle tanks and other heavily armored targets. Nag can be launched from land and air-based platforms. The land version is currently available for integration on the Nag missile carrier (NAMICA), which is derived from a BMP-2 tracked infantry combat vehicle. The helicopter-launched configuration, designated as helicopter-launched NAG (HELINA), can be fired from Dhruv advanced light helicopter (ALH) and Hal Rudra (ALH WSI) attack helicopter.

The Nag anti-armor guided weapon's airframe is built with lightweight and high-strength composite materials. The missile features top-attack capability and has high immunity to countermeasures. The missile is equipped with four foldable wings and has a length of 1.85m, a diameter of 0.20m, a wingspan of 0.4m, and a weight of 43 kg. A blunt nose cone houses the guidance system, while the middle portion accommodates a compact sensor package and the main charge of the warhead. A booster rocket motor is located towards the rear. Four tail fins are fitted at the rear to stabilize the missile while in flight. A real-time image processor with fast and efficient algorithms is installed next to the guidance section to provide automatic target detection and tracking capabilities. The digital autopilot offers guidance, stability, and control for the missile during the flight. Nag is also outfitted with an electric actuation system for flight control. NAG is a third-generation Anti-Tank Guided Missile with Fire and Forget top attack capability, which has strengthened the Indian defense system.

KALI Weapon

Kali 5000 is India's warfare weapon under development which can stop missiles, aircraft, and enemy satellites from anything with an electric circuit inside it. KALI stands for Kilo Ampere Linear Injector. It is a linear electron accelerator being developed by DRDO (Defence Research and Development Organization) and BARC (Bhaba Atomic Research Centre). KALI was developed by keeping an industrial mindset but later when the developers understood the great potential of KALI as a weapon, they researched further into the subject, and now they are working towards fulfilling it. It is designed to work in such a way that if a missile is launched in India's direction, it will quickly emit powerful pulses of Relativistic Electrons Beams (REB). India now is one of the most powerful countries in the world with its world-class weaponry and missiles. India's great missile man APJ Abdul Kalam and his mentor Vikram Sarabhai are the visionary pioneers of Indian defense.

Strong Economy

The economic health of a country is indicated by its Gross Domestic Product (GDP), which refers to the total market value of all the goods and services a nation produces in a given year. It comes to light from a report of the Business Insider India (13 April 2022) that India is the world's sixth-largest economy by nominal GDP, and the third-largest by purchasing power parity (PPP). From 2014 to 2018 India was the world's fastest-growing economy. In the last nine years, India's GDP grew from 2.04 lakh crore to Rs. 3.75 lakh crore. Further, it is interesting to note that India's economic health has improved in the current year: "India's GDP has reached $3.75 trillion in 2023, from around $2 trillion in 2014; moving from 10th largest to 5th largest economy in the world. India is now being called a bright spot in the global economy" (Jain, Forbes India, 12 June, 2023). Now we will have a look at the global position of India in terms of GDP and Per Capita Income of the top 10 economies in the world (IMF data (as of November 4, 2024), https://www.forbesindia.com/article/explainers, and IMF, 2023, and CEIC, Singapore National Government Debt).

It is evident from the IMF (Nov, 2024) data that, India's current (2024) GDP is $3.89 trillion and its GDP Per Capita Income is $2.7 thousand. With this economy, India ranks fifth position in the world. Due to India's large population, India's GDP per capita income is lower than other top economies. Despite this fact, it is the hardest reality that, the USA is the richest country in the world with a GDP of $29.17 trillion while Per Capita Income is $86.6 thousand. On the other hand, China is rising very fast, and it is predicted to reach or supersede the US economy in no time. China's economy is the second largest at $18.27 trillion, but its per capita income is much lower ($12.97 thousand) than that of the USA. The third position is occupied by Germany with a GDP of $4.71 trillion, while the GPD Per Capita Income is $55.52 thousand. Last year (in 2023) Japan was the fourth largest economy, but it has made a robust increase in its GDP and per capita income. Germany's external debt is moderate with $2.81 trillion. On the other hand, Japan, a small country that was devastated during the Second World War, rejuvenated its economy, and now it is the world's fourth-largest economy with a GDP of $4.07 trillion and its GDP Per Capita Income is $32.86 thousand. But Japan has an external debt of $4.34 trillion (as of June, 2023). India holds the fifth position with a $3.89 trillion economy. The size of India's economy might be smaller than the other top four countries, but India's external debt is much lower than that of the other top four countries in the world. The sixth position is occupied by the United Kingdom, our former colonial master, who basically looted us and took away cash and goods worth a few billions of dollars. However, today the UK's economy is behind India with a GDP of $3.59 trillion and their Per Capita Income is $52.42 thousand. Interestingly, the UK's total external debt was $3.13 trillion in October, 2023. The other top four countries are France (7th), Italy (8th), Canada (9th), and Brazil (10th). The most interesting thing is that the USA's total external debt is $32. 9 trillion (August, 2023), which is more than that of the total external debt of other top 5 economies ($30.94 trillion in 2024) in the world.

Ease of Doing Business in India

The economy of a country is related to the participation of its people in economic activities and the production of goods, assets, and services. Foreign direct investment also held a significant role in increasing one country's GDP. India, in recent years, has taken steps to enthuse young people to be entrepreneurs and do business. Also, India facilitated the industrialists both foreign and Indian through the formulation of various trade policies and programs. India dreams of being a "Manufacturing Hub" of the world by replacing China. For this purpose 'ease of doing business' is important. In 2021 India held the 63rd position on the 'Ease of doing business' index, and the country ranks the 68th position on the Global

Competitiveness Report (The Economic Times, 18 Sept. 2021). Further, India's "rank in ease of doing business according to World Bank report has improved from 142 in 2014 to 63 in 2022 and reduction in compliances is now a major focus" (The Economic Times, 6 July, 2022). This report is prepared based on a survey of 190 countries.

Apart from the size of the economy in terms of GDP, India's economic strength can be gauzed by the gold reserves of the Reserve Bank of India. Indian big temples are repositories of gold, silver, diamond, and other jewelry. Not only those, but there are Indian households particularly women who purchase the highest amount of jewelry every year in the world. There are rarely households in India that do not possess a certain quantity of gold and silver.

Gold Reserve in India – both Institutional and Personal

The Reserve Bank of India emerged as the second-largest buyer of gold among the world's Central Banks in 2021. The largest buyer, the Central Bank of Thailand, bought 90 metric tonnes of gold while RBI bought 77.5 metric tonnes taking its total gold reserve to 754.1 metric tonnes at the end of December 2021. The worth of India's gold reserves is US$ 41 billion, which amounts to 6.22 percent of India's foreign reserves (Fortune India, 8 Feb 2022). Many Indian temples are very old and affluent. A few years ago, the World Gold Council estimated gold holdings with temples in India would be 3000-4000 tonnes. Much of this is what is termed "idle" gold – resting just in lockers or vaults. One Padmanabhaswamy Temple in Kerala, a 16th-century temple, has around 1300 tonnes of gold jewelry with $ 22 billion worth at the price of 2011. Take another example of Sri Venkateswara Temple, Tirumala, Andhra Pradesh, popularly known as Tirupati temple which gets around 100 kg. of gold every month or 1.2 tonnes a year as offerings. It comes to light from a newspaper report that "A record 130 kg of gold was offered in July - biggest ever in a single month - this year by devotees of Lord Venkateswara at the hill shrine of Tirumala...the Tirumala shrine gets around 100 kg of gold and 2,600-3,000 kg of silver ornaments and articles every month in the form of offerings and donations from pilgrims across the country" (The Times of India, 1 Sept, 2019).

Indian people, particularly women, are fond of gold and diamond jewelry. From a report by *The Financial Express* (2019), it is estimated that households in India may have piled up around 24,000 to 25,000 tonnes of gold, remaining the world's largest holders of the precious metal. The value of the holdings in 2019 international price was as much as $1,135 billion, or the equivalent of more than 40% of India's nominal gross domestic product (GDP) 2019 (Pattanayak, Financial Express, 20 May 2019). The Europeans, particularly the British merchants and traders, had looted tons of gold and jewelry from India. Despite that, India has so much gold, diamond, and other precious stones that any country in the world can be envious of its precious stones and jewelry.

India's Trade & Commerce and Industries

India might have a huge gold reserve, but this phenomenon is confined to a small number of people only. This type of richness is not required at all. What we need is a holistic development, where every Indian citizen will have a certain quantity of gold and decent employment or work. It is a fact that no government in India could ever be able to provide government jobs to all its university pass-out youths. Hence, a strong industrial base is the demand of time. India's dream of being an 'industrial hub of the world' needs the Government's encouragement, entrepreneurship training, and assistance to its youths as well as the affirmative mental makeup of our students, youths, guardians, teachers, and above all political leaders. At present, the contribution of India to international export is discouraging. India holds the 15th position with a total world export of all products with a total value of US$455,513,136.00 thousand (2021), which is only a 2.10 percent share of the world. The first position is occupied by the United States of America with US$2,827,816,679.94 thousand (13.06%) the worth of total exports of all countries to the USA; China with US$ 2,158,872,201.26 (9.97%) thousand stands in second position. The third position is occupied by Germany with US$ 1,353,626,272.54 thousand (6.25%) worth of total exports to Germany (wits. World Integrated Trade Solutions, worldbank. org/ country Profile/ en/ Country/).

The latest picture of India's foreign trade indicates that India is doing well in exports and imports. In September 2023, the worth of India's total exports was $37.47 billion, while this amount was a little less (US$35.39 billion) than that of the previous (2022) year. On the other hand, India's imports have been reduced from $63.37 billion in 2022 to $53.84 in 2023, which indicates that India is gradually approaching "Atmanirvar Bharat" i.e. self-sufficient India. India's service sector is getting better with more exports and fewer imports. Total exports of services have increased in 2023 to $29.37 billion from $29.22 billion in 2022. The level of dependency on other countries is reducing. Also, it is a positive sign. While the total trade balance was US$ -15.03 in 2022, it has now been reduced to US$-4.92 billion.

In 2024, India's overall trade deficit reduced to $US 78.1 Billion from 121.6 billion in FY2023.

Foreign Direct Investment in India

FDI or foreign direct investment is an important component of the Gross Domestic Product (GDP) of a country. Often we hear about FDI. But what is FDI? To answer this question we can say that, FDI or foreign direct investment is the investment by an entity - either individual or firm - based outside the country where the investment is being done. Recently India's foreign direct investment has increased due to some positive reasons including a stable government, government's welcoming attitude, a business-friendly environment, ease of doing business, policy or reducing corporate tax rates, addressing liquidity issues in non-banking financial companies and banks, India's relations with foreign investors, India's contemporary role in global politics and above all internal peace and tranquility. As a result, "Foreign Direct Investment (FDI) flows into India rose by 10 percent to $49 billion in 2022, making it the third largest host country for announced greenfield projects and the second largest for international projects finance deals, according to a report released by United National Conference on Trade and Development" (Chitravanshi, Business Standard, 5 July, 2023). FDI is increasing in India year after year. It is reported by the Press Information Bureau, Government of India that "In FY 2023-24-, total FDI inflows amounted to $70.95 billion, with equity inflows reaching $44.42 billion, underscoring India's growing appeal as a global investment destination" (Press Information Bureau, 10 Sept, 2024).

Foreign direct investment and foreign affiliate sales have a confirmed positive and significant relationship. In this regard Fukui and Lakotos (2012) said that "FDI statistics can be considered an appropriate measure of the aggregate business activity of foreign affiliates while, at the same time, they warn against potential biases that may arise to cross-country and cross-industry analysis" (IMF Working Paper, June 2023, p. 24). FDI in India has actually started to rise since the 1990s after the liberalization of the economy by Dr. Manmohan Singh, the then-finance minister. But the rate of inflow was very low. "FDI into China has taken off, while FDI into India has trickled in. In 2004 India received FDI inflows of around 0.5 percent of GDP, whereas China received FDI worth 3.2 percent of GDP. In dollar terms, China received 16 times the FDI than India in 2004" (Jain-Chandra, IMF E-Library, p. 1). However, India is now a skilled country. Let us now examine how skilled the present India is.

India is Now a Skilled Country

Skill is attained through training and educational attainment. Training comes through participation in academic and training institutions. Training and skill development is the sine qua non of the 21ˢᵗ century. Education is the backbone of any country. With general education and skill training with the help of information and communication technology, only young people can make themselves prosperous, developed, and economically well-established. With the development and growth of every individual, national growth and development will be ensured. The rate of education and skill development has a direct and clear relationship with the economic prosperity of a person as well as a nation. It comes to light that India's total literacy rate in 2023 is 77.7 percent including a male literacy rate of 84.7 percent and a female literacy rate of 70.3 percent (The Global Statistics, 2023). Further, the Wheebox India Skills Report 2023 finds that "...in contrast with last year's employability figures of 46.22%, 50.3% of young people were found to be highly employable overall, which is a significant improvement. The percentage of the employable women workforce has increased to 52.8%, compared to 47.2% for men" (India Skills Report 2023, The Economic Times, 29 December 2022). While the world is aging, India's educated and young youths are the greatest strength for India. Experts predict that India will become the talent powerhouse and one of the largest English-speaking, hard-working, sincere, and honest contributors to the global workforce.

India's Small-Scale Manufacturing Industries

India is gradually approaching to become the world's manufacturing hub. At present, there are 1,05,21,190 micro, small, and medium enterprises spreading over the length and breadth of 35 districts and Union Territories in India (Ministry of Micro, Small and Medium Enterprises, Govt. of India, 31ˢᵗ July, 2023).

About 55% of these units are located in rural areas and over 44 lakhs (42.26%) are in the total Small Scale Industries (SSIs) while the remaining 61 lakhs (57.75%) are Small Scale Service and Business (Industry related) Enterprises (SSSBEs). Further, according to Hurun's Global Unicorn Index 2023, "India has some of the highest numbers of unicorns and gazelles...India bagged the third spot with 68 new unicorns, which is third only to the US' 666 unicorns and China's 316...India also had the third-highest number of gazelles" (Madhukalya, Upstart, 18 April, 2023). India's fintech industry is also thriving rapidly. We may discuss about the fintech industry in a nutshell below.

Fintech Industry in India

The Government of India has demonstrated to the world a unique model of public-private partnership by building a strong public infrastructure in the India Stack that facilitates and enables private sector innovation. Despite the slowdown in the economy due to the COVID-19 pandemic in 2020, the Fintech Industry in India continued to showcase growth by capitalizing on the digitization opportunities posed by pandemics and leveraging public digital infrastructure among other things. "India is one of the largest and fastest-growing Fintech markets in the world with more than 2100 Fintechs and is the third-largest Fintech ecosystem in line after the US and China. India has a fintech adoption rate of 87 percent which is the highest in the world with a global average of around 64 percent. As of December 2021, India has over 17 fintech companies, which have gained 'Unicorn Status' with a value of over US$1 billion, India's market was US$ 50-60 billion in 2020 and it is expected to grow to US$150 billion by 2025, as per a recent study conducted by the Boston Consultancy Group" (Srinivas, Yojana, April 2022, p. 212). Additionally, India is the USA, UK, and China combined when it comes to real-time online transactions, with $25.5 billion in real-time payments recorded in 2020.

India is Now Digital

India is growing as a global hub for technology and innovation in the digital economy. By any number of key matrices, from 834 million total internet users to 4617 million total UPI transactions, India's fintech revolution is at a population scale, exceeding most of the global countries. According to Debjani Ghosh (Yojana, April 2022, p. 25), "India's massive digital infrastructure played a key role in driving India's tech adoption with public digital platforms and open-source architecture becoming the core foundation of digital India." Today India has more than 80 percent bank account holders. India created the requisite infrastructure to reach more than 1.41 billion populations living in sprawling, varied, and sometimes inaccessible territories by assigning a unique number, "Aadhaar". The new bank accounts were linked with Aadhaar and mobile phones. The National Payments Corporation of India has developed a soft infrastructure – the Aadhaar Payment Bridge (APB), which has become the catalyst for India's cash transfer programs. The Central Government used APB-enabled direct benefit transfers for 314 programs/schemes and different state governments used these digital rails to deliver benefits to 450 programs. "India's digital consumer base is the second largest in the world, and the benefits of technology are being felt by all segments of people" (Garg, Yojana, April 2022, p. 22). In March 2019 Mckinsey Global Institute recognized 'India's rapid digitization.' The launch of *Pradhan Mantri Jan Dhan Yojana* in 2014 encouraged digital payments. Indians have already opened some 44.58 crores of Jan Dhan bank accounts (as of 26 January 2022). This proves India is gradually approaching digital and economic empowerment of people. It is to be noted that "India has pioneered uniquely innovative digital projects, implemented population scale transformational projects, and ensured digital inclusion - with an objective of providing affordable access to digital services to all citizens. India's digital transformation journey has left an indelible mark in all walks of life, and is ensuring digital access, digital delivery of services and digital inclusion of all, based on technology that is sustainable, affordable and transformative" (Digital India, mygov.in/campaigns/digital-India).

Agriculture and Strong Rural Economy

India has been an agro-based economy for a long past. The farmers of our country keep us alive. Without their contribution, the very existence of the country will be in jeopardy. Indian economy, though largely shifted from agriculture to service, the importance of agriculture has not decreased at all. Though India has developed a lot, still agriculture and its allied sectors are the largest sources of livelihood in India. The majority of people in rural areas are completely dependent on the farm and farm-related activities. India produces a huge quantity of food grains every year. Draught, floods, and other natural disasters are common in India, but Indian farmers avoiding all challenges keep on producing better quality food crops for us and our children. As a result of their dedication and hard work, "during the 2019-20 crop years, India produced approximately 295.67 million metric tonnes (MT) of crops in 201-20" (The Economic Times, 15 May, 2020). What does it mean? 295 million metric tonnes (in numbers 295000000) is equal to 295000000000 kg of food grains. One metric tonne is equal to 1000 kilograms. If India has a population of 137.13 billion (in numbers 1371360350), what is the per head food grain of each person in India? It is about 464 grams per head. This suggests that India is having surplus food grains to feed its people. The Government of India still wants to improve the food production and health of farmlands. Through the Union Budget of 2022-23, the Government of India proposes to use 'Kisan Drones' to help farmers assess crops, digitize land records as well as spray insecticides and nutrients. The introduction of 'One Nation One Registration' software will promote a uniform registration process and allow people to register deeds and documents anywhere. These are just revolutionary steps for the vibrancy of Indian farms and farmers. These comprehensive programs of the Union Government have encouraged the farmers, and in turn, food production in India has been increased.

The Food Corporation of India has so much food grain in its stock that it distributes cooked food to all the students from primary to elementary level aged between 6 to 14 years and studying in government, government-aided, or sponsored schools. During the lockdown period, the government of India decided to distribute free of cost 5 kg of food grains to every person and one kg of pulses per household under *PM Garib Kalyan Anna Yojana* initially for three months, and it was extended up to November 2020, later the deadline was extended. About 80 crore people in India have benefitted, so during the coronavirus-induced shutdown period, Indian people were not in starvation, rather they had excess food in their stock. Let me tell you two facts. The maid-servant of our own house received so much rice and food grains from government ration shops and local clubs that she offered it to the security guard of our building. This happened in Kolkata. In another incident, one retired school teacher at Fulia in the district of Nadia gained so much rice and coarse flour from the ration shop that he poured the coarse flour into the pond to feed the fish, while many such people in India and particularly in West Bengal sold the excess rice to open market at an excess price. The quality of rice was good and the supply was also smooth. All this was possible only because of excess food production by our farmer friends.

In India, more than 70 percent workforce lives in rural areas. The Ministry of Rural Development (MoRD) is the nodal ministry that looks after the welfare of the rural people. Realizing the maxim "Without rural development, India's development will not be possible," the MoRD has taken several steps to increase livelihood opportunities, provide social safety nets, and improve infrastructure in rural areas for rapid growth. Not only that, the Ministry of Rural Development has been provided the seventh-largest allocation across all ministries in the Union Budget for the financial year 2022-23. Its current allocation shot up to Rs. 1,38,204.00 crore (in 2022-23). Budgetary allocation to certain centrally sponsored schemes such as Mahatma Gandhi National Rural Employment Scheme (MGNRGS), *Pradhan Mantri Awas Yojana – Gramin (PMAY-G)*, Pradhan Mantri Gram Sadak Yojana (PMGSY), National Rural Livelihood Mission (NRLM), National Social Assistance Program (NSAP) and Shyama Prasad Mukherjee Rurban Mission

(SPMRM) is Rs. 1,35,539.00 crore (Ministry of Rural Development, Demands from Grants, 2021-22 to 2022-23).

Among various schemes of rural development, the Mahatma Gandhi National Rural Employment Guarantee Scheme (MGNRS) is the most momentous because it strengthened the livelihood resource base by providing 100 days of guaranteed wage employment per year to every rural household whose adult members volunteer to do unskilled manual work. This rural employment scheme is prevalent in all 716 rural districts of India. Under this scheme during the year 2021-2022, assets worth Rs. 6.12 crore were created through the generation of 276.89 crore person days benefitting 6.81 crore households up to February 10, 2022 (Kurukshetra, March 2022, p. 38). The Deendayal Upadhyay-National Rural Livelihood Mission (DAY-NRLM) aims at creating diversified and gainful self-employment for the rural poor through sustainable livelihood enhancements and improved access to financial services. This scheme promotes and strengthens the Self-Help Groups which in turn mediate the livelihoods of the poor people in villages. At present, the scheme covers 707 districts spread over 2,55,928 gram panchayats and 7,17,496 villages in the country. The National Social Assistance Program provides public assistance to citizens in case of unemployment, old age, sickness, or any form of disability. *Shyama Prasad Mukherjee Rurban Mission*, a unique program launched in 2016, aims at developing a cluster of villages that preserve and nurture the essence of rural community life with a focus on equity and inclusiveness. It bridges the rural-urban divide viz. economic, technological, and those related to modern facilities for stimulating local economic development with emphasis on employment generation in rural areas. *Pradhan Mantri Matru Bandana Yojana* and the 'Ease of Living' program have evolved the rural ecosystem and facilitated women's empowerment in Indian villages. Under the aegis of 'Ease of living' clean cooking fuel and drinking water are provided to all rural households through the schemes of *Pradhan Mantri Ujjwala Yojana* (PMUY) and Jal Jeevan Mission. All these programs are meant to make 'Vibrant India' through the making of 'Vibrant Villages.' Rural people are now technologically as well as economically empowered. The ambitious projects of BharatNet (National Optical Fibre Network) and Digital India have also transformed a large population in rural India. Thus, India is transforming significantly, and it is hoped that by the time India celebrates its centenary year of independence, India will be a very prosperous and technologically advanced country. Along with agriculture and the economy, now the Indian health system is also in a better position. Let's examine hereunder.

Indian Health

There is a proverb in India, "Health is wealth." The government of India is very much concerned with the health and well-being of the people. It addresses the broader indicators of health and focuses on the comprehensive and interrelated aspects of physical, mental, and social health and well-being. India has taken the initiative to achieve Sustainable Development Goal No. 3 which seeks to "Ensure healthy lives and promote well-being for all at all ages." Health is related to other SDGs such as poverty, hunger, education, gender equality, clean water and sanitation, work and economic growth, climate action, etc. India adopted its health policy in 2017 that seeks to invest in the primary healthcare system to facilitate 1,50,000 Health and Wellness Centers (HWCs), which are intended to become the main points of contact for communities within the public health system. The Centers cover about 70 percent of the out-patient care, including non-communicable diseases and maternal and child health services. The government also launched the Ayushman Bharat program to include the health insurance component, and the Pradhan Mantri Aarogya Yojana, a women empowerment scheme.

Thus, Indian Maternal Mortality Rate is now as per a UNICEF report the lowest ever at 113 per 1 lakh live births in 2016-18 (Maternal Health, UNICEF). The latest National Family Health Survey, India (NFHS, Round 5, 2019-21) indicates that the Total Fertility Rate (children per woman) is 2.0 (Urban – 1.6, and Rural – 2.1), and the Infant Mortality Rate has been lowered to 35.2/1000. Institutional birth has also been increased to 88.6% (Urban – 93.8%, and Rural – 86.7%), and home births by skilled health personnel have been reduced to 3.2%. Moreover, 76.45% of children aged 12-23 months are fully vaccinated. Nowadays the number of doctors has increased. The ratio is 1:1445. India has about 11 lakh allopathic doctors who are registered with the Medical Council of India. These vast medical practitioners are providing service to the entire population in India. Along with them, an additional 7.88 lakh Ayurveda, Unani, and Homeopathy (AUH) doctors are providing health care in the country. Taking together both AUH and allopathic doctors, the doctor-patient ratio stands at 1: 860. India has successfully reduced HIV/AIDS infection. At present only 21 lakh people are living with the deadly disease. The government immunized the majority of unimmunized and partially immunized children against vaccine-preventable diseases.

Towards achieving universal health coverage, a health insurance cover of INR 100,000 (USD 1,563) has been extended to all poor families.

The National Credit Fund for Women - The *Rashtriya Mahila Kosh* - was set up in 1993 to make credit available for lower-income women in India. The *Pradhan Mantri Mahila Vandana Yojana* is a conditional Maternity Benefit sponsored by the national government to pregnant and lactating women aged 17 and over for the first two live births. Rajiv Gandhi Scheme for Empowerment of Adolescent Girls i.e., Sabla is an initiative launched in 2012 that targets the empowerment of adolescent girls. The Indian government has introduced several such schemes for empowering women and girls.

The use of technology for transforming healthcare service is a new area in contemporary India. 'Digital Health' is a new terminology in the repository of the health sector. Digital health encompasses software, hardware, and services in an integrated platform; it is "the cultural transformation of how disruptive technologies that provide digital and objective data accessible to both caregivers and patients lead to an equal level doctor-patient relationship with shared decision-making and the democratization of care" (Verma, Yojana, May 2023, p. 28). As per the Precedence Research report (May, 2022), "The global medical devices market was estimated at US$577.26 billion in 2022 and is expected to reach around US$ 850 billion by 2030." Through the digital system nowadays individual citizens can access easily and quickly to medical counseling, and specialist care from the confines of their homes. The introduction of telemedicine is greatly useful for people. "One can save time and energy, especially in rural areas, who need not travel long distances to obtain consultation and treatment. The population cohort, including children, older adults, and individuals with disabilities, also stands to benefit from e-health services. This is also accompanied by reduced financial costs associated with travel as travel for seeking healthcare by marginalized and disadvantaged communities is often accompanied by loss of work hours, loss of wages, and lower productivity. As per a recent impact study by an NGO, each tele-consultation at an Ayushman Bharat Health & Wellness centre saves an average of a journey of up to 21.58 km, and more than Rs. 941 as Out-of-Pocket-Expenditure on healthcare" (Verma, Yojana, May 2023, p. 28).

Distribution of Vaccination During COVID-19 Pandemic

India was one of the pioneering countries that produced its indigenous vaccines. The government of India supplied free of cost to all the states and Union Territories two locally manufactured vaccines, Covishield and

Covaxin. India is also using the Russian vaccine, Sputnik. India is always an expert in the vaccine manufacturing industry; Indian scientists, manufacturers, and medical researchers are world-famous. India's largest vaccine maker, the Serum Institute of India (SII) manufactured 250 million doses of Covishied a month. Bharat Biotech, the manufacturer of Covaxin, makes 50-60 million doses a month. As of 6 May 2022, a total of 1,89,81,52,695 doses of vaccines were administered to the people in the country (Ministry of Health and Family Welfare, Government of India). As of 30 October 2023, 008:00 IST, "India's total vaccination is 220,67,74,807" (Ministry of Health and Family Welfare, Govt. of India, 30 Oct. 2023). Around 90% of India's total adult population had been fully vaccinated. The government has also launched a program to conduct at-home inoculations. The government has announced jabs for children aged 12-14, and 15-18 years and a booster program for health workers, election workers, teachers, and those above 60 years with other health conditions. The prompt action of the Health Ministry of the Government of India has helped prevent the death of people during the world's worst pandemic.

Bountiful Physical Infrastructure

In the modern era infrastructure is defined as facilities that support and accelerate modern life. There are two types of infrastructure viz. physical and social. The development of physical infrastructure is very vital for rapid economic growth. Physical infrastructure comprises transportation, communication, power, and telephones. It was revealed in a study (Bose and Bhanumurthy, 2013) that the estimated value of the capital expenditure multiplier is 2.45. "This implies every one rupee spent as capital expenditure creates Rs.2.45 income in the economy. Considering the necessity and significance of investment in infrastructure to promote economic growth, the Government of India has spent $1.1 trillion from 2008 to 17. India launched the National Infrastructure Pipeline (NIP) with a project cost of $1.5 trillion during the pandemic in 2020 (up to 2025) to provide world-class infrastructure across the country and improve the quality of life of all citizens (Sharma, Kurukshetra, March, 2022). The government has adopted the *Pradhan Mantri Gati Shakti program* to boost the physical infrastructure through seven engines such as (i) Roads, (ii) Railways, (iii) Airports/Aviation, (iv) Ports, (v) Mass Transport, (vi) Waterways, and (vii) Logistics Infrastructure.

India has the world's second-highest road network in the world with 63.71 lakh km (2019), and everyday road construction is increasing. In

2020-21 the new road construction was 36.5 km per day. The Union budget of 2022-23 has allocated Rs.1,99,107.71 crores for the Ministry of Road Transport and Highways. The Master Plan aims to complete 25,000 km of expressways and national highways by 2022-23. An average of 1835 km per year of new track length has been added through the new line and multi-tracking projects during 2014-2021. 400 new generation high-speed Bande Bharat trains are targeted to be adopted within 2025, and 100 PM Gati Shakti cargo terminals will also be developed by the same year. The domestic air traffic in India has reached 137 million in 2019-20. The development of regional airports through the UDAN program is a commendable step by the Government of India as part of the Regional Connectivity Scheme (RCS). Under the RCS-UDAN, 153 RCS airports including 12 water aerodromes and 36 helipads have been identified for the RCS flights.

India has a rich history of trade through ports and seas. The development of seaports is very vital to India now. As a result, the Government of India has released its 'Maritime India Vision 2030,' to develop world-class mega ports, transshipment hubs, and infrastructure modernization. Logistical facilities are also crucial for the efficient delivery of goods and services. Four multi-model logistic parks with the PPP model are planned to be made to bring India at par with global supply chain networks and enhance competitiveness.

Impressive Innovation in Technology

Aiming to seed, nurture, and scale up scientific and industrial Research and Development (R&D), and create a vibrant & innovative ecosystem in Quantum Technology (QT), the Union Cabinet has recently approved the National Quantum Mission (NQM) at a total cost of Rs. 6003.65 crore from 2023-24 to 2030-31. This will accelerate QT-led economic growth, nurture the ecosystem in the country, and make India one of the leading nations in the development of Quantum Technologies and Applications (QTA) (Yojana, May 2023).

India began its journey with the launch of its first rocket on 21 November 1963 from Thumba. Then the rocket, payload, radar, and computer all that was required for the first launch, came from outside the country. After six decades "The latest member of ISRO's rocket family is the Small Satellite Launch Vehicle (SSLV) a three-stage launch vehicle. Solid stages and a liquid propulsion-based velocity trimming module made SSLV capable of launching a 500 kg satellite into a 500 km planar orbit in a quick turn-around time" (Somnath, Yojana, May 2023, p. 7). India's space technology has developed tremendously in the last few decades. India's "Capability in the remote sensing has grown from the coarse resolution of 1 km to the fine resolution of 25 cm with day and night and all-weather capability. The communication transponders have also proportionally grown from a mere single unit to 317 numbers. Altogether, ISRO has mastered the capability of making satellites of 2000 kg with 1 kw power to 6000 kg with 14 kW power, operating in various frequency bands and with wide, shaped, and highly focused spot capability for communications, sub-meter resolution, optical, mufti-spectral, and microwave imaging for earth observations, and progressing from payload-based navigation solutions to a satellite constellation – VavIC (Navigation with India Constellation). The present space infrastructure includes 25 Earth observation satellites, 22 communication satellites, 7 navigation satellites, 2 space science satellites, and experimental, small, and student satellites" (Somnath, Yojana, May 2023, p. 8).

ISRO has successfully sailed to the reach of the Moon and Mars, opening the era of planetary explorations and beyond. After Chandrayan I, the first lunar orbiter mission, India launched Chandrayan-II on 22 July 2019 from Satish Dhawan Space Center, Sriharikota. "ISRO continues to explore Mars with the first ever interplanetary mission to the red planet, called Mars Orbiter Mission (MOM), aka Mangalyaan. It made India the first Asian nation to reach the Martian orbit and the first nation in the world to do so in the maiden attempt" (Somnath, Yojana, May 2023, p. 9). Human Space Exploration is the latest entrant to the programmatic verticals of ISRO. At present, "ISRO is actively pursuing the maiden human spaceflight mission – Gaganyaan to send astronauts to space and safely return to Earth. Gaganyaan is yet another very complex mission, involving the development of major technology elements such as human-rated launch vehicle, Crew space systems, Habitable orbital module, Life support system, and Crew management activities for the safety of humans onboard, to name a few" (Somnath, Yojana, May 2023, p. 10).

India's Latest Lunar Mission: Chandrayaan 3

India created history recently by sending its Chandrayaan-3 on the Moon's south pole. The Indian Express reported that "India's Moon mission Chandrayaan -3 scripted history by successfully landing on the lunar surface at 6.04 PM on August 23. With the Lander accomplishing a 'soft landing' on the Moon's south pole, India becomes the only country to have ever done so" (The Indian Express, 29 August, 2023). The Chandrayaan-3 spacecraft was launched from Satish Dhawan Space Centre at Sriharikota in Andhra Pradesh. The main objectives of the mission were to demonstrate a safe and soft landing on the lunar surface; to demonstrate rover roving on the moon and, thirdly to conduct in-situ scientific experiments for collecting invaluable scientific data. India's successful Chandrayaan-3 mission made India the fourth country to successfully land on the moon, after the former USSR, the United States of America, and China. It is to be remembered that, no country in the world has ever succeeded in sending a spacecraft to the south pole of the Moon which is full of water and ice, while some parts are dark, and the temperature can go below 230 degrees Celsius. This great event was praised by every Indian citizen. Prime Minister of India congratulated all the scientists and people associated with the ISRO, and said, "It was a new chapter in India's space odyssey." Further, it is interesting to note that, NASA administrator Bill Nelson expressed his willingness to learn from the Indian mission. In this regard we may point out that "Russia's first moon mission in 47 years failed over the weekend when its Luna-25 spacecraft crashed into the moon" (Reuters, August 23, 2023). Also, a private Japanese space startup, ispace (9348.T), failed an attempted lunar landing in April, 2023.

Benefits of India

After the successful landing of the Chandrayan-3, India has emerged as a space power. This will continue to give benefits to India for hundreds of years from now. India's private space companies would increase their share of the global launch market by five-fold within the next decade. Prime Minister Narendra Modi said that the government is also looking to spur investment in private space launches and related satellite-based businesses. But India created history by "Doing so showcases a spacecraft's technical capabilities. The landing site is near the south pole of the moon at 70 degrees latitude" (The Indian Express, 29 August, 2023).

Emergence of Education Technology System

In the last 1 decade, EdTech, or Education Technology has provided affordable learning at a large scale to the students of India. The classrooms now have moved from bricks and mortar to clicks and portals. Indian ICT, Information and Communication Technology industry has been growing rapidly since the last quarter century. In the financial year 2022, the industry crossed US$200 billion in total revenue and 5 million in total workforce. By the end of 2023, it is predicted to spend US$144 billion on ICT. There has been an enormous increase of Smartphone users in India from 34 million in 2010 to 931 million in 2022, and it is expected to rise to 1.53 billion by 2040. In this post-COVID era, "Technology has made education inclusive and affordable for all strata of students and learners. Catalyzed by India's digital revolution, EdTech has enabled accessibility by reaching the remotest parts of India" (Gupta & Shah, Yojana, May 2023, p. 20). Not only that, India's EdTech sector is one of the largest in the world, with about 400 startups operating across its various sub-sectors. These startups have cumulatively raised more than US$10 billion over the last decade. As of March 2023, 7 out of 30 global EdTech unicorns were from India" (Gupta & Shah, Yojana, May 2023, p. 22). It is to be remembered that a unicorn is a privately held startup company with a value of over $1 billion. It is commonly used in the venture capital industry.

India Is Gearing up to Leverage the Quantum Computing Wave

Quantum computing differs from traditional computing, which uses 'bits' – binary digits of 0s and 1s – to represent information. It is quantum computing that uses quantum bits, or 'qubits', which can exist in multiple states simultaneously, instead of just two states (i.e., 0 and 1). "This property of qubits, known as 'superposition' allows quantum computers to perform many computational calculations orders of magnitude faster than classical computing" (Dwivedi & Kar, Yojana, May 2023, p. 38). In India, industries are slowly and steadily gearing up to leverage the quantum computing wave through strategic collaborations and investments in research and innovation. "Quantum computers can perform certain types of calculations significantly faster than classical computing logic. As these types of computations increase in scope and scale, this could enable faster data analysis for business problems in the era of big data. Particularly for large datasets created with high velocity. Machine learning algorithms are increasingly being used for predictive capabilities and enhanced data-driven decision-making. In the era of cognitive computing, these algorithms may focus on complex data types like images and videos for solving business and social problems through areas like computer vision. Quantum computers could potentially improve machine learning by enabling more efficient optimization of these algorithms so that computer vision capabilities become more efficient, accurate, and fast" (Dwivedi & Kar, Yojana, May 2023, p. 39).

Quantum computing has the potential to create architectures that analyze real-time additions to the web of knowledge in the digital world. The outcome of these capabilities would translate to the development of driverless cars, automated management of smart city infrastructure, and digital public services. Moreover, "Realization of industrial maturity levels such as Industry 4.0 and beyond, through platforms like digital twins would be enabled through quantum computing. The Distributed computing networks, federated learning, 'Internet of Everything', blockchain, and related technologies can be envisioned to become more efficient in terms of achieving their desired objectives computationally as well as in terms of quality of outcome"(Yojana, May 2023, p. 40).

Use of AI Chatbots in India

Chatbots are not a very old phenomenon. Hence it is necessary to understand what it actually is. In simple terms, a bot is a piece of code, a program, or an application that can conduct pre-defined tasks using a database of pre-existing responses or a limited knowledge base. The recent emergence of chatbots is a clear indication that India is progressing. "The new-age chatbots utilize AI and Natural Language Processing (NLP) to simulate human-like conversations and automate responses to customer queries, making it easier for users to find information without human intervention" (Dadhich, Yojana, May 2023, p. 46). Chatbots are gradually used in different important fields such as healthcare, finance and banking, education, customer service, e-commerce, human resources, marketing, and social media. E-commerce companies are mostly using AI chatbots to help their customers locate products that match their needs by asking questions about preferences and showing relevant products. They can also help them navigate relevant processes such as placing orders and making payments. Education is another area where AI chatbots are becoming increasingly relevant. They have also been helping institutions and educators manage personalized learning recommendations and dealing with academic administrative queries. The banking sector uses AI chatbots as a way of reducing costs and enhancing customer satisfaction. The primary reason for their popularity is that they can minimize the expenses of providing initial support. Chatbots can address basic customer queries, while complex ones can be forwarded to human agents for further assistance. Thus the use of AI chatbots is found in different fields, which will foster growth and control cost of the organizations and institutions.

India is Using Technology in Urban Planning

India is moving fast towards urbanization. An article in the *Yojana* (Aulukh & Sahni, May 2023, pp. 63-65) highlights that "Urban planning is the process of both developing and designing open land, urban areas, and the built environment...Urban planning is a many-sided process involving infrastructure like physical and social, utility systems, communication networks, distribution chains, and more." By using the technology in urban planning our city planners make our environment clean and healthy by planning good streets, parks, public spaces, and such. In modern India city planning is challenging work. The use of Information Technology has helped urban planners in many aspects, especially with software based on GIS (Geographic Information System). Now various apps have been developed for city planners that use contemporary technologies as well as open data to build up comprehensive and lively spaces for inhabitants and commercial businesses. Moreover, several fundamental IoT (Internet of Things) tools are already being used to make comprehensive and comfortable city planning. "They include intelligent streetlights that automatically turn off to conserve energy. On top of those answers, urban planners can create ideas that improve the infrastructure of cities. Urban planners may employ technology to establish self-management strategies to create smarter cities and put more emphasis on growing communities and neighborhoods. Cities achieve more financial stability, independence, and provision of green space this way. These instances demonstrate how technology may be utilized to develop smarter city plans and foster more community participation." Technology has become the main key for city planners in planning smart cities efficiently and effectively.

India Revolutionized Digital Payments

India's economy is now digital. In the last few years, only India has revolutionized in attracting the attention of global leaders in e-economic activities. In January 2023, "about eight billion transactions worth nearly $200 billion were carried out on the Unified Payment Interface (UPI)." This is a great achievement for India. The use of digital payments has significantly increased mainly during the COVID-19 period. Nowadays Indian people are making even small payments digitally to buy vegetables or groceries. It is learned from an article published in the Yojana (May 2023, p. 67) that "The value of instant digital transactions in India last year was far higher than in the United States, Britain, Germany and France" It has made daily life more convenient, expanded banking services like credit and savings to millions more Indians, and extended the reach of government programs and tax collection. "India and Singapore have launched cross-border linkage using their respective Fast Payment Systems, namely Unified Payments Interface (UPI) and PayNow. The UPI-PayNow linkage enables users of the two fast payment systems in either country to make convenient, safe, instant, and cost-effective cross-border fund transfers. Now funds can be transferred to/from India using just the UPI ID, mobile number, or Virtual Payment Address (VPA). This has revolutionized the financial relations between the two great economies. This interlinkage aligns with the G20's financial inclusion priorities of driving faster, cheaper, and more transparent cross-border payments and will be a significant milestone in the development of infrastructure for cross-border payments between India and Singapore" (Yojana, May 2023, p. 67).

It is a fact that India has already attained feats in economy, trade, infrastructure, military, agriculture, health, science & technology, space research and development, and other sectors. But this is not all. If India has to reach the top, it needs a lot more policy initiatives, manpower development through education and skills, political stability, reform in political structure, and the outlook of the policymakers and the executive officers. Finally, the mental makeup of all the stakeholders needs to be changed. However, the next chapter deals with the achievements of some top economies and technologically developed countries that might help our policymakers and readers transform India into a Viksit Bharat by 2047.

References:

1. INDIAN FOREIGN POLICY. *Pakistan Horizon*, vol. 36, no. 2, 1983, pp. 18–25. *JSTOR*, http://www.jstor.org/stable/41394186. Accessed 6 Dec. 2024.

2. Jaffe, E. & Nebenzahl, D. (2001). National Image and Competitive Advantage: The Theory and Practice of Country-of-Origin Effect, Copenhagen Business School Press, Copenhagen. Quoted by Fetscherin, M. (2010, July). The determinants and measurement of a country brand: the country brand strength index. *International Marketing Review.*

3. Fetscherin, M. (2010, July). The determinants and measurement of a country brand: the country brand strength index. *International Marketing Review.*

4. Kapur, D. & Mehta, B.P. (2006, January). *The Indian Parliament as an Institution of Accountability.* United Nations Research Institute for Social Development.

5. Reddy, N. D. (2017, November 8). Demonetization, corruption and black money. *The Front Line.*

6. Measures to combat corruption. (2021, February 10). Ministry of Personnel, Public Grievances and Pensions, Government of India posted, *PIB.*

7. Mustafa, F. (2019, August 6). Explained: What are Articles 370 and 35A? *The Indian Express*, 6 ugust, 2019.

8. What is Article 35A? (2023, October 8). *Business Standard*.

9. Rajagopal, K. (2023, August 28). Article 35A took away fundamental rights while giving special rights to permanent residents of J&K, says CJI. *The Hindu*.

10. Chaturvedi, A. (2021, August 5). 2 years of abrogation of Article 370: 5 big changes in Jammu and Kashmir. *The Hindustan Times*.

11. Mehta, D. (2015). The Ayodhya dispute: The absent mosque, state of emergency and the jural deity. *Journal of Material Culture*.

12. Dixit, P. (2023, July 9). Ram temple work in full swing, completion nears. *The Hindustan Times*.

13. Sengupta, S., Munjal, T., Dhuria, A., and Vaish, A. (2020, May). A Study of Goods and Services Tax (GST) [Conference Paper]. https://www.researchgate.net/publication/347910918.

14. Nayyar, A. & Singh, I. (2018). A Comprehensive Analysis of Goods and Services Tax (GST) in India. *Indian Journal of Finance*, Vol. 2, p. 2.

15. Sharma, K. (2017, June 30). India's traders protest in the hours before GST. *Nikkei Asia*.

16. About 82 per cent decline in triple talaq cases since law enacted by Modi govt: Mukhtar Abbas Naqvi. (2020, July 22). *The Economic Times*.

17. The Muslim Women (Protection of Rights on Marriage) Act, 2019, cited by Prime Minister during Independence Day Speech. (2019, August 15). *Ministry of Information and Broadcasting, Government of India*.

18. Mandal, K. (2010). Empowerment of Women and Panchayati Raj: Experiences from West Bengal. *Sarat Book Distributors*.

19. Jha, G. (1993, July-December). Seventy Fourth Constitutional Amendment and the Empowerment of Municipal Government: A Critique in Urban India. *A journal of the National Institute of Urban Affairs*, XIII(2), p. 68.

20. Manoj, C.G. (2023, September 19). Handing fire for 27 years: How Women Reservation Bill kept lapsing through its tumultuous journey. *The Indian Express*.

21. India passes law to reserve seats for women legislators. (2023, October 4). UN Women.

22. PRS Legislative Research. (n.d.). *Ministry of Law and Justice, Government of India*. https://prsindia.org/billtrack/the-constitution-one-hundred-twenty-eighth-amendment-bill-2023

23. Deka, K. (2019, December 23). Everything you wanted to know about the CAA and NRC. *India Today.*

24. US has world's most powerful military, Pak in 7th place, Bhutan weakest. Is India in top 10? LIST. (2023, July 10). *The Hindustan Times.*

25. Johnson, D. E. et al. (2009). In *Preparing and Training for the Full Spectrum of Military Challenges* (1st. ed.). (n.d.). Preparing and Training for the Full Spectrum of Military Challenges: Insights from the Experiences of China, France, the United Kingdom, India, and Israel. Rand Corporation.

26. Population of India. (2023, October 18). Worldometer, https://www.worldometers.info/world-population/india-population.

27. Sharma, R., (2023, August 5). Arjun Tank: India Pitches Its 'Hunter-Killer' Arjun MBT To African Countries As Indian Army Places Its Last Order. *The Eurasian Times.*

28. Singh, A. (2023, August 14). India's maritime power is growing, but challenges loom. *Observer Research Foundation.*

29. BrahMos. (2023, October 24). *Aerospace.* https://www.brahmos.com/content.php?id=10&sid=10

30. Top 10 largest economies in the world. (2022, April 13). *Business Insider India.* https://www.businessinsider.in/top-10-largest-economies-in-the-world/articleshow/70547252.cms.

31. Jain, S. (2023, June 12). *Forbes India.* https://www.forbesindia.com/article/news/indias-gdp-growth-surges-to-72-in-2023-outpacing-major-economies/85645/1

32. World Economic Outlook: Navigating Global Divergences, International Monetary Fund. (2023, October). *Washington DC.*

33. Suneja, K. (2021, September 18). No irregularities found in World Bank's 'Doing Business' data on India. *The Economic Times.*

34. Ease of doing business: Govt. working on to reduce compliance issues. (2022, July 6). *The Economic Times.*

35. Singh, R. R. (2022, February 8). India in global gold buying spree; RBI 2nd largest buyer of yellow metal. *Fortune.*

36. Golden devotion: Tirumala gets record 130 kg yellow metal in July. (2019, September 1). *The Times of India.*

37. Pattanayak, B. (2019, May 20). In gold we trust: India's household gold reserves valued at over 40% of GDP. *Financial Express.*

38. Transforming India into a Global Manufacturing Powerhouse. (2024, September 10). Press Information Bureau, Ministry of Commerce and Industry, Government of India.

39. Chitravanshi, R. (2023, July 5). FDI inflows into India rise 10%, outflows shrink 16% in 2022: Unctad. *Business Standard.*

40. Fukui, & Lakatos. (2012). cited by Casella, B., Borga, M., and Wacker. (2023, June). K. M. Measuring Multinational Production with Foreign Direct Investment Statistics: Recent Trends, Challenges, and Developments. *International Monetary Fund, Working Papers.*

41. Literacy Rate in India 2023. (n.d.). *The Global Statistics.* https://www.theglobalstatistics.com/literacy-rate-in-india/?expand_article=1.

42. India Skills Report 2023: Indian employable talent leaps from 46.2% to 50.3%. (2022, December 29). The Economic Times.

43. Ministry of Micro, Small and Medium Enterprises. (2023, July 31). *Govt. of India.* https://www.dcmsme.gov.in/ssiindia/census/ch6.htm)

44. Madhukalya, A. (2023, April 18). India has 3rd-highest number of unicorns, gazelles: Hurun's Global Unicorn Index 2023. *bt Upstart.* https://www.businesstoday.in/entrepreneurship/news/story/india.

45. Srinivas, I. (2022, April). Fintech Beyond Boundaries. *Yojana, 66*(4), p. 21.

46. Ghosh, D. (2022, April). Fintech Revolution. *Yojana,* 66(4), p. 25.

47. Garg, S. (2022, April). Digital Identity. Yojana, 66(4), p. 22.

48. India's foodgrains production to touch record 295.67 MT in 2019-20 crop year. (2020, May 15). *The Economic Times.*

49. Demands from Grants. (2021-22 to 2022-23). *Ministry of Rural Development.*

50. Samanta, D. (2020, March 22). Infrastructure Development. *Kurukshetra.*

51. Maternal Health. (n.d.). *UNICEF.* https://www.unicef.org/india/what-we-do/maternal-health

52. National Family Health Survey (NFHS - 5) 2019-21, Compendium of Fact Sheets. (n.d.). *Ministry of Health & Family Welfare, Government of India.*

53. Verma, M. (2023, May). Leveraging Technology for Transforming Healthcare. *Yojana, 67*(5), p. 28.

54. Precedence Research Report. (2022, May). https://www.precedenceresearch.com/medical-devices-market

55. Verma, M. (2023, May). Leveraging Technology for Transforming Healthcare. Yojana, *67*(5). p. 28.

56 Ministry of Health and Family Welfare, Govt. of India. (2023, October 30). https://www.mohfw.gov.in/

57. Sharma, H.L. (2022, March). Strengthening Rural Economy. *Kurukshetra*, 70(5) pp. 27-32.

58. National Quantum Mission. (2023, May). *Yojana*. 67(5), 3.

59. What is a soft landing, why did India send Chandrayaan – 3 to the Moon's south pole and what happened after the landing was accomplished? We explain. (2023, August 29). *The Indian Express*.

60. Bhattacharya, N. (2023, August 23). Chandrayaan – 3: what to know about India's moon landing mission. *Reuters*.

61. What is a soft landing, why did India send Chandrayaan – 3 to the Moon's south pole and what happened after the landing was accomplished? We explain. (2023, August 29). *The Indian Express*.

62. Gupta, R. & Shah, S. (2023, May). Potential of India's EdTech Sector. *Yojana*. 67(5), pp. 19-37.

63. Dwivedi, Y.K. & Kar, A.K. (2023, May). Transforming Technology. *Yojana*, 67(5), pp. 38-44.

64. Dadhichi, B.S. (2023, May). AI Chatbots: Future and Challenges. Yojana, *Yojana*, 67(5), pp. 45-56.

65. Aulukh, R.S. & Sahni, S. (2023, May). Use of Technology in Urban Planning. *Yojana*, 67(5), 63-65.

II

India's Take from Others

I had been contemplating for a long time why India is remaining behind some of its counterparts, which got freedom almost simultaneously from their colonial masters, in terms of infrastructural progress, technological advancement, and economic growth. Intending to search for the answer, I started studying the available literature at the Indian National Library and on the Internet. My study of the world economy, growth statistics, politics, education, and people's empowerment helped me to grasp the ground situation in the world, particularly in India. In this chapter, I would like to highlight the story of the progress of a few countries that have made astounding developments in science, technology, economy, infrastructure, military, space, and environment. The first name that comes to mind of the majority of Indians is China. Why does China appear first? Because it is the country that is mostly discussed as well as criticized from the international development discourse to tea-table debates across the globe; it is the country that has been sprouted as an alternative to the most powerful Western economies viz. the USA, the UK, or Germany; it is the only most powerful communist country in the world; it is the world's second most populous country. It is a recusant country and it has given (re)birth to bipolarism in the post-World War II global politics.

Now the question is how strong is China in the second decade of the 21st century? Many of you are well aware of it, while millions of people are not fully aware of the power China holds in the global economy, politics, defense, and space. Chinese military and economy are so robust that it dares to talk keeping an eye to eye contact with the USA, the most powerful country in the world. Chinese advancement is so spectacular that, very few democracies have been able to match with it. Evelyn Cheng and Yen Nee Lee in an article wrote, "China is set to overtake the United States as the world's largest economy a few years earlier than anticipated due to the Coronavirus pandemic. In the pandemic period though the gross domestic product of the U.S. contracted by 2.3% to $20.93 trillion in current-dollar terms, China's GDP was expanded by 2.3% in 2020 to 101.6 trillion Yuan, which is about $14.7 trillion, and that puts China's economy at only $6.2 trillion behind the U.S., down from $7.1 trillion in 2019" (Cheng & Lee, CNBC, 31 January, 2021). It was predicted that China's size of the economy might increase to a great extent, but the real milestone will be when China can overtake the US in terms of GDP per capita. In November 2024, China's per capita GDP rose to around $12.97 thousand, while this figure in the U.S.A. is five times more than that of China. As per the latest report of Forbes India (4 November, 2024), the United States of America is the largest economy with a GDP of $29.17 trillion and GDP Per Capita Income of $86.6 thousand, whereas China holds the second position with the GDP of $18.27 trillion. The GDP Per Capita Income of China ($12.97 thousand) is much lower than the USA. India, though became the fifth largest economy, its a GDP of only $3.89 trillion, and its GDP Per Capita Income is merely $2.7 thousand. Hence, it is clearly understood that India is far behind the USA and China. Japan with a GDP of $4.07 trillion came down to the fourth position and Germany with $4.71 trillion rose above Japan to become the third position. Now the question is - how the USA, China, Germany and Japan achieved this success? What are the methods and strategies did they adopt to attain the top four positions? As we always follow the best persons in society, so we need to follow the best economies in the world. Hence, the following part will attempt to search for the answers as how these countries became the top economies in the world. Let us begin with China, our contemporary as well as as competitor.

Tracing the Origin of Contemporary China

Before learning from a country, it is always better to learn about the origin of the country. In this endeavor, I chose to find rare books on China in the National Library of Kolkata. I found a very useful book entitled *A General Description of China, Containing the Topography of the Fifteen Provinces Which Compose This Vast Empire, That of Tartary, the Isles, and Other Tributary Countries: Vol. II* (1788). I came to learn that Chinese sovereignty was basically patriarchal. However, the author (translator) Grosier Abbe beautifully narrated the sovereignty authority of China in the sixteenth-seventeenth century. "The Chinese government brings to our remembrance that of the patriarch. Whatever authority these had over their families, the same is exercised in the fullest manner by the emperor of China over his subjects. It, besides, evidently appears, that the monarchical government, taken to its utmost extent, is founded upon the patriarchal; and in this view, we consider it when we speak of that of China. No potentate on earth possesses so unlimited power as the sovereign of this numerous nation. All authority is vested in him, and him alone. He is the undisputed master of the lives of his subjects, yet he seldom employs this prerogative, but to provide for their safety and promote their happiness. No sentence of death pronounced by any of the tribunals can be executed without his consent: a wonderful care in an empire so populous and extensive, but at the same time necessary, to render the tribunals more cautious and circumspect in their conduct. Those therefore of China seldom venture to give a rash decision in matters of so great importance. Every verdict in affairs purely civil is subject to the same revision; and no determination is of any force until it has been confirmed by the emperor" (Abbe, Grosier, (translator), 1788, pp. 1-2).

How Did China Overcome India in the Last 70 Years: A Lesson for India

India and China were almost at an equal stage when both countries became republics in the forties of the previous century. Wen Zhou, a Professor at Yunnan Normal University, China, compared the economic growth of China and India in an article. In that article, he elaborately highlighted the strategies and policies taken by the Chinese government in the post-independence period that helped them to excel in India. Professor Zhou wrote, "In the early stages following the foundation of the People's Republic of China (PRC), the national economies of China and India were at similar levels. In 1950, India's gross national product (GNP) was 49.5% higher than that of China, and as for the per capita GNP, India's was 2.3 times higher than that of China, while the Chinese per capita gross domestic product (GDP) was only 43.5% of India's" (Zhou, World Review of Political Economy, 2014, p. 455). But the situation began to deteriorate in India, and the Chinese economy made rapid progress, and notable achievements subsequently were recognized as the "Chinese Miracle". India's growth and development were uneven; but attained noticeable progress after a series of economic reform policies since 1991.

Zhou further wrote, "Chinese economic reform and development have taken a traditional road of industrialization, in which manufacturing industry has been established as the core force to drive the development of other industries and to eventually accelerate the development of national economy and promote the adjustment, optimization, and upgrading of industrial structure. Chinese economic development has experienced a process of enhancing the domestic manufacturing industry and accordingly the general industrialization of the country by considerably expanding investment demand (by domestic investment and foreign direct investment (FDI) entry) and export demand (with huge trade surplus)... Mckinsey & Company claims that the development of the manufacturing industry has made the Chinese mainland a "world factory" within a short period of 20 years, and China has found a sustainable development pattern for the manufacturing industry. China has gained great success in opening up as well. First, the introduction of foreign capital has gained notable achievements. By 2010, the Chinese FDI mounted up to US$105.7 billion, ranking second in the world, the fourth in 2005, its proportion in the world rising from 7.3% in 2005 to 9.4% as well. China has already become one of the world's most attractive FDI countries. Until now, with over 30 million foreign companies carrying out business activities in China, China has become the second FDI inflow country, ranking only second to the US in the past 5 years. Almost all Fortune 500 companies, with a small exception of companies that are not allowed to invest in China due to Chinese restrictions on foreign access to certain industries, have invested in the Chinese mainland. Second, Chinese foreign trade has maintained rapid development. At present, China's volume of total imports and exports ranks the second largest in the world. Third, China's foreign investment has made considerable progress. By 2009, China's FDI outflows had maintained steady and rapid growth for 8 consecutive years, with an average annual growth rate of over 50%, ranked fifth after America, France, Japan, and Germany in the world. Fourth, the national per capita income is also increasing rapidly. The gap in gross national income (GNI) per capita between China and the developed countries' average level has reduced significantly. China's per capita GNI ratio to developed countries' average level has increased from 24.8% in 2005 to 41.8% in 2009, narrowing the gap by 17% within 5 years.

Fifth, the total scale taken in the world economy has been increasing. Chinese GDP ranking in the world increased from fifth in 2005, to fourth in 2006, third in 2007, and surpassed Japan to be the world's second-largest economy for the first time in 2010. The proportion of China's GDP in the world has increased year by year, from 5% in 2005 to 9.5% in 2010. Meanwhile, the gap between China and the USA gradually reduced; the ratio of US GDP has risen from 17.9% in 2005 to 40.2% in 2010. If the total GDP in 2010 is taken as the base, the American economy develops at an average annual growth rate of 2%, while China's GDP grows at an annual rate of 8%; without consideration of exchange rate changes, it is estimated that China's GDP will reach nearly US$20 trillion by 2025" (Zhou, World Review of Political Economy, 2014, pp. 456-57). However, Zhou and Lin in an article in 2011 predicted that, " in 2025, China's GDP will rank alongside or outpace America's.

Further, Zhou has indicated the poor performance of India's economy. He said, "India's economy performed poorly during the 1950s-1970s, so India has got into the Hindu equilibrium with a low-speed economic development (3% - 3.5%). In 1950, India's per capita income was about 40% higher than China's, while in 1978 the two countries almost had equal per capita income. In the 1980s, India's economy began to speed up and the economic growth accelerated in the 1990s. In 1999, China's per capita income increased to twice that of India's. India's economic growth reached 6% during 1980-2002, and 7.5% during 2002-2010, while China's average annual GDP grew by 10% in 1978-2010" (Zhou, World Review of Political Economy, 2014, p. 457).

India in the last nine years from 2014 to 2022 made a striking advancement in her GDP growth. The latest World Bank data (GDP growth (annual % - India, China) reveals that in 2014 both China and China had an annual GDP growth rate of 7.4%. But it gradually started to grow and in 2016 India's annual GDP growth became 8.3%, while in China this rate was 6.8%. Further, in 2017 in China, it decreased by one point to 6.7%, and in India, it turned lower than China to become 6.5%. During the COVID-19 period in 2020, China's annual GDP growth rate came down to 2.2%, and in India it became -5.8%. This indicates that India suffered a lot from the Coronavirus pandemic. However, India recovered soon in 2021 and 2022 respectively. India succeeded in attaining 9.1% and 7% annual growth to its GDP in 2021 and 2022 respectively, while this rate for China was only 8.4 and merely 3% during the same period. Now India is the fastest growing economy in the world. Despite this fact, it is an undenying fact that at present (in Oct., 2023, IMF) China's GDP ($19347 billion) is five times more than that of India ($3,750 billion), and her (China's) GDP Per Capita Income (US$13.72 thousand) is also five times more than that of India with only US$2.6 thousand. But the question is how did China attain this success, while India could not do so? We have discussed several issues above. Now we may discuss some other challenges in the following part.

China's Philosophy is Competition

China and India have attained independence almost at the same time. Still, India remains much behind China on several fronts. Why is this lagging? There might be several reasons behind it. But, have you ever thought of a simple concept prevalent amongst most of us? What is that view? In this regard, I will share a personal and general statement of an average Indian citizen, which is reflected in the words of my friend Debasish (Santra), who once told me that, it is because of Indian philosophy. Our forefathers, our parents, and teachers have taught us "Not to win, but to take part," while Chinese philosophy is "play the game to win." Immediately I recall my childhood and school days when I was a sportsperson. In all of my nearly 40 certificates that I won in games and sports during my school days, it is written on the top: "NOT TO WIN BUT TO TAKE PART" in red or blue ink. All of our teachers including the Head Master and Games Teacher used to highlight the same sentence in their concluding lecture at the annual sports meet. Since our childhood, we grew up with the philosophy of taking part in an event only for the sake of 'participation,' and not for winning the prize. Unfortunately, today being the Head Master of a High School, I find the same quotation in many of our guests and colleagues in their lectures in various competitions – may that be a drawing competition, or sports or elocution competition. This difference in the attitude and mental makeup of average Indian teachers, parents, and the general public holds a deciding factor.

We were not taught to be competitive, rather we were taught to refrain from any type of competition. We were taught to leave the battlefield for the others. This 'leaving the battlefield for others' attitude amongst the majority of our rural, semi-urban, and even urban Indian students and youths poses a tremendous hindrance to our accomplishment in difficult and top-notch positions in different fields from economy to education, and from agriculture to astronomy. It is necessary to strengthen the mental makeup of our students, inspire them, and assist them in their preparations for the achievement of great, well-paid, and respectful positions through competition. Healthy competition is always good, beneficial, and encouraging. Without a competitive environment, one gets demoralized sometimes, and we fail to judge our exact strength and position in comparison with our competitors. So, it is our duty to create as much healthy competitive atmosphere as possible for our students in both educational institutions and homes. When there is competition among friends, siblings, neighbors, and countries, it always produces good results. Look, always there are two types of people - one who tries and others who are 'genius.' "Kanazawa makes a distinction between 'genius' and 'effort', which united is observable 'productivity'. It is an effort that is driven by competition, rather than genius" (Sealy, materialstoday, Sept. 2003, editorial). It seems to me that, when a good boy reads and makes an outstanding performance in the examination, the next-door average-merit boy's mother compares her son with the next-door good boy, and tells her son to work hard and do better. Likewise playing the role of a mother here, I must tell my beloved Indian students to awake from hibernation, get ready to take up the challenge of hard work, and jump into action for turning our motherland from the present good place into a better place by 2030 and to the topmost place by 2047.

Other Lessons from China

We are contemporaries, we are friends, and we are brothers. China is not our rival and not our enemy; the country is our friend, and the people there are our brothers. When they have made stupendous progress in economy, science, technology, research, agriculture, infrastructure, space, and sports, we may learn many lessons from our colleagues there, we may apply those ideas and knowledge to India to achieve the same or excel them. The UPSC CSE (Union Public Service Commission Civil Service Examination), NEET (National Eligibility cum Entrance Test for medical students), or WBCS (West Bengal Civil Service) aspirants always watch the videos, read the blogs of the previous years' toppers, and make a strategy for their own. Likewise, we should learn the lessons and make our strategy according to our social, political, geographical, and economic conditions. China took 70 years to emerge from isolation, and now it is one of the world's greatest economic powers. How did China do so? A lot of fundamental principles were adopted by the People's Republic of China and the Communist Party of China (CPC) to bring about astonishing and spectacular transformation in the country and the life of its people.

The Communist Party is basically a party of the proletariat - a party of the laborers and farmers. The party was 'very very poor' when the country got independence. Why I am talking about the Communist Party of China? It is because the State is completely controlled by the Communist Party. Hence, India needs a strong political party like the CPC to rule the country. There must be a strong government of a single political party. The government should be run with the aid and advice of the Party's joint leadership. Now, you may ask - what will be the constitutional provisions of democracy in India? Remember, the originator of democracy Aristotle himself considered democracy as the worst kind of rule. Secondly, if a system does not help in bringing affirmative changes in people's lives, what is the use of worshipping the system? If democracy means the enjoyment of certain rights (Right to Freedom of Speech and Movement, Article 19) such as obstructing, protesting, and shouting slogans only for the sake of opposing the government's development agenda, why should people of this country adore and preserve it? If democracy means opposing the government "without ethical base" and without considering the "public benefit", why people should maintain and protect it? How far Indian citizenry should bear with the misdemeanor, shouting, and child-like debates of many Members of Parliament in the shrine of democracy? So, my first proposition is the introduction of a single-party rule or at best two-party or two-major alliance-led governance system from the existing multi-party system.

The ruling party would be elected directly by the people based on popular votes. Only they will be considered as an opposition party in Parliament, which will attain at least 20 percent seats of the total strength of the house. If any party or alliance fails to attain the minimum 20% seats, they will lose certain privileges, and they will have to function for the development of the people of their constituency merely and assist the government in its functioning. However, they might do constructive criticisms and propose alternative and better policies to the electorate. I advocate for the limited role of the Opposition, and the major role of the elected government in India. Otherwise, India could not touch the top 3 economies of the world in terms of GDP, and GDP per capita income. India's dream of being a superpower will also remain merely a hallucination. The state governments will work according to the existing constitutional provisions with minor changes in favor of a strong Union Government. The election of State and Union Governments will be considered as two separate subjects. The responsibility of the Union Government will be only military help, border security, and natural calamity. The subject of Education should be withdrawn from the concurrent list, and it must be brought completely under the Union Government. As the Union Government is responsible, they should formulate a uniform Education Policy. The State boards will be the only implementing agencies. The procedure of passing a bill will remain the same as it now exists. The role of the Opposition Party will only be advisory in nature, and they must not enjoy any power to obstruct any bill. However, the Education Department of the Union Government may welcome the good suggestions of the Opposition Parties. Strict disciplinary action, even cancellation of membership, might be introduced against the unruly members for any nuisance as is now being seen in the holy place of Parliament. The alliance or majority party being the Ruling party/alliance will hold all primary decision-making power. It is not the government only responsible to the general public, but the political party will also be equally responsible to the people for its performance. People generally love or hate a party. So, let the ruling party be as strong as the Chinese Communist Party. Today's ruling party is tomorrow's opposition party. The Opposition parties will have to work hard, and present alternative and better policies for the growth of GDP, per capita income, and people's safety and security. Then people will ultimately decide who will win the next elections and rule the country.

However, the party along with the government must keep up diplomatic relations with neighboring countries and various regions inside or outside of the country. There should be a representation of scientists (social, political, and applied) and current researchers, doctors, authors, teachers (primary, secondary, and higher), farmers, and businessmen in the core committee, who will actually "aid and advice" the party from time to time. Both party men as well advisers will be highly qualified in different fields with proven track records. The total number of members must not be more than 50. Based on the suggestions by scholars, the ruling party (or major party of the coalition) will guide the Prime Minister and the Council of Ministers, who must abide by those guidelines of the party. All the new policies will be made by the core committee members on the basis of authentic research, and the same should be kept in record, both electronically and physically.

The new party guides could be designated as "Ambassadors of Vision 2047." Let India adopt the policies of Perestroika, a political movement for reformation within the Communist Party of the Soviet Union undertaken during the 1980s by Mikhail Gorbachev, and Glasnost, i.e. the openness in policy reform. India needs more market reforms to open up trade routes and investment flows intending to pull hundreds of millions of people out of poverty and deprivation. What Mao Zedong attempted in the 1950s, India needs to do that now. India should heartily welcome all the multinational companies, research institutions, big and best universities, and their students in India. Yes, India is now welcoming the world's best higher education institutions and companies in India. I also ask earnestly them to come to India, and learn and invest knowledge, expertise, and money to make personal profit and transform the infrastructure, life, income, and longevity of Indian people.

To achieve the national goal, Mao Zedong initiated the Cultural Revolution in the 1960s. But I do not support for Cultural Revolution of Mao that sought to get rid of the Communist Party from his rivals. It only destroys the country's social fabric. Rather, I believe in the united strength of people of all communities and beliefs in a country. All the communities of India must come forward to boost India's goal of achieving supremacy in the economy, academy, sports, agriculture, industry, science, and other fields. I especially believe in the combined strength of both the Hindu and the Muslim communities. When both of them are united, India becomes a very strong country in the world. Not only that our relations with Pakistan and Afghanistan are required to be improved through cultural exchange, sports, movies, and academic exchange programs. Muslims in Bangladesh, Pakistan, and Afghanistan are our neighbors and they are our brothers. In India, all the minorities are our valuable human resources. They also require benefits from government schemes to improve their academic, economic, spiritual, and cultural base. But the only thing I would like to emphasize is that all Indian students must learn basic education on the basis of the National Education Policy 2020. It will not harm any people; it would only help all students to flourish and learn happily and enthusiastically to make them updated, modern, and sophisticated to adjust to the outer world beyond our borders. All these are possible through dialogue, affirmative attitude, and goodwill. I urge all communities and parties to extend their hands of friendship and goodwill toward the Union Government and respective state governments for making this beautiful country the best place by 2047. Make this country the "Workshop of the World." All people have been granted equal rights in India as per the Constitution of India. So, take advantage of it and swing into action to improve your standard of living and income through educational attainment and skill development. Making ties, inviting others to our country for investment, and creating job opportunities for our students and youths will help India grow and flourish. All the people with sound knowledge and good rapport with foreign businessmen tradesmen or investors might pursue them to set up industries individually or jointly in India with foreign money, technology, expertise, and know-how.

China removed all barriers to the inflow of investment in the country. Similarly, India should explore the avenues for the removal of all kinds of trade barriers and odd tariffs. With these two components, Indian quality goods with lower and competitive prices can have the potential to go to any market in the world. India might see real magic in lifting major trade barriers and with reasonable tariffs. Necessary tax reforms, if any further requirements should be done immediately. We must explore roads to become the "workshop of the world." Now China is the largest trading nation in goods in the world. Why does India fail to do so? What hinders us from being so? Why cannot we lift our poor people from the vicious cycle of poverty? I sincerely appeal to the policy experts of our country to ponder over these questions and act accordingly. There are certain works that an individual performs, while there are other works that are done by other employees. But my mantra is very simple: every Indian must love his country first, give priority to the country first, and work for the development of the country, must not use any negative words and acts against the interest of India either inside or outside of India. The government must save its people from all dangers of war, pandemics, and any natural calamities; at the same time, it would be very strict in matters of complying laws of the land. The policy of carrot and stick should be applied in both civil and police administration.

Both China and India are the world's two most populous countries. There is an affinity of culture, mental make-up, and social system between these two countries. Despite this fact, there is a vast difference between these two countries. China adopted the One Child Policy at the end of the seventies of the previous century to control its population by requiring citizens to have only one child. The rationale behind the policy was to reduce the population growth rate, which the government perceived as too rapid. As a result, it is estimated that soon the country began to grow as the first old country. Its population will peak just below 1.5 billion in the next decade and then slowly shrink to about 1.3 billion by mid-2050. Do you know what would happen then? China's "dependency ratio" i.e. children and the aged people will double from 35 percent to 70 percent. This will put massive pressure on China's welfare economy and health system.

On the other hand, India's population is expected to be about 1.7 billion during the middle of the present century; the largest population in the world. India is now a country of young people. Over the next 35 years, its dependency ratio will actually decline from a bit over 50 percent today to under 50 percent in 2050. With more affluence and educational attainment, people's consciousness levels will increase a lot, and the birth rate will come down considerably. But Indian fertility will remain high by all but African standards, and this will be a great foundational resource for the Indian economy. India's growing demography is, thus, will not be a burden; rather it would be a boon to India's economic productivity and growth. Average Indian people's standard of living and longevity will also be much higher than today.

Though India liberalized its economy in the 1990s, China brought reform and opened up its economy by the end of the seventies. China's socialist market economy was led by Deng Xiaoping, who is often credited as the "General Architect" of reforms of China, which had gone into stagnation after the military crackdown on students' protest movements at Tiananmen Square (1989). On the other hand, Indian economic liberalization led by Dr. Manmohan Singh in 1991 opened up the economy with the goal of more market service-oriented, and expansion of private and foreign investment. Earlier attempts at liberalization made in the sixties and eighties were unsuccessful, but the new industrial policy to liberate the economy, increase employment opportunities, boost production and productivity, make central public sector units more competitive, and encourage foreign investment never looked back, and it continued without any hitch.

Despite this fact, China has been able to accelerate its economy, while India has remained weak comparatively. China was able to attract some of the world's largest investments, which has enabled the country to turn its infrastructure into new cities, high-speed rail lines, airports and ports, and manufacturing industries. For the last two decades, China has been the world's factory. Its ability to move things quickly and efficiently - may it be a land acquisition or declaration of the compensation package or rehabilitation arrangements for the affected people - has been a critical component in its growth miracle. Besides, the investment of China and the corporate from around the globe in the country is almost fifty percent of its total economy, while India invests about thirty percent of its GDP. Not only that China has the world's best physical infrastructure outside the Western world, but India has concentrated on infrastructure development only recently where about a 30-kilometer road is being constructed daily. India is endeavoring to attract more investments both from Indian industrialists as well as foreign companies. India is well aware that without infrastructure development, it would not be possible to attract investors from both India and abroad.

Indian democracy is so vibrant that all people enjoy their Right to Freedom of Speech and Movement and other five Fundamental Rights. They are fond of cricket and politics. It is often criticized that there is too much democracy in India. What China can do, India cannot do in terms of land acquisition for setting up industries. China can acquire land and move ahead to compensate the adversely affected people without much delay. It seems easier for China to acquire land; while in India, too much politicking obstructs the land acquisition process in almost every state. If there is the same party rule in the Centre and state, still the state faces protests from opposition parties of the concerned state (and other states). China rarely retreats from a major project whatever obstacles might come in its way. The Three Gorges Dam considered the world's biggest hydroelectric power generator, can be cited as the best example. India cannot even think of it in its most sound dreams. It is only because of an ironic complaint – "too much democracy." The new rail lines, hydroelectric power systems, road expansion, airport building projects, car factories, and thermal power projects are, no doubt, set up for national development. All these serve the interests of all the people of India. Despite that, vehement protests, long shouting processions, strikes, demonstrations, sit-ins, shutdowns, and violence are common scenes in India. All these have been barring the Indian infrastructure-building initiative. That is why all major entrepreneurs, industries, and institutions are compelled to remain satisfied with the infrastructure and the facilities they receive. The government also gets dejected by the unreasonable protests and violent movements. Therefore, many infrastructural development projects are postponed in the half-way. And for lacking good and smooth infrastructure foreign direct investment gets stuck. As a result, the growth and development of India is hampered. Hence, the governments - State and Union – must adopt a humanistic approach regarding rehabilitation and reasonable compensation for the evicted people, and on the other hand, suppress any unethical, anti-developmental, and narrow politically-aimed movements. It is really a challenge for the Government in India to earn more revenue and increase its GDP. However, the Indian government is committed to changing all of this. The government has already given priority to infrastructure building and strengthening national income. It is a welcome step for the government.

Finally, I would like to conclude this part with the suggestions of Michael Mandelbaum, a Professor of American Foreign Policy at The Johns Hopkins School of Advanced International Studies. He asserted in 2014 in the World Economic Forum that, "Now, however, the new government must try to match the superior economic progress that China has achieved over the last three decades. To do so, it will have to foster, in a different political context, two key ingredients of China's economic success. The first ingredient is a robust industrial sector composed of manufacturing industries that use unskilled labor, which would offer a route out of poverty for India's hundreds of millions of rural laborers and their families. It is the route that China, and other countries before it, has taken. In India, by contrast, the underdevelopment of the industrial sector has kept the country from realizing its full economic potential. The second ingredient is the infrastructure that all economic growth requires: roads, bridges, ports, and schools, as well as reliable supplies of electricity and clean water. Poor infrastructure hinders the growth of the industry in India. Factories need reliable supplies of power to operate effectively, good roads and railways to source inputs and distribute products, and, if they are to export those products, ports for cargo ships and airports for high-value items and business travel. China has these things in abundance. India does not" (Mandelbaum, World Economic Forum, 21 May, 2014).

Lessons from the USA

Today the U.S.A. is the most prosperous country in the world. It is the oldest democracy too, and the country's military and economy are the strongest in the world. But now the question is how and why the USA is always so rich. In this regard, a very interesting article was written by David Brooks in *The New York Times Magazine* (9 June, 2002). It is important for both Indian people and policy makers. He wrote that "No nation on earth has ever tried as hard, and failed as utterly, in its efforts not to become rich as America has." He further said, "We're big earners. We're big spenders. We're huge borrowers. Risking sin and perdition, we're rich...American standards of living actually surpassed European standards of living around 1740... American workers are still the most productive on earth, two-thirds more productive than our counterparts in Great Britain, for example, American technology is still the envy of the world, and her universities are the queens of learning...America is now the undisputed great power of the globe...They spent less on entertainment and more on education, housing, transportation, and computers...We can't take a vacation for a week without bringing our laptops along, let alone laze away at health spas for weeks on end slicing sausages, the way the Germans do...Despite leadership from the top, we haven't really learned to relax about adultery, and serious sex surveys do not depict a nation of serious kinkiness and sensuality...The abundance mentality starts with the unconscious premise that there exists, at all times, close by, a happy hunting ground, a valley where acres of diamonds are there for the picking. In the land of abundance, work is worth it, because it is often rewarded. In the land of abundance, a person's lower-class status is always temporary. If the complete idiot next door has managed to pull himself up to the realm of Lexus drivers, why shouldn't the same thing happen to you?...the most obvious feature of the land of abundance is that people work feverishly hard and cram their lives insanely full. That's because the candies are all around, looking up and pleading to you, "Taste me, taste me, taste me." People in this realm live in a perpetual aspirational trance. They are bombarded from first waking to nighttime's last thought by images, messages, novelties, improvements, and tales of wonder... In this way, abundance electrifies and motivates. Life becomes a vectorial thrust toward perpetual gain and aspirational fulfillment."

Further, Martin S. Feldstein, the George F. Baker Professor of Economics at Harvard University and President Emeritus of the National Bureau of Economics Research, wrote in the *Harvard Business Review* that, "Each year, the United States produces more per person than most other advanced economies" (Feldstein, Harvard Business Review, 2017). Further, he raised a question and answered the same himself. He questioned why the US remains richer than its peers. And thereafter points out 10 features that distinguish America from other industrial economies. He enumerated: "**An entrepreneurial culture:** Individuals in the U.S. demonstrate a desire to start businesses and grow them, as well as a willingness to take risks. There is less penalty in U.S. culture for failing and starting again. Even students who have gone to college or a business school show this entrepreneurial desire, and it is self-reinforcing: Silicon Valley successes like Facebook inspire further entrepreneurship. **A Financial system that supports entrepreneurship:** The U.S. has a more developed system of equity finance than the countries of Europe, including angel investors willing to finance startups and a very active venture capital market that helps finance the growth of those firms... **World-class research universities:** U.S. universities produce much of the basic research that drives high-tech entrepreneurship. Faculty members and doctoral graduates often spend time with nearby startups, and the culture of both the universities and the businesses encourages this overlap. Top research universities attract talented students from around the world... **Labor markets that generally link workers and jobs unimpeded by large trade unions, state-owned enterprises, or excessively restrictive labor regulations:** Less than 7% of the private sector U.S. labor force is unionized, and there are virtually no state-owned enterprises. While the U.S. does regulate working conditions and hiring, the rules are much less onerous than in Europe... **A growing population, including from immigration:** America's growing population means a younger and therefore more flexible and trainable workforce. Although there are restrictions on immigration to the United States, there are also special rules that provide access to the U.S. economy and a path to citizenship (green cards), based on individual talent and industrial sponsorship... **A culture (and a tax system) that encourages hard work and long hours:** The average employee in the United States works 1,800 hours per year, subsequently more than the 1,500 hours worked in France and the 1,400 hours worked in Germany (though not as much as the 2,200+ in Hong Kong, Singapore, and South Korea). In general, working longer means producing more, which means higher real incomes...**A supply of energy that makes North America energy independent:** Natural gas fracking in particular has provided U.S. businesses with plentiful and relatively inexpensive energy. **A favorable regulatory environment:** Although U.S. regulations are far more perfect, they are less burdensome on businesses than the regulations imposed by European countries and the European Union. **A smaller size of government than in other industrial countries:** According to the OECD, outlays of the U.S. government at the federal, state, and local levels totaled 38% of GDP, while the corresponding figure was 44% in Germany, 51% in Italy, and 57% in France. The higher level of government spending in other countries implies not only a higher share of income taken in taxes but also higher transfer payments that reduce incentives to work. It's no surprise that Americans work a lot: they have extra incentive to do so. **A decentralized political system in which states compete:** Competition among states encourages entrepreneurship and work, and states compete for business and individual residents with their legal rules and tax regimes. Some states have no income taxes and have labor laws that limit unionization" (Feldstein, Harvard Business Review, 2017).

America is a land of abundance, and it is a land of hard-working and self-motivating people. The people are rich and the country is prosperous because the Americans do not waste time idly and in adultery. In a word, they are mostly workaholics, i.e. *karma yogis*. The country assists entrepreneurs and gives incentives for the work they do. The universities are the queens of research and innovation.

The states compete with one another to grow and excel in others. It is healthy competition. They work for longer hours than most of the other countries in the world. There is little problem of Marxist-Leninist trade unionism such as in India. Now let us turn our eyes to their achievement in the Olympics and Nobel Prize. America is not only rich in economy and defense; it is also the recipient of the highest gold medals in the Olympics and a producer of Nobel Prize winners. In the 2021 Olympics, "Team USA led for the most overall medals, having secured 113 medals. China followed with 88 overall medals" (Carlisle, Time, 8 August, 2021). Also, the USA has been dominating the Nobel Prize-winning race since its inception in 1901. In 2021, out of a total of 13 Nobel Prize winners, eight were American citizens, The Deccan Herald reported (October 12, 2021). From 2001 up to 2021, the USA racked up 400 medals, followed by the United Kingdom with 138 and Germany with 111. What is India's position? India won only a total of 7 medals including one gold in the 2021 Olympics, and so far India won 12 Nobel prizes with 5 Indian citizens and 7 recipients with Indian ancestry or residency. On the other hand, how does America perform such stupendously? If you explore the American Universities and research facilities, you will find that in the USA there are ample opportunities as Ardem Patapoutian, the co-winner of the 2021 Nobel Medicine prize said at a press conference after his win, "I'm really appreciative of the opportunities that have been given to me in his country" (Deccan Herald reported, October 12, 2021). It is learned that behind American Nobel Prize success there are 'public-funded Universities;' one researcher has ample freedom 'to go where his curiosity led him;' 'American emphasis on basic research'; and 'The US has built a phenomenal culture of welcoming'. Also, philanthropy and private endowments play an ever-growing role in financing universities and research institutions. India has more than fifty thousand higher education institutions with approximately one thousand good universities. But only three universities – Indian Institute of Science (IISC), Bengaluru; Indian Institute of Technology (IIT), Bombay; and IIT Delhi ranked in the top 200 positions in the latest QS World University Rankings of 2022. This is the pathetic picture of India's higher educational institutions. India's failure can be traced to the fact that it does lowly embrace people affiliated with multiple countries. Moreover, in Indian Universities public funding is scanty; private funding is nil; there is no welcoming attitude or indifferent attitude of Indian political masters as well as academic *gurus* toward serious scholars from both India and abroad; except in a few institutions and universities, research culture is very poor; research infrastructure is nominal; often the quality of professors is not up to the mark; gender bias and caste bias are clearly noticeable.

Indian universities and particularly research institutions need more public funding like the USA. Academic freedom can be given to researchers and professors to go where their curiosity leads them, which is another key to success. Peace and space study should be encouraged. More people from out of the University campus should be allowed and encouraged to do research with government financial assistance. Funding for basic research, defined as a study to improve scientific theories or understanding of subjects, is at the heart of America's wins, considers David Baltimore, co-winner of the 1975 Nobel Prize in medicine. Without strong fundamental research institutions, India cannot compete with its rival countries in the field of Nobel Prizes such as the USA, the United Kingdom, and Germany. Philanthropy and private endowments also play an ever-growing role in financing in the USA, which is very much lacking in India. Recently (Pawar, Science, 23 August, 2023), India's Parliament has approved Anusandhan (Innovation) National Research Foundation, which aims to inject only $6 billion into basic and applied research over the next 5 years. India has created this independent funding agency on the model of the U.S. National Science Foundation. This is a very small amount of research in the field of science and technology. A comparative analysis of the top 10 countries reveals that India's R&D spending is the 7th highest globally. The USA tops the list with $679.4 billion, China holds the second position with $551.1 billion, and the third rank is occupied by Japan with $182.2 billion. Germany ($143.1 billion), South Korea ($106.1 billion) and France ($68.5 billion) are ahead of India ($65.2 billion). But in terms of share of GDP India's condition is very poor. Israel with 4.8% spends the highest percentage of GDP on research and development; South Korea spends 4.5%; Switzerland spends

3.7%; Germany and Sweden both spend 3.31% of their GDP; but India spends only 0.65% of their GDP on research and development (Murty, Businessline, 15 Aug. 2023). On the other hand, according to America's research and development statement "Science, technology, research, experimentation, and innovation have been critical to America's long-standing as a global leader, to our economic strength and shared prosperity because they allow us to expand what is possible and to solve seemingly intractable problems" (Research and Development, White House, 13 March, 2023, p. 51). So, the picture is clear before us. India needs more budgetary allocation in research and development to become a global leader. Kiran Majumder Shaw, the executive chairperson of Biocon & Biocon Biologics also considers that "If India is to deliver on its aspiration of becoming a $10 trillion economy by 2023, we will need to pursue value-added growth. And research and innovation are fundamental to driving this kind of value-added growth. Fostering a robust research ecosystem can boost India's intellectual capital, thereby driving the kind of innovation that helps improve the lives of ordinary Indians and creates lasting global impact...India will need to raise GERD to the long-promised level of 2% of GDP if it wants to consolidate on the gains made so far in Science and Technology" (Shaw, The Times of India, 18 Jan, 2023).

India must give it serious thought. Indian universities must attract top talents of the world through scholarship, freedom of research, and international standard facilities. Another important message for the Indian government is that a scientist must be provided with job opportunities not only in academics, but also in industry, government labs, and other institutions according to his choice. What else India can do? India can build a phenomenal culture of welcoming like that of the USA. There must not be any trend of hate, or xenophobia in nationalism, in research institutions, and workplaces. With these rewards and opportunities, young and bright researchers could be attracted to India. Scientists and researchers have a great role in transforming India. Zero level of tolerance for corruption and manipulation in higher education; rigorous competition in admission and administration etc. can prove magic for India. Hard-working mentality; zero copy-paste tolerance; and zero tolerance for anti-national activities are some lessons that can be learned from the USA. Military power, economic power, intelligence power, and soft power of India have to be developed at the fastest speed. For all these, industrialists should work together with the government in harmony. The government alone can't do all these works;

let the industrialists and multinational companies come forward to achieve India's big target of a superpower.

Regarding corporate responsibilities Livia Gershon in an article (Justor Daily, Nov. 2, 2016) wrote that "In the 1980s, the first public relations professionals began advising wealthy on how to use philanthropy to placate the public. Many Gilded Age industrialists, like John D. Rockerfeller and Andrew Carnegie, donated money to support cultural institutions and scientific advancement. Hammer suggests that these men were motivated not just by public relations concerns but also by their own moral codes." The American industrialists also donate to churches and other social causes. It is not that Indian companies, Industrialists, film actors/actresses, individuals, and non-government organizations are not donating anything. During the COVID-19 pandemic, Tata Group had pledged to donate Rs. 1500 crores; Adani Foundation humbly contributed Rs. 100 crores to the PM Cares fund. Even Reliance Industries opened a hospital for coronavirus treatment in Mumbai. Similarly many individuals like Sonu Sood, Salman Khan, Amir Khan, and others have donated as per their capacity. Many chief ministers and non-profit organizations have also donated to the government to fight against the pandemic. In India, about 90 percent of companies are spending 2 percent of their net profit on corporate social responsibilities. It is a good sign. But India is a very big country and the numbers of illiterate, poor, and unhealthy people are about 300 million in India. It can never be possible for the government alone to send all the children to the classrooms of government schools. Similarly, all people cannot be treated freely to the government hospitals; and poverty cannot be removed by the government and philanthropic organizations alone. Indian temples are very rich. Some Indian industrialists are also very rich. The newly added billionaires in India must spend at least 3 percent of their income on building school rooms, and rich industrialists must set up more hospitals in rural areas. Either by selling or by mortgaging the gold and jewelry of the temples, the management committee of the temples should set up only school buildings and hospitals. What is the use of gold? Let us serve people - the poor, unhealthy, and unprivileged - to serve God. Give them nutritious food, teach the poor children, and serve the poor, rural, and unwell people. God will be satisfied. When God will be happy, you will also be happy and immortal. So, please start doing good work and service to mankind from tomorrow, nay from today itself. Japan is another country wherefrom we can learn a lot of things. Let us read the following part on Japan.

Lessons from Japan

When I am talking about the mantras for India's gigantic growth and development, it remains incomplete if I do not take the example of Japan, a small island country located in the northwest Pacific Ocean. How a country after major destruction in the Second World War survived is a story of inspiration for others striving to achieve success and prosperity. "The transformation of Nazi Germany and imperial Japan into peaceful, prosperous, vibrant democracies remains to this day the gold standard of nation-building" (Dobbins, Poole et. al. No. date, p. 11). The country lost millions of lives and faced the devastation of major capital stock. The story of Hiroshima and Nagasaki is well known to students all over the world. How was it? "On August 6, 1945, during World War II (1939-45) an American B-29 bomber dropped the world's first deployed atomic bomb over the Japanese city of Hiroshima. The explosion immediately killed an estimated 80,000 people; tens of thousands more would later die of radiation exposure. Three days later, a second B-29 dropped another A-bomb on Nagasaki, killing an estimated 40,000 people. Japan's Emperor Hirohito announced his country's unconditional surrender in World War II in a radio address on August 15, citing the devastating power of "a new and most cruel bomb" (History.com editors, 18 April, 2023). Japan was almost ruined and crippled in the Second World War. "World War II destroyed Japan's economy, killing millions of its people and destroying about 40 percent of its capital stock" (Powell, Japan, https://www.econlib.org/library/Enc/Japan.html#).

Despite that, the archipelago of 6852 islands defied its geographically odd position and foreign attacks, it became one of the world's most developed countries. After suffering defeat in the Pacific Ocean and two atomic bombs, Japan had to surrender to the Allied powers and remained under the Allied powers for seven years. Before that, the country had also suffered from various ups and downs. However, since 1947 when Japan adopted a new Constitution, it started to support a unitary parliamentary constitutional monarchy with a bicameral legislature, the National Diet. The Allied forces almost destroyed Japan, but they could not destroy their spirit and hard-working mentality. Today Japan is the world's third-largest economy with nominal GDP and the fourth-largest by the PPP (Purchasing Power Parity). It is a global leader in the automotive and electronics industries. Its science and technology are envious of the world's other big economies like that of the USA, UK, Germany, China, France, etc. It is ranked "very high" on the Human Development Index, and interestingly the country's people live the longest years on earth. Moreover, its culture is well-known to the world. The sober demeanor, and bowing down head before seniors and others are known even to a school student across the world. This is today's Japan what we see before our eyes.

Japan has many similarities with the Indian political system; the only difference is that it has a constitutional monarchy. Like our President, the Emperor of Japan also enjoys ceremonial powers only, but the real power or executive power is vested with the Prime Minister and his cabinet, whose sovereignty is ultimately vested in the Japanese people. India is also having the same system. In Japan, the Opposition Parties try to win concessions from the ruling party by refusing to participate in legislative proceedings or using other delaying tactics. This approach takes advantage of the shortness of Diet sessions and the tendency of the media to criticize the ruling party if it railroads a bill through the legislature. Benjamin Powell wrote about the rise and fall of the Japanese economic growth story from the middle of the last century. But our concern is how Japan grew so fast and so smartly after losing millions of people and about 40 percent of its stock capital. What are the factors that contributed to Japan's rapid economic growth? Let us examine the factors, which might be helpful for India to learn.

Is it the case of low levels of privilege-seeking of its people that helped them to grow faster? Unlike India, the Japanese people, and its special interest groups do not seek special privileges from the government. When a privileged group seeks special benefits from a government, it causes losses to society to a large extent. The level of the interest group's gains is much lesser than that of the overall losses to society whereas the economic growth rate of the government also turns low. With the demand for special privileges by the interest groups, the economic growth of a country gets slowed. Hence, we learned that we must not seek any special privileges from the government and our institutions, where we are working, except for a very emergency need. We have to grow such mental makeup. Our students must be inculcated this lesson from their schools and childhood days. India will surely be a superpower with the selfless works of millions of today's students, who will be turned into tomorrow's adult citizens. A country becomes great only when its citizens become toilsome, patriotic, spiritual, inquisitive, and great.

India must pay more attention to the savings of its people so that the country can fund its investments through domestic savings. Besides, the habit of small savings is good for families too. It comes into use in times of crisis. All families must save a certain amount of money according to capacity every month from their earnings. This will help them in meeting the needs of their children's education, family health issues, and other challenges. The Japanese government encouraged its citizens the habit of savings by not taking away the incentive to save. The economic policy of India is required to be modified a little by paying interest to its citizens on their savings. Savings bank account interest rates in different banks are very low at present and this must be hiked to encourage saving habits to citizens. This habit of savings should be encouraged at the school level. The government may initiate an increasing rate of interest and decrease the period of maturity of its various schemes such as the National Savings Certificate, Kisan Vikas Patra, etc.

Japan quickly embarked on recovering its economy and national wealth. "During the following decades and long into the twentieth century, Japan underwent a torturous modernization process. Industrialization and urbanization swept through the country. Large multi-faceted corporations came into existence, many supported by modernizers in the Japanese government who looked to Germany and the United States as exemplars of commercial and manufacturing economies. Liberals in Japan were impressed by British parliamentary democracy and the social reforms of the Victorian and Edwardian years, and pushed for Japan to become more democratic, less hide-bound by religious and patriarchal traditions." This helped them to recover and turn into a modern democracy" (Clapson, M. 2019, pp. 97-98). Also, "Japan funded its investment and capital accumulation through high rates of domestic savings. As a result, gross private savings rose from 16.5 percent of GNP between 1952 and 1954 to 31.9 percent in 1970 and 1971. Average domestic savings from 1960 through 1971 averaged 36.1 percent of national income. The United States, by comparison, averaged only 15.8 percent from 1961 to 1971. The Japanese government encouraged saving. The tax code allowed for a portion of savings to earn interest income tax-free in an employer-run savings plan. In addition, interest on the first thirteen thousand dollars in each postal savings account was tax-free, and many people had multiple accounts" (Powell, Japan, https://www.econlib.org/ library/Enc/ Japan. html#). When people have more money, they will tend to invest, and businesses will have a greater incentive to exploit opportunities since they will reap the rewards. Like Japan, India must be the freest economy in the world. There should be special privileges for certain categories of industries that would bring more profit and increase the Indian Gross National Product. However, this prioritization must be based on good market research and without obstructing the interest of other industries. Manufacturing in automobile and electronic industries such as electric and solar bicycles, electric and solar cars, high-quality laptops, mobile phones, software, robots, drones, airplanes, ships, rockets, spare parts, etc. should be encouraged more by providing special incentives. Where are automobile companies like Nissan, Toyota, or Honda in India? Similarly, do we find any Indian companies like Sony and Funai Electronic Company (electronics, manufacturing, consumer goods, and manufacturing), Marubeni (metals and minerals, mining, metals, and mining), Mitsubishi Corporation (chemicals, petrochemicals, motor vehicle parts) or Elematec (personal computers, and peripherals, consumer electronics, and optical equipment)? Yes, we do have Reliance industries; Tata Consultancy Services, Infosys, Hindustan Unilever, etc., and our top manufacturing companies are Ashok Leyland, Hero Honda Motors, Maruti Suzuki Limited, Mahindra and Mahindra Limited, Larsen and Toubro Limited, Godrej, Dabur India, etc. India has much more scope for exploring manufacturing companies. Indian automobile scientists might form small groups and set up manufacturing companies. There is no dearth of talent and money, what we need is encouragement from the part of government, and all hassle-free facilities to set up industries and companies to cater job opportunities to the young graduates passing out from thousands of engineering colleges in India. The finance, industry, and environment ministries together should formulate policies for facilitating the startups, and not playing a distorting role in start-ups. After setting up industries by the entrepreneurs, there should be 'relatively low government interference and high economic freedom', so that they may assist the nation to grow more rapidly. Further, it can be added that "...low taxes and low levels of government intervention were the main policies driving that growth" (Powell, Japan, Econlib).

Japan made large warships and advanced airplanes about nine decades ago. But after its dreadful defeat in 1945 following the use of atom bombs by American President Truman, the Japanese decided to give up their militarism and focused mainly on their economic development. When they started making small cars, the Westerners laughed at them. But today the number one and number two best-selling four-door cars in the United States are Toyota and Honda. Have our Maruti and Nano been able to tap the Western markets in such a style as Japan did? If not, then please explore the possibilities and attune every credible avenue to surpass Toyota and Honda.

Japanese people love and respect their own culture and almost nobody speaks English in Japan. It does not mean that they are not modern. They attempt to improve themselves through their own culture and focusing on their internal positives. India, despite its multiculturalism and multi-religionism, should adopt and promote its own culture and heritage more holistically among the people, especially among the students, who are the future citizens of this country. Another very important factor is that both Japan and Korea turned away from hating their respective neighbors and their minorities. Presently, large numbers of Koreans live in Tokyo and Osaka; and similarly, many Japanese people live in Seoul. It is necessary to highlight here that, Japan occupied Korea for many years till 1945, and even Japanese soldiers abused tens of thousands of Korean women during that period. Now both Korean and Japanese elites avoid English. Their nationalism has not focused on hating and harming their minorities. From Japan and Korea, India should learn a very good lesson that without equal participation of all communities, castes, and genders in national developmental programs, there can be no comprehensive and complete development. Secondly, by increasing enmity with Pakistan, we could not prosper properly. Pakistan should also change its outlook and stop all kinds of cross-border terrorism, violence, and tension. All religions are the same and respectful. Let us live happily together like our own brothers as we happened to live in the pre-independence period. Our religious minorities are our brothers and they should get equal and respectful treatment from both Union and all State Governments. What have Japan and Korea achieved in the last 30 years, can India not achieve likewise after 3-decades of economic liberalization? Let India and Pakistan be good friends, good partners, and good neighbors. I don't find any difference between my Pakistani brother and my own brother. We are the same. The only difference I find is in our language, food habits, and place of residence. Rest is equal. So, in place of enmity let there be mutual respect and cooperation with each other. Let us help each other, let us call each other 'Brother and Sister.'

The success story of Japan is not merely observed by Western people. "Observers from the world often fasten with wide-eyed enthusiasm on the mysterious workings of "Japan, Inc.," that fabled edifice of business-government cooperation" (Drucker, Harvard Business School, Jan 1981). Japan's continual flow of industrial miracles can be ascribed to its continuous application of single-minded energy. The dedication of people towards achieving success in business and trade is an asset of the country. Moreover, they have unity and this sense of unity comes not from above, rather it comes from within. In Japan, one could find harmonious industrial relations. Both Japanese and Western companies try to keep the same kind of equable labor relations except in the public sector, only where unions are strong, there is no sign of the fabled harmony.

Japanese People Take Competitiveness and National Interest Seriously

Japan's political parties have habits of good political behavior. They generally consider thoroughly a proposed policy's impact on the productivity of Japanese industry, on Japan's competitive strength in the world market, and on Japan's balance of payments and trade. How great are the policymakers and opposition leaders there! This has become almost second nature for Japanese policymakers in the ministries, in the Diet, and in business as well as for analysts and critics in the popular newspapers and economics departments in universities. The Harvard Business Review reports that this is the general tendency of every responsible political party in Japan, and they take it seriously. Indian policymakers should also develop such serious and national mental makeup. The opposition party leaders can take lessons from leaders of Japanese Opposition Parties.

Estimating the impact of various policy alternatives on Japan's competitive position in the world economy is only one of the habits of behavior expected of Japanese leaders. They are also expected to start with the question "What is good for the country?" rather than the question "What is good for us, our institution, our members, and our constituents?" (Drucker, Harvard Business School, Jan 1981). Let Indian statesmen and all political leaders learn this behavior and attitude from Japanese leaders.

Foundational Principle of Japanese Leadership

Interest groups in Japan are very strong and they have an endless array of economic federations, industry associations, professional societies, trade groups, special interest clubs, and guilds. They also try to influence the policymaking process, but every group must start in its deliberations by considering the national interest, not its own concerns. Indian leaders also often cite national interests, but those are mostly for their narrow political gain. Japan is still guided by Confucian tradition that believes self-sacrifice is natural. Therefore, "Each group is, however, expected to fit its self-interest into a framework of national needs, national goals, national aspirations, and national values" (Drucker, Harvard Business School, Jan 1981). How religiously do Japanese people follow a good principle? A substantial proportion of Japan's business leaders have for 100 years subscribed to the rule that the national interest comes first, a rule first formulated by the nineteenth-century entrepreneur, banker, and business philosopher Eiichi Shibusawa (1840-1931). On the other hand, Indian businessmen, entrepreneurs, and policymakers are mostly guided by the Western philosophy of the "self-interest first" approach. Further, in the Japanese model, both leaders and special interests derive their legitimacy from their stewardship of the national interest, which might better serve the unavoidable pluralism of modern industrial society.

Public Relations is Very Important in Japan

Irving Shapiro, chairman, and CEO of E.I. du Pont de Nemours, the world's largest chemical company, was widely quoted in the U.S. press in recent years for having pointed out that he now had to devote four-fifths of time to "relations" with policymakers in the Congress and the Washington bureaucracy, and could only spend one-fifth to manage his company. This is most surprising to the Japanese CEOs because very few CEOs of large Japanese companies have any time available to manage their companies. They spend most of their time building public relations with the employees, vendors, suppliers, trading company people, and managers of subsidiaries. "The top people spend their time sitting, sipping cups of green tea, listening, asking a few questions, then sitting some more, sipping more cups of green tea, listening and asking a few more questions" Drucker, Harvard Business School, Jan 1981). They even sit with top people working in other companies in their groups. They often sit with people from the banks, with senior bureaucrats from the various ministries, and with people from their own companies in after-hour parties in Ginza bars. They sit on half a dozen committees in half a dozen economic and industry federations. They sit and sit and sit. In these sittings and meetings, they do not, like their Western counterparts, have conversations pointlessly; rather Japanese top business leaders discuss with their employees on different issues – it ranges from issues of economic policy to personal concerns, from the other fellow's questions and problems to the topics of the day, from expectations for the future to reappraisals of the past. Through these, they try to solve anything but to establish mutual understanding.

Japanese People Follow Mutuality of Interest and Love for Peace

The Japanese people have developed very good habits. "The last of these habits of Japanese economic behavior is to base human interactions not solely on adversarial relations but also on common interest and mutual trust" (Drucker, Harvard Business School, Jan 1981). Japanese people make sure that their relationships have at their core a mutuality of interest. Then, whatever conflict or disagreement exists can be subsumed in the positive bond of broadly shared concerns. Great care is taken by all the people and parties so that there is no damage done to the common interest. Another very interesting lesson we can learn from Japan is that there is no final victory over the individuals or groups with whom one has to live and work. The Japanese people believe and abide by the maxim that, to win such a war is to lose peace. Though these are mostly followed by the majority of top business leaders, it is not fully abided by some most successful entrepreneurs and companies such as Honda, Matsushita, Panasonic, or Sony. Modern industry demands time for up-gradation of skills, maintaining relations with government departments, looking after marketing, finance & sales, and supervising plants and works regularly.

Japanese Industrial Policy

Government policy facilitates fostering the economic growth of any country. "In the second half of the twentieth century, Japan experienced unprecedented economic growth, with gross domestic product (GDP) rising from $44 billion in 1960 to $5.45 trillion in 1995, a 123-fold increase" (Gerstel & Goodman, 2020, p. 5). This miracle has happened only for the direct state intervention in the private markets to direct resources to targeted sectors. How was the policy of the Government of Japan? Japanese economist Masahiro Okuno-Fujiwara and U.S. economist Laura D'Andrea Tyson identified three phases of Japanese industrial policy to describe the unprecedented growth, which may be briefly mentioned hereunder.

1. "1945-1960: postwar reconstruction, when officials directly regulated private sector activity through price controls, rations, and priority production for coal and steel;

2. 1960-1973: support for strategic industries through "hard" measures like tax advantages, subsidies, preferential financing, and trade protection; and

3. 1973-1990: support for strategic industries through "soft" measures including administrative guidance, state-facilitated industry research coordination associations, and structural adjustment assistance for supply and foreign exchange shocks" (Gerstel & Goodman, 2020, p. 5).

Behind Japan's amazing economic growth, the policymakers of Japan played a significant role. "Throughout the postwar period, Tokyo engaged in both strategic and corrective industrial policy to promote the development of targeted sectors and fix market failures, respectively. Japanese officials often targeted industries associated with future productivity growth, such as semiconductors and supercomputers, although they also selected industries to boost employment or based on political motivations" (Gerstel & Goodman, 2020, p. 5). Japan's Ministry of International Trade and Industry (MITI) also adopted a system of deliberation councils, or *shingikai* to direct support to favored industries. Indian Ministry of Commerce and Industry should also need all kinds of support to develop industries. The recently started initiative by the government of India, and particularly the Prime Minister to foster business dynamism and strong entrepreneurial spirits is a positive step. But the officials and political leaders of all parties need all types of cooperation and support in case of trade and business growth and national development. "To further spur development, the Japanese state organized temporary joint research projects and inter-firm coordination, most notably through the Very Large Scale Integration (VLSI) Technology Research Association" (Gerstel & Goodman, 2020, p. 8).

Japanese Art and Culture

Japanese camera is famous in the world. They are fond of art. "In 1851, Westerners had known little about the floating kingdom. Since the early 17th century, Japan had been completely isolated from the West, save for a few Dutch traders who conducted business around Nagasaki. Then, in 1853, the American commodore Matthew Perry forced Japan to trade with the West under threat of naval bombardment. Kinonos, fans, and especially woodblock prints by the great Japanese artists flooded European markets...The "Japanese effect" was most prominent in art. As Japanese art entered European salons, French artists were beginning to experiment with Impressionism. Painters like Monet, reaching in part to the industrialization of Europe and the rise of photography, were interested in capturing how light interacted with a certain object at a given moment in time. In Japanese woodblock prints, they found the simplicity and the ethereal quality that they strove to create in their art" (Abou-Jaoude, The History Teacher, 2016, p. 57). Harold W. Stevenson (Sept., 1991, p. 109) considers that "The Japanese population has become one of the most highly educated of any country in the world. Illiteracy has been almost completely eliminated, and Japanese students consistently are among the top performers in cross-national studies of academic achievement."

Japan gives too much importance to family bonding and values education. Value education starts from school in Japan. It comes to light from the work of Gail R. Benjamin (1997, p. 203) that students in Japan "... think about their own society, education is seen as the key to personal and family success. No Japanese parents or teachers seem to question the idea that education is crucial for each individual." Further, "The term *kizuna* was originally used to describe various types of intimate and personal bonds involving people and places, such as the love for one's family or hometown, rather than public relationships....kizuna has also been used to sentimentalize and standardize positive and heart-warming bonds or relationships between Japanese people today - an attitude that may be summed up simply as 'caring for others and working together, which is almost synonymous with Nihonjinron keywords such as 'group-oriented and 'community'. This broadened conceptualization is especially useful for the Japanese authorities, who wish to unite Japanese people in the effort to reconstruct the nation" (Mihik, 2020, p.14). The Japanese government encourages and propagates the term kizuna through media and national discourse. The Japanese people have a sense of ownership of their country. They feel "Japan as (Still) Number One", and 'Japan as one team'. Indian people should also have a similar feeling and sense of ownership of the motherland. "All the Indian people including students and youths should work hard for the growth and development of India, live happily for India, praise India, and speak at least a few good words or write a few lines praising India because India is our mother, she is our protector, she is our caregiver, she is our educator, she is our nurse, she is our feeder, she is our healer, she is our all" (Face book post https://www.facebook.com/profile.php?id=100086835397863, dated 09.11.2023).

Lessons from Germany

At present Germany is a member of the European Union. From 1949 to 1990 there were two Germanys - the German Democratic Republic and the Federal Republic of Germany. "East and West Germany existed well before World War II...East and West Germany were differentially affected by the war and by the dismantling of infrastructure and reparations to the occupying forces in the immediate after-war period...roughly one-fifth of the East German population moved to West Germany between 1945 and the building of the Berlin Wall in 1961" (Becker, Mergele, and Woessmann, 2020, Journal of Economic Perspectives, p.144). After that, both the countries have merged into a single Germany. This country is now the fourth-largest economy in the world. "Germany is the EU's center of gravity - its most influential country" (Puglierin & Franke, 2020, p. 4).

Why Germany is so rich has been beautifully highlighted by David S. Landes, a Harvard Professor of the Department of Economics in a journal article in *The American Economic Review*, where he began his writing by asking why they are rich and others are so poor. Landes continues "One says that we are so rich and they so poor because we are so good and they are so bad; that is, we are hardworking, knowledgeable, educated, well-governed, efficacious, and productive, and they are the reverse. The other says that we are so rich and they are so poor because we are so bad and they are so good: we are greedy, ruthless, exploitative, aggressive, while they are weak, innocent, virtuous, abused, and vulnerable" (Landes, 1990, p. 1). The answer lies within the above remarks of Landes. The German people are rich only because of their hard-working mentality, knowledge, education, discipline, skill, and productivity. I also crave for these qualities to be developed and cultivated by our youths and students. At the same time, we have to be selfless, greedless, and virtuous. We must be patriots, disciplined, hard-working, sincere, ethical, honest, and competitive.

As a result of Germany's hardworking mentality and discipline, they have been able to develop their economy and industry. These have paved the way for their living standards. According to OECD Report (February, 2014, pp. 2-3), "The German economy has performed exceedingly well given the context. GDP per capita has risen above the pre-crisis level and has converged to that of the best-performing OECD countries. Unemployment is lower now than before the crisis, having fallen from 11.3% in 2005 to 5.3 in July 2013, well below the OECD average of 8%. Falling unemployment helped eliminate government deficits by reducing social spending needs and raising tax revenues. This improvement in public finance was supported by the introduction of a "debt brake" rule adopted in 2009. This has in turn helped maintain financial market confidence. Advances in German living standards have been sustained and impressive." Further, according to the OECD well-being framework, "German households enjoy a relatively high level of economic welfare. Germany performs above the OECD average in jobs, earnings, wealth, and housing. Moreover, non-monetary measures of quality of life are high by OECD standards, notably concerning environmental quality and personal security - two areas where Germany is among the top performers" (OECD Report February 2014, p. 3).

What Can India Learn from Israel?

Israel, comparatively new and very small, is one of the top technologically developed countries in the world. Since the beginning, India has had a very good relationship with Israel. The founder of Israel, Ben-Gurion had great respect for our "Father of Nation" Mahatma Gandhi. Despite that, our diplomatic relationship is only three decades old, though the Jewish nation was established just one year after ours. However, India and Israel are always natural allies. In 2009 the country became India's largest defense supplier. "In the past decade alone Israeli defense sales to India were more than $10 billion and the exports are expected to grow faster in the coming days... Nobody can beat Israelis in peddling weaponry." The price for cutting-edge technology is also very competitive (Ullekh, The Economic Times, 24 September, 2012). Indian scientists and entrepreneurs must learn how to be more diligent and smarter in peddling weaponry. Their cutting-edge technology is world-famous now. Israel's secret technology is so strong that it can detect secret tunnels across the border with our neighboring country. This is called smart technology. Why India cannot manufacture such technological devices? What holds India back? Are our scientists not so sound, innovative, and skilled? Or, are our industries or defense research centers not interested in innovation? Or, is there a crunch of funds in research and development? How our neighboring countries are trying to dig tunnels even to supply arms and terrorists through the tunnels? It is a matter of concern. India must learn from friendly countries to deter the evil attempts of our non-friendly countries.

Further, through bilateral agreements and academic collaborations India can learn from Israel about how to manage water and health, bring innovation in technological research, improve medical machines, and build modern communication models, and electronic equipment. Also, India has the opportunity to learn smart manufacturing by utilizing artificial intelligence, big data science, machine learning, 3D printing, 5G communication, the Internet of things, drones cloud computing, etc. It is not that India is not exploring the opportunities for technological and research collaborations; many Indian big industries have already signed MoUs (Memorandum of Understandings) with Israeli companies. But what I want to say is that India must learn from them in different sectors, and try to improve that indigenously, and use the same for the advancement of our country. After that, India should supply the indigenously made technology to the least developed countries, and earn a lot of dollars. Indian technological institutions and universities may give some special scholarships to students who wish to study in Israel. In addition to this, Indian students must give a bond to the sponsoring institution regarding coming back and working in India for Indian farms. Another thing can also be done. Indian Universities can sign more MoUs with Israeli companies and their Universities for student exchange programs at the Master's Degree level or they may conduct joint research projects. Cultural exchange programs between various academic institutions of both countries can be started more seriously for India's development. All academic and business ties must aim at a definite goal- the goal of national growth and development. Skill development programs for Indian youths can be intensified through alliances and partnerships with Israeli industries and institutions.

It is not yet a mystery that Israel has greatly encouraged and welcomed start-ups in their country. Like India's startup state of Bangaluru, Israel selected Silicon Wadi to symbolize the location of its tech business hub. But that is not the question. The moot question is what drove that region to become a software-centric startup nation of young companies, and why Israel has shown its mettle in the tech market. The existing literature suggests that it is their "...local mindset, mentality and morals – after all, the country is well accustomed to fighting for its place. The wider answer is the combination of resources (largely human, not natural ones), higher education, the widespread use of English, and the steadfast grasp of the nettle attitude that typifies the local culture" (Adrian, 2020, February 21). How Israel Became A Technology Start-Up Nation. *Forbes.*). Moreover, Jon Medved, CEO of OurCrowd, a Jerusalem-based global venture investment platform organization, points out, "We don't have huge natural resources, so we have worked hard to develop our skills base in the country. I don't want to overplay the Jewish rhetoric, but there is a certain mentality that leans towards risk acceptance here... and people develop that from a young age. In my view, great achievements (in life- and in technology) are made by taking lots of risks, but in a calculated way with a diversified approach to everything" (Adrian, 2020, February 21). Can the Indian Ministry of Electronics and Information Technology take similar measures to develop startup companies like the OurCrown umbrella that develop technology software applications that focus on everything from AI-enabled smart driving sensors to MedTech, Health Tech, and SportsTech innovators?

It is a fact that Israel has a longstanding tradition of turning their curses into blessings. During the Israel and Palestine recent war, many young military officers are found to do their duties. How does it happen? How do the Government train them, and how do the young people learn the art of warfare at that young age? And, how they turn their odds into opportunities can be found in the worlds of Dr. Applebaum, the chief scientist of the Israeli Innovation Society. He considers that "The mindset of military service excellence is instilled in every citizen from childhood. You (as an individual) know that you will be stretched to the extreme limits of your abilities...a good deal of that drive has to stay with people throughout adolescence and as they enter the workforce. The army teaches you teamwork and the skills to make life and death decisions" (Adrian, 2020, February 21).

Let us now learn how Israel became a technologically developed country. Liran Grinberg, Partner and Co-founder of Team8 Company feels that "Much has already been made of Israel's high-tech industry stemming from graduates that have completed drafts in the country's elite military intelligence units such as the Unit 8200 Intelligence division. While most Western software developers may not feel like they have too many parallels with the armed forces in any part of the world, there are actually a lot of shared skills" (Adrian, 2020, February 21).

What Indian Government-sponsored Schools cannot imagine is being practiced in Israel, which fosters their technological growth and innovation in science and technology. We come to learn from an article published by Forbes. It indicates that: "There are fairly advanced computing studies as early as middle school (aged 12-14), through to college matriculation (entering university). That is why Israel has become a 'startup nation.'

Both Israel and India became sovereign countries almost simultaneously. In the last seven decades, Israel's standard of living has risen from 30 percent of the USA's standard of living at the time of its foundation to 60 percent in the year 2018. This is a great achievement. We need to know how they achieved this success so that we can learn and apply the same strategy to become a Viksit Bharat, i.e. a developed nation by 2047. The Times of Israel highlights that "A lack of natural resources pushed its dwellers to find alternative ways to cope, leading to the development of drip irrigation and water desalination plants – technologies that are now sold globally. The wars the country has fought have led the nation's military to develop cutting-edge technologies that have also permeated the civilian sphere, creating the basis of Israel's thriving tech scene" (Solomon, 2018, April 18). In the 1950s Israel's economy grew by about 13% each year, and in the subsequent years into the 1960s it grew by 10 percent. Similarly, the Indian government will have increased its GDP at least by 10 percent per annum by 2047. In Israel, the rate of unemployment is almost nil. The government provides jobs and sets up infrastructure projects using money from overseas, mainly from Jews living across the world, which helps Israel build and develop roads, ports, and trains. But inflation and other problems seized Israel from the 1970s to the 1980s. However, it recovered its economy and came out of hyperinflation hit in the 1990s through the formulation of better fiscal policies by Shimon Peres, the Finance Minister, in association with the US Secretary of State George Shultz and IMF economist Stanley Fischer. They devised a program that took some stringent measures to reduce public debt, curb government spending, and start a spurt of privatization of government-owned companies. They also liberated their economy opened Israeli markets to imports and lifted curbs on the currency. These measures produced fruits. The program froze prices and wages and thus stopped inflation. Thereafter, in 1990, the country introduced a program named "Yozma, which helped creat a local venture fund industry that invested in burgeoning Israeli technologies." The internet boom broke all the geographical barriers and entrepreneurship in Israel started to grow. Israel is a small country and it has no local market. Despite that, the country revolutionized in technology sector and became a developed tech nation.

Today Israel has the highest number of start-ups of any country in the world. Israel attracts investment from all the countries in the world. As a result in 2017, "There were 365 active foreign R&D centers operating in Israel, including giants like Google Inc., Facebook, Intel Corp, and Apple. Intel's massive $15.3 billion acquisition of Mobileye, a Jerusalem-based developer of advanced vision and driver assistance systems, in March 2016 is a testament to the mark Israeli technologies have made globally" (Solomon, 2018, April 18). From 1950s rationing to modern high-tech boom: Israel's economic success story, The Times of Israel). Behind Israel's present growth story, its strong fiscal policy has a great role. "The Israeli governments have been managing a responsible fiscal policy – staying within the budget and lowering government deficit, without breaking out of the set framework" (Solomon, 2018, April 18). Education plays a major role in shaping the Israeli economy, science and technology, and entrepreneurship. Students are taught seriously science and maths in Schools. Israel has always been improving its educational achievements in international examinations and tests. It was revealed from the report of Nachum Blass, the Principal Researcher and Education Policy Program Chair (Blass, 2018) that "Israel's improvement on international exams has been larger than the average improvement in all countries, and larger than the average improvement of countries that participated in the first and last tests examines in the study. In fact, Israel was one of the top three countries in terms of improving test scores for the PIRLS and IMMSS tests evaluated in the study and ranked first in reducing gaps on the PIRLS test and the PISA test in math and sciences."

From the above discussion, we learned thatIsrael is a very small country with only nine million populations, which is smaller than New Jersey in the USA and even less populous than the Indian city of Kolkata. The Biblical Holy Land of Jerusalem is regarded as the most sacred site to the Jews, Christians, and even Muslims. It is a vibrant democratic country in the Middle East with nuclear capacity. Just imagine, how a country even smaller than Kolkata became the third country with the most NASDAQ-listed companies after the US and China. It is even the world's sixth most innovative country as per the Bloomberg Innovation Index of 2020. Why India and its different states cannot do this? Why do Indian states of Tamil Nadu, Karnataka, Uttar Pradesh, West Bengal, and others fail to perform like Israel? When I study Israel, I find that it is regarded as the world's "start-up nation," and not France, Germany, or Japan. If Israel can do this; why not India? What hinders us from achieving our big targets? But for this, we have to make a big target. I have discussed it in detail in the 11th and 12th chapters. Do you have any big targets really? If yes, how sincere are you in attaining the goals? Remember, every individual has a role in transforming India. The time has come to think about it and find reasonable solutions. Therefore, let us think positively and aggressively to attain our goal. Now, we will focus our attention on the policies that the government of India has taken to achieve the goal of a Viksit Bharat.

References:

1. Evelyn, C. & Nee, L.Y. (2021, January 31). New chart shows China could overtake the US as the world's largest economy earlier than expected. *CNBC*.

2. The top 10 largest economies in the world in 2024. (2024, November 4). *Forbes India*.

3. International Monetary Fund. (2023, October 16). https://www.imf.org/external/datamapper/

4. Grosier, A. (translator). (1788). *A General Description of China, Containing the Topography of the Fifteen Provinces Which Compose This Vast Empire, That of Tartary, the Isles, and Other Tributary Countries* (Vol. II). J. Robinson.

5. Zhou, W. (2014, Winter). Comparing the Economic Growth of China and India: Current Situation, Problems, and Prospects. *World Review of Political*

Economy, 5(4), p. 455.

6. The World Bank data (GDP growth (annual % - India, China). (n.d.). https://data.worldbank.org/

7. Sealy, C. (2023, September 2003). Healthy competition. *materialstoday*, *Elsevier Ltd*. p. editorial.

8. Mandelbaum, M. (2014, May 21). The two things India can learn from China. World Economic Forum.

9. Brooks, D. (2002, June 9). Why the US Will Always be Rich. *The New York Times Magazine*.

10. Feldstein, Martin S., 'Why the US is Still Richer Than Every Other Large Country,' Harvard Business School, 20 April, 2017.

11. Feldstein, M.S. (2017, April 20). Why the US is Still Richer Than Every Other Large Country. *Harvard Business School*.

12. Carlisle, M. (2021, August 8). Here's How Many Medals Every Country Won at the Tokyo Summer Olympics. *Time*.

13. Why the United States dominates the Nobels. (2021, October 12). *The Deccan Herald*.

14. Pawar, A. (2023, August 23). India creates new research funding agency, but doubts linger. *Science*.

15. Murty, R. N. (2023, August 15). India's R&D needs a boost. *The Hindu Businessline*.

16. Research and Development. (2023, March 13). *White House*.

17. Shaw, K.M. (2023, January 18). Budget 2023 can boost India's march to global leadership in research & innovation. *The Times of India*.

18. Gershon, L. (2016, November 2). The Social Responsibility of American Industrialists. *Jstor Daily*. https://daily.jstor.org/the-social-responsibility-of-american-industrialists/

19. Dobbins, J., Poole, M.A., Long, A. and Runkle, B. (n.d.). After the War: Nation-Building from FDR to George W. Bush. In *Post-World War II Nation-Building: Germany and Japan*, p. 11. RAND corporation. https://www.jstor.org/stable/10.7249/mg716cc.10

20. Bombing of Hiroshima and Nagasaki. (2023, April 18). *History.com editors*. https://www.history. com/topics/world-war-ii.

21. Powell, B. (n.d). *Japan, The Library of Economics and Liberty*. https://www.econlib.org/library/Enc/ Japan.html#:

22. Clapson, M. (2019). *The Blitz Companion: Aerial Warfare, Civilians and the City since 1911*. University of Westminster Press.

23. Powell, B. (n.d). *Japan, The Library of Economics and Liberty.* https://www.econlib.org/library/Enc/ Japan.html#:

24. Drucker, P. F. (1981, January). Behind Japan's Success. *Harvard Business Review.*

25. "GDP (Current US$) - Japan", World Bank. Quoted by Gerstel, Dylan, and Goodman, Matthew P. In *Japan: Industrial Policy and the Economic Miracle.* Center for Strategic and International Studies (CSIS), (2020), p. 5.

26. Okuno-Fujiwara, M. (1991). Quoted by Gerstel, Dylan, and Goodman, Matthew P. In *Japan: Industrial Policy and the Economic Miracle.* Center for Strategic and International Studies (CSIS), 2020, p. 5.

27. Gerstel, D., & Goodman, M.P. (2020). *Japan: Industrial Policy and the Economic Miracle.* Center for Strategic and International Studies (CSIS).

28. Abou-Jaoude, A.L. (2016, November). A Pure Invention: Japan, Impression, and the West, 1853-1906. *The History Teacher, 50*(1), p. 57. https://www.jstor.org/stable/44504454

29. Stevenson, H.W. (1991, September). *Japanese Elementary School Education, in The Elementary School Journal.* The University of Chicago Press. https://www.jstor.org/stable/1002079

30. Benjamin, G.R. (1997). *Education in Japanese Society. in Japanese Lessons: A Year in a Japanese School Through the Eyes of An American Anthropologist and Her Children.* NYU Press. https://www.jstor.org/stable/j.ctt9qfg52.13

31. Mihik, T. (2020). *Japan after Fukushima in Re-imagining Japan after Jukushima.* ANU Press.

32. Facebook post. (2023, October 9). [Love for Motherland] Facebook. https://www.facebook. com/profile.php?id=100086835397863

33. Becker, S. O., Mergele, L., and Woessmann, L. (2020, Spring). The Separation and Reunification of Germany. *Journal of Economic Perspectives, 34*(2), p.144.

34. Jana, P. & Franke, U.E. 2020). *The Big Engine That Might: How France and Germany can Build a Geopolitical Europe.* European Council of Foreign Relations. URL: https://www.jstor.org/stable/ resrep25380).

35. Landes, D.S. (1990, May 2). Why are We So Rich and They So Poor? *The American Economic Review, 80*(2), p. 1.

36. "Better Policies" Series Germany Keeping the Edge: Competitiveness for Inclusive Growth. (2014, February). *OECD Report,* pp. 2-3.

37. Ullekh, N.P. (2012, September 24). $10 bn business: How Israel became India's most important partner in arms bazaar. *The Economic Times.*

38. Adrian, B. (2020). How Israel Became A Technology Start Up Nation. *Forbes.*.

39. Solomon, S. (2018, April 18). From 1950s rationing to modern high-tech boom: Israel's economic success story, *The Times of Israel.*

40. Blass, N. (2018). The Israeli Education System: An Overview, Taub Center: For Social Policy Studies in Israel.

III

Public Policies of India

"Policy-making, decision-taking, and control: These are the three functions of management that have intellectual content."
- Anthony Stafford Beer

Public policies are framed and implemented by every government to achieve certain goals. These policies are changed from time to time to meet the needs of the day. The formulation of a policy needs an extraordinary amount of research to gauge its impacts on society. In India, the background framework of a policy is prepared by various scholars, bureaucrats, and ministers. Finally, the draft is placed in the form of a Bill by an MP or a Minister in a House of Parliament. It goes through the process of reading, referring to the Committee, and subsequent discussions and debates in the House, and finally acceptance of the bill and sending it to the other House in Parliament. In the end, after getting the presidential nod, the Bill is passed and it turns out to be an Act. India has a long history of policy formulation since the time of Chandragupta Maurya. Chanakya, a great scholar and political philosopher at first formulated public policy in his seminal work *Arthashastra*, which is still a unique policy document followed by various statesmen across the world.

According to the Indian School of Public Policy, the concept of "Public policy is a set of laws, regulations, directives, and budget allocations that governments or their representatives put in place to achieve public good goals. This process is an iterative one, with many players involved, leading to a policy determined by various interests and options...It usually consists of six steps: agenda setting, policy formulation, adoption, implementation, evaluation, and policy maintenance" (Indian School of Public Policy, 2023).

Since its Independence, India has adopted various policies on the social, economic, educational, agricultural, and industrial development of our country. Different governments have different ideologies, and they adopt unique ways and methods of socio-economic development of the country. Whatever the ideologies of the respective parties and governments, they all had one goal fixed, i.e. the development and growth of India as a whole. The upliftment of the standard of living is another stable goal. Governments may go and come, but the basic policies remain almost the same. It is the government's domestic policies that either progress a country or regress the development of a country. Let us examine the rule of various governments since Independence.

From the very beginning of a sovereign government in India, the Indian National Congress Party and its allies have served the country for 54 long years by some famous Prime Ministers such as Jawaharlal Nehru, Indira Gandhi, Rajib Gandhi, P.V. Narasimha Rao, and Dr. Manmohan Singh while the Bharatiya Janata Party and its allies have been serving for a total of 16 + years including Atal Bihariji's 13 months from 1998 to 1999, followed by a full term from 1999 to 2004. All the previous 17 Prime Ministers from different political parties have attempted to raise the country ahead with their capacity, competence, and caliber. The 14th and the existing Prime Minister is Sri Narendra Modi (from 2014 to till date).

Under his leadership, economic growth has been robust, digitalization has been popularized, Indian borders are safe, and India's status in the eyes of Western leaders is graceful. Hence, Narendra Modi's popularity and fame have skyrocketed both in India and abroad. Now every Indian either living within its territory or elsewhere in the world feels secure and proud of India as Thomas A. Barkland writes almost the same about the people of America (Birkland, 2011, p. xiv) that, "...the Internet boom seemed, to some, an unlimited engine of growth and innovation, and Americans felt reasonably secure at home and abroad." Food security, economic security, and border security give the Indian government the luxury to bring about necessary reforms through the legislature to strengthen Indian federal democracy, ensure people's empowerment, improve the ecosystem, space research, trade & commerce, agriculture, etc. Public policy plays a conducive role in transforming the status and dignity of a country. How India's public policies under various governments have changed the socio-economic status of the people of our country is the main content of this chapter. Before going to discuss it, in detail, the policies of different governments up to 2014 may discussed in brief. Thereafter, the public policies and programs adopted by the present Government under Prime Minister Narendra Modi will be presented in detail. However, it is necessary to understand the concept of 'public policy.' Let us discuss briefly about public policies in the following part.

Conceptualizing Public Policy

Public policy is different from private policy, which is made by individuals for their families or institutions. Here, we will discuss the policies that are made by a government for the greater number of people in a country. Public policies are formulated by political authority, where general electors or the public is the source of that authority and the public has to act on behalf of the general electors. In India, public policies are made by different authorities – Union Government at the national level and State Governments/Union Territories at the state or Union Territory level. The local bodies act according to the policies made in the form of laws and regulations by the national and state governments.

Though the term politics is as old as Aristotle, the concept of public policy is a new concept. "Daniel McCool argues that modern policy studies began in 1922 when political scientist Charles Merriam sought to connect the theory and practice of politics to understanding the actual activities of government" (Birkland, 2011, p. 7). Over the last few decades, some political scientists have tried to define the term according to their perceptions. Clarke E. Cochran et al consider that, "The term public policy always refers to the actions of government and the intentions that determine those actions" (Clarke E. Cochran et al., 1999). Further, it can be said that "Public policy is the outcome of the struggle in government over who gets what." On the other hand, Thomas R. Dye conceptualizes the term as "Whatever governments choose to do or not to do" (Dye, 1992). Further, B. Guy Peters stated most simply, "Public policy is the sum of government activities, whether acting directly or through agents, as it has an influence on the life of citizens" (Peters, 1999). Basically, we can say that, "Public policy consists of political decisions for implementing programs to achieve societal goals" (Birkland, 2011, p. 8). In a word, public policies are a group of policies of the government made from time to time to fulfill the aspirations and demands of people as well as the government itself. From the above definitions, we can draw some characteristics of public policy. These are as follows:

- "Policy is made in response to some sort of problem that requires attention.
- Policy is made on the public's behalf.
- Policy is oriented toward a goal or desired state, such as the solution of a problem.
- Policy is ultimately made by governments, even if the ideas come from outside government or through the interaction of government and non-governmental actors.
- Policy is interpreted and implanted by public and private actors who have different interpretations of problems, solutions, and their own motivations.
- Policy is what the government chooses to do or not to do" (Birkland, 2011, pp. 8-9).

Despite having different jurisdictions of different governments, we will discuss here primarily the policies formulated by the Union Government headed by PM Modi during his last 10-year terms in office. If public policies are government statements; they are often found in the Constitution, statutes, case laws (judgments of the Supreme Court), rules, regulations, and even leadership decisions. Public policy is directly related to public interest, as it touches different people in some way or another. Similarly, it is not a fact that all of us are affected equally by every policy or leadership decision. Different sections of people are affected by different laws; though there are certain decisions or laws that affect all of us. For example, during the COVID-19 pandemic, a nationwide lockdown was imposed. Hence, it affected all the people of the country. On the other hand, the withdrawal of Articles 370 and 35A affected directly the people of Jammu & Kashmir and indirectly the people of the rest of India. Similarly, the Indian government declared the Muslim Women (Protection of Rights on Marriage) Act consisting of Triple *Talaq* illegal and unconstitutional and made it a punishable offense from 1 August 2019. This Act saved all Muslim women from the *Talaq-e-Biddat* or Triple Talaq that was practiced in Islam, whereby a Muslim man could divorce his wife by merely pronouncing *talaq* three times.

While the first decision of the Prime Minister regarding the imposition of the lockdown affected all the people living in India; the next two Acts mainly touched the Muslim minority community and especially women. But the point is how far the national policies formulated by the present government are instrumental in making India a global superpower and how far the public policies, welfare schemes, government Acts, and leadership decisions have transformed the lives of the general public in India, and how far these policies will have an impact to turn Indian into a Viksit Bharat will be examined in the following part. However, prior to that at first, we will discuss briefly the political scenario of India from 1947 to 2014 and some important government policies that helped India to grow and develop its socio-economic condition. Here, I must confess that within this small chapter, it is not possible to discuss all the policies of every government. Therefore, a few significant policies, programs, and schemes of the Pre-Modi governments are examined hereunder.

From 1947 to 2014: Political Situation and Public Policies

National development and international recognition are correlated. Both are interdependent. It is a well-known fact that without ensuring the empowerment of domestic people, without the skill development of Indigenous people, without the increase of business and trade, without foreign direct investment, and without achievements in science, technology, engineering, and mathematics – in a word, without the national development India's position in the global arena would not be established and recognized. How far Indian Prime Ministers have been successful to exploit the full potential of its people and take India to a new height is a matter of debate. Let's examine, in brief, the political stability and performance of our top leaders under different governments since Independence.

India, from 1947 to 1964 witnessed a robust and visionary Prime Minister Pundit Jawaharlal Nehru for 18 years. After two years of internal political turmoil in Congress, the next 11 years (1966-1977) under Mrs. Indira Gandhi India regained some international recognition, despite remaining under the clutch of poverty, ill health, malnutrition, lower educational performance, bad infrastructure, internal conflicts, and many more ailments. The short tenure of Morarji Desai (1977-1979) and Charan Singh (1979-1980) as Prime Ministers was unstable, loose and unpredictable. Again, Mrs. Indira Gandhi and her son Rajib ruled for 9 years (1980-1989). After a brief period of coalition governments under V.P. Singh (343 days) and Chandra Sekhar (223 days), India found better leadership in P.V. Narasimha Rao. Further, from 1996 and 1997 India saw three Prime Ministers. This proves India's political bankruptcy. No single party was strong enough to run a full-term government. What a pity! Under the veteran leadership of Atal Bihari

Vajpayee, the National Democratic Alliance formed and continued government for 6 years (1998-2004). However the Vajpayee-led NDA government could not come back in power in the next elections; instead, a hotchpotch government under the leadership of Dr. Manmohan Singh came to power in 2004.

In the 2004 general elections, not a single party got a two-thirds majority. Hence, the United Progressive Alliance was formed by Indian National Congress Party with support from left-leaning political parties. "The Congress won 145 seats in 2004 –barely four more than it had won in 1998 (141 seats) when it was defeated by the Vajpayee-led BJP. More significantly, in 2004, the Congress won just seven seats more than the BJP (138). Had it not been for the Left Front which gave it outside support with its block of 60 seats, there would have been no UPA-1 – and perhaps none of UPA-1's scams: 2G spectrum, Coalgate, Commonwealth Games, Agusta Westland, Scorpene, etc." (Merchant, 2013). The unfaithful, hostile, and disgusting alliance of the UPA government was headed by Dr. Manmohan Singh, a world-famous economist; chaired by Sonia Gandhi, a foreigner by birth; guided by Prakash Karat and Sitaram Yechuri, two comrades and vanguards of 'destructive politics,' and dictated by a political nincompoop and milk-sucking child-like person – Rahul Gandhi. Consequently, it took no time to turn it into a 'corrupt,' 'confrontational,' and 'paralytic' government. People were fading up with the bad governance of the UPA-I & II, and earliear coalition governments; they sought a one-party-ruled strong government. The desire of the people became true in the year 2014 when the NDA alliance came to power with a thumping majority. Before examining the policies of the Narendra Modi-led NDA Government, we require an exploration of some important public policies formulated by various Prime Ministers before 2014. Let me begin with the policies of Pundit Jawaharlal Nehru.

Government Policies From 1947 to 2014

Pundit Nehru is considered the maker of modern India. The first landmark law formulated by his government was the Minimum Wages Act enacted on 15 March 1948 to improve the decent standard of living of industrial workers in India. In 1948, another very comprehensive law – The Factories Act - was passed by the Union Government under Nehru regarding the protection of workers' interests in factories. However, the law was amended at least 7 times before 2016. The Factories (Amendment) Bill, 2016 was turned into the Factories (Amendment) Act, 2016 that provided a landmark arrangement in Section 65 under the Principal Act that "...further extend the total number of hours of overtime work in any quarter up to one hundred and twenty-five in the public interest" (The Factories (Amendment) Act, 2016). In 1949 the Nehru Administration enacted the Banking Regulation Act with a view to give powers to the Central Bank, the Reserve Bank of India, to issue license banks, regulate shareholding and voting rights, lay down instructions for audits and liquidation, and even impose penalties. It was further amended in 1965 to include the cooperative banks.

One of the most significant contributions of the Nehru Government was the creation of the Planning Commission in 1950. Further, the Finance Commission was constituted in 1951. These Acts were urgently required by the Government at that time to smoothly run a newly set-up government. If these were the good laws, the Industries (Development and Regulation) Act, 1951 was a bad one as it gave birth to the Licence Raj in India, which obstructed the industrial growth of the country. Nehruji nationalized Air India in 1953. The government of India took over the Imperial Bank of India through the enactment of the State Bank of India Act, 1955. Another very important policy was taken by the Government in 1955, which is called the Essential Commodities Act, which sought to regulate the production, supply, and distribution of essential commodities such as drugs, oils, kerosene, coal, iron, steel, and pulses. The Nehru Government took a bold step to formulate an Industrial Policy in 1956. The resolution indicates that the state will "assume a predominant and direct responsibility for setting up new industrial undertakings" (Chikermane, 2018). The Life Insurance Corporation was nationalized in 1956. One of the greatest achievements of Nehruji was to enact the Institutes of Technology Act, 1961 which facilitated to constitute of five eminent institutes of technology such as Kharagpur (1950), Bombay (1958, with assistance from UNESCO, and the Soviet Union), Kanpur (1959, with a consortium of US universities), Madras (1959, with the government of West Germany), and Delhi with the help of United Kingdom. Food Corporation of India was set up in 1965 to purchase, store, move, distribute, and sale of food grains and other food. Nehruji's foresightedness is reflected in his creation of Special Economic Zones in 1965 started with the setting up of a special Free Trade Zone at Kandla in Gujarat. It is the first free trading zone in Asia for which India can boast of.

Smt. Indira Gandhi nationalized the banks in 1969 to control the economy. Further, coal was nationalized in 1971. After 2 years, the Foreign Exchange Regulation Act, of 1973 was enacted to have a controlling mechanism "to regulate certain payments, dealings in foreign exchange and securities and the import and export of currency and bullion" (ibid, p. 55). After several years of Independence, India abolished the Bonded Labor System (Abolition) Act of 1976. This abominable system was going on in different states, especially in the Southern states of Tamil Nadu, Karnataka, and Odisha where around 282,429 bonded laborers were released and rehabilitated by 20th July, 2016. The Right to Property was abolished in 1978. Sanjay Gandhi, son of Prime Minister Indira Gandhi, is remembered for setting up Maruti Motors Limited on 4 June, 1971. It was nationalized by Smt. Indira Gandhi after his plane crash, but further Maruti Udyog was privatized.

Corruption is an age-old evil system in India. Every government tries to regulate either through verbal instructions or through legal mechanisms. However, the first anti-corruption law in independent India was the Prevention of Corruption Act of 1947, which was further extended its periphery in 1988 through the enactment of the Prevention of Corruption Act. The young and energetic Prime Minister, a well-educated person with a foreign degree, enacted the National Highways Authority of India Act on 16 December 1988 to consolidate and look at highways as an enabler of economic growth in India. He realized that India's development lies in the construction of smooth and better infrastructure. The first robust Industrial policy was enacted in 1991. The Foreign Investment Promotion Board was also established in 1991. These steps were taken to expedite India's economic development. The P.V. Narasimha Rao and Dr. Manmohan Singh duo opened the door of the economy to the investors of the world. In 1991, Dr. Manmohan Singh disinvested public sector undertakings. In 1996 a Disinvestment Commission was also set up to recommend and supervise the process of disinvestment. Out of 72 Public Sector Enterprises, "the Commission recommended disinvestment in 58 and Rs. 4704 crore was brought in" (ibid., p.86). Securities and Exchange Board of India (SEBI) was established by an administrative order in 1992. It was created mainly to protest the interests of investors in securities and to promote the development of, and regulate, the securities market. At that time, Harshad Mehta, a share broker, diverted funds to the tune of over Rs. 3500 crores which exposed the loopholes in the banking sector in India. Rao Government also created Debt Recovery Tribunals in 1993. It was another successful attempt of the government to reform the public sector banks. Indian National Stock Exchange was established in 1994. Further, the National Telecom Policy was undertaken in 1994. It was set up to fulfill the desire of the people to have telephones on demand. This policy provided scope to the private players to enter the telephone market. During this time the Government also opened services of e-mail, voice mail, data, and audio and video text services. This was a revolutionary step of the government of India at that time that opened the Indian door to the global people.

Much later in 2000, Information Technology Act was formulated after the mushrooming of India's information technology industry in the late 1990s. It needed government regulation; hence, the new law was formulated. With the advancement of the economy, India's problems also started to increase. Hence, to plug the problems and challenges, India had to come forward with new laws and schemes. In 2002, the Prevention of Money Laundering Act was made. India was facing threats of illegal money and dirty money, which were being whitewashed later. National Policy on Airports was framed in 2003. This policy authorized the Airports Authority of India to allow private players to operate and manage existing airports. There appeared the Private and Public Partnership model. The government realized that it was not possible for the government alone to control everything. Further in 2008, the Airports Economic Regulatory Authority of India Act was enacted by Dr. Manmohan Singh's Government to regulate tariffs and other charges and to monitor the performances of private players. As a result, the airport authority began to increase profitability.

One of the most revolutionary Acts formulated by the UPA-I government under the Prime Minister of Dr. Manmohan Singh was the Mahatma Gandhi National Rural Employment Guarantee Act in 2005, which was later renamed in 2009 to honor the 'Father of the Nation.' This Act was the extension of Nehruji's Community Development Program (1952), and the Food for Work program was renamed as the National Rural Employment Program in 1977. However, the MGNREGA for the first time guaranteed at least one member from every rural landless family for up to 100 days of unskilled work in a year. The UPA-II Government formulated a policy on foreign direct investment (FDI) in the multi-brand retail sector. But the attempt was held hostage due to protests by a small group of traders. However, the FDI policy was changed from time to time. In 1991, the policy statement on FDI allowed only for exports. Thereafter, in 1997, "100 percent FDI was permitted for exports, and cash and carry wholesale trading....Five years later, on 20 September 2012, the government allowed 100 percent FDI in single-brand retail" (Chikermane, 2018). Further, in 2013, the UPA-II Government allowed 51 percent FDI in multi-brand retail, while the Modi government approved 100 percent FDI in single-brand retail under the automatic route. The (in)famous 1894 land acquisition law was amended in 2013 to address the compensation and rehabilitation, and resettlement issues of the affected people. There are more than one hundred important such laws that were enacted by various governments to transform India from an underdeveloped country to a developing country. Now, we will explore the policies and schemes that were initiated by the NDA Government led by Narendra Modi from 2014 to till date for improving the standard of living, ease of doing business, economic growth, developing infrastructure, agricultural production, trade and commerce, foreign direct investment, research and development, science and technology, space research and military power, etc. The foreign policies will be discussed in the following chapter only. However, let me explore the domestic policies of the Modi Government that aim to make India a Viksit Bharat by 2047.

Policies of Modi Government that Transformed India: from 2014 to 2024

Unlike his predecessors, the current Prime Minister Sri Narendra Modi, possesses and nourishes a clear vision for India's economic growth and development, and he sets his development agenda accordingly. He always likes to walk an extra mile and think out of the box. By doing so, he substantially developed the state of Gujarat as its chief minister (from 2001 to 2014). After his overwhelming and boisterous victory in the general elections of 2014, he took every effort for the holistic development and economic growth of India. He calls himself '*Pradhan Sevak*' of the people. This indicates his deep sense of patriotism and respect for the country and its people. We find here the reflection of Swami Vivekananda's 'Call to the Nation' where he said, "What we want is this *Sraddha*. Unfortunately, it has nearly vanished from India, and this is why we are in our present state...What makes one man great and another weak and low is this *sraddha* (respect)" (Vivekananda: His Call to the Nation, 2013, p. 60). The same expression of *sraddha* came to light when he bent down on the steps of the main entrance of Parliament, when he for the first time entered in the Central Hall of Parliament. However, he gave an outline of his vision in his maiden speech at the 68th Independence Day from the rampart of the historic Red Fort. Unlike his predecessors, he delivered his speech without written script.

The Prime Minister, a devotee of Swami Vivekananda, believes that "Our duty to others means helping others; doing good to the world....The good life for others alone. The wise man should sacrifice himself for others.' He devoted his life to the service of his fellow countrymen. He works himself day and night and thus possesses the audacity to tell the countrymen - "If you work for 12 hours, I will work for 13 hours." He knows that a country grows and sustains only with the economic growth and skill development of its people, and no person, no family, and no society can develop without hard work. There is no alternative to hard work. Hence, he gave a target to the countrymen particularly the youths to work at least 12 hours a day without wasting time uselessly.

The Prime Minister realized that poverty is a curse and it's a great challenge to the development of the world. India is such a vast and multi-layered country where millions of people cannot afford to eat a square meal whereas thousands of young boys and girls suffer from malnutrition and the majority of women are anemic. Therefore, he told the people: "We were together during the freedom struggle and we won, it is the need of the hour to fight poverty in a similar way." He wants to fight poverty on a war footing. He observed that millions of Indian people are lacking toilets mainly in rural areas across the country. Hence, he gave emphasis on building toilets and maintaining cleanliness. He knows the maxim: "Cleanliness is next to God." Further, PM Modi sought to change the perception of the Western people about India. The majority of Western people particularly the British and American people considered India as a very backward, primitive and barbarian country. Philip Goldberg writes that in the 19th century "India was perceived by most as a backward outpost of the British Empire, and Hinduism as a primitive, polytheistic, idol-worshipping religion in need of Christian missionaries" (Goldberg, 2020).

It was Swamiji who transformed the misconception of the Western people by setting up the Vedanta Society in the USA in 1894. Today there might be the Vedanta Society and other organizations that are spreading of Indian culture and spirituality; Indian students might be studying and doing research in thousands of higher educational institutions; Indian scholars might win Nobel Prizes; many of the professors might be teaching in hundreds of higher educational institutions; out of Fortune 500 companies in the world there might be more than 10 percent CEOs from India alone, still India remains in the subordinate position in the eyes of millions of Westerners. Narendra Modi understood this hard and bitter reality. He himself felt the heat of discrimination and hatred while he was denied American visa even being the chief minister of Gujarat after the

Godhra episode in 2002. Hence his aim was to change the perception of western people about India. He said, "Earlier, we were considered a country of snake charmers, but our IT professionals changed the country's image." He keeps faith in Information and Communication Technology and Science, Technology, Engineering, and Mathematics (STEM).

PM Modi ascertained that China is the world's manufacturing hub. So, to beat China India needs to focus on the manufacturing industries. He said in his first speech as the Prime Minister of India "We should be able to export more than we import and be a manufacturing hub." If we do not produce more what would we export? Hence, we have to manufacture more and export more to earn revenue more and to make our country a developed one. He also gave top priority to the safety, survival, and education of women and girls. He expressed his concern with the gradual increase in violence against women. The Prime Minister voiced concern over cases of female feticide and stressed that they should be stopped and warned the doctors against becoming a partner in such crimes against humanity. He also emphasized on the suicide cases of the farmers and sought to stop that because the farmers are our food-makers and food-givers. PM Modi gave a clarion call to all the neighboring and SAARC countries to work "shoulder-to-shoulder" to remove poverty from the region, leaving behind the world of death and killings. He observed that people have mobile phones but the same people had no bank accounts. Hence he considered that a bank account should be opened for every Indian citizen. In his address from the Red Fort, he told the people that, he wants India to emerge stronger as a country so that it can contribute significantly to the betterment of the world (The Indian Express, 2014).

His vision and mission as the Prime Minister of India are well understood from his maiden speech at the Red Fort in 2014. His vision is very clear that is to develop the country's status, position and dignity through the positive transformation of human life, infrastructure, GDP growth, and increase of per capita income. Now we will focus on some specific schemes, policies, decision and Acts formulated during his last 10 years that were instrumental to the human development in India. There are hundreds of schemes and policies that were formulated by the NDA Government under the leadership of Narendra Modi, and many hundreds were either merged or abolished. It is quite impossible to discuss all of them in this small chapter. Hence, a few major public policies that have transformed the economic, educational, health, agriculture, science &

technology, military, and political image of India will merely be highlighted hereunder. Let us begin with the empowerment of women and girls.

1. *Beti Bachao Beti Padhao* (Save Girls and Educate Girls)

Prime Minister began his service to the nation through the empowerment of women and girls. He realized that every fetus must see the light of the Sun. As per his indication in his maiden speech from the Red Fort, he launched the *Beti Bachao Beti Padhao* scheme on 22nd January 2015 to address the declining Child Sex Ratio in India. The key elements of the scheme include Enforcement of PC & PNDT Act (Pre-Conception and Pre-Natal Diagnostic Techniques Act, 1994), nation-wide awareness and advocacy campaign and multi-sectoral action. Girls' safe birth in hospitals, their nutrition, and education were given the topmost priorities by PM Modi. As a result of his initiative, the sex ratio at birth for children has risen from 919 (2015-16) to 929 (2019-21) (The National Family Health Survey – 4 & 5, 2022).

2. Pradhan Mantri Ujjwala Yojana

Empowerment of women is another topmost priority of Narendra Modi. The Prime Minister experienced that women in most of the rural areas use traditional cooking fuels such as firewood, dry leaves, coal, cow-dung cakes, etc. Usage of these traditional cooking fuels had detrimental impacts on the health of women, who carry us, nourish us, and make us what we are today. Fumes and smoke cause cancer in mothers and children. It affects the aged persons badly. Therefore, he introduced the *Pradhan Mantri Ujjwala Yojana* in 2016 as a flagship scheme with the objective of making clean cooking fuel such as LPG (Light Petroleum Gas) free of cost to rural and deprived households. The release of 8 crore LPG connections under the scheme has also helped in increasing the LPG coverage from 62% on 1st May 2016, the day of launch, to 99.8% as of 1st April 2021 (Pradhan Mantri Ujjwala Yojana 2.0). The number has increased to 10.33 crore in December 2024 (Ministry of Petroleum and Natural Gas, https://pmuy.gov.in/ accessed on 18.12.2024).

3. Jan Dhan Yojana (JAM) and Liking of Aadhar and Mobile

The Prime Minister created history in the economic empowerment of people. It was a financial inclusion scheme of the government that was not thought of by any government earlier. PM Modi realized the urgency of bank accounts for all students, farmers and other adult citizens of India for their economic empowerment. Under the scheme, the country has witnessed significant progress in financial inclusion in recent years. As per the latest National Family Health Survey, the population covered with bank accounts increased from 53 percent in 2015 to 78 percent in 2019-21 (The Economic Survey, 2022-23, p. 30). The Pradhan Mantri Jan Dhan Yojana was launched in 2014 by the Prime Minister. This scheme created an unprecedented response from the citizens. Earlier bank officials were unwilling to open bank accounts for the poor and marginal people; but it was PM Modi who told the banks to do so. As a result of such a government scheme just within a few months, the scheme has radically transformed the lives and futures of millions of Indians. In just over a year, 19.72 crore bank accounts were opened and 16.8 crore Rupay cards have been issued so far. Not only that, there have been deposits worth Rs. 28,699.65 crores in different banks in India (PM India).

How did the scheme transform the lives of people? The available data on the Progress Report of the Ministry of Finance (Department of Financial Services, Government of India, Pradhan Mantri Jan-Dhan Yojana) shows that as of 11th December 2024, a total of Rs.2,39,323 crore was deposited in 54.19 lakh beneficiaries's accounts. Out of these, the total number of rural-urban female beneficiaries is 30.16 crore equivalent to the total population of the USA. What are the benefits of Jan Dhan Account holders? The benefits can be enumerated one by one hereunder:

(a) One basic savings bank account is opened for unbanked persons.

(b) There is no requirement to maintain any minimum balance in PMJDY accounts.

(c) Interest is earned on the deposit in PMJDY accounts.

(d) Rupay Debit card is provided to PMJDY account holder.

(e) Accident Insurance Cover of Rs. 1 lakh (enhanced to Rs. 2 lakh to new PMJDY accounts opened after 28.8.2018) is available with RuPay card issued to the PMJDY account holder. Not only that,

(f) an overdraft facility up to Rs. 10,000 to eligible account holders is available (Pradhan Mantri Jan-Dhan Yojana, https://pmjdy.gov.in/scheme).

4. Make in India Scheme

The 'Make in India' is a flagship program of the Government of India that aspires to facilitate investment, foster innovation, enhance skill development, and build best-in-class manufacturing infrastructure (Ministry of Commerce and Industry, 2022). This initiative was taken up by the dynamic leadership of the Prime Minister in September 2014. PM Modi realized that India does not lack entrepreneurial energy, but the energy was not explored earlier. Therefore, after assuming office, Narendra Modi decided to harness the energy of our youth.

The 'Make in India' project recognizes 'ease of doing business' as the single most important factor to promote entrepreneurship. Indian people found a complete change in the government's mindset. This shift was such that the Prime Minister himself declared his tenet of 'Minimum Government, Maximum Governance.' Due to this innovative 'Make in India' scheme, various sectors have opened up for foreign direct investment, such as defense, manufacturing, railways, space, single-branded retail, etc. To quicken the start of the business and investment, the Government has introduced the ease of doing business, under which regulatory policies have been relaxed to facilitate more investments. India's 'Ease of Doing Business' scheme ranked 130th earlier by the World Bank. Today, unnecessary compliances have been removed, and many permissions can be obtained online. Consequently, "India ranks 63rd in the World Bank's Doing Business Report (DBR), 2020, published in October 2019 before its discontinuation by the World Bank. India's rank in the DBR improved from 142nd in 2014 to 63rd in 2019, registering a jump of 79 ranks in a span of 5 years" (Ministry of Commerce and Industry, 2024, February 7).

The 'Make in India' scheme focuses on key sectors like semiconductors to achieve India's vision of an *Aatmanirbhar Bharat*, i.e., a self-reliant India. Production Linked Scheme (PLI) gives a huge boost to localized manufacturing in India. This project has encouraged Indian entrepreneurs and consequently, India's export of toys registered tremendous growth, i.e. 636% in April-August 2022 over the same period in 2013 (Ministry of Commerce and Industry, 2022). India is celebrating the 10th anniversary of the Make in India project in 2024. Under the Make in India 2.0 scheme, a total of 27 sectors have been included. These sectors can be divided into two segments such as manufacturing and service. Under the manufacturing head, the most important sectors are: Aerospace and Defence, Automotive and Auto Components, Pharmaceuticals, and Medical Devices, Bio-Technology, Capital Goods, Textile and Apparels, Chemicals and Petrochemicals, Leather & Footwear, Electronics System Design and Manufacturing (ESDM), Gems and Jewellery, Shipping, Railways, Construction and New and Renewable Energy. On the other hand, the service sectors include Information Technology & Information Technology enabled Services (IT & ITeS), Tourism and Hospitality Services, Medical Value Travel, Transport and Logistics Services, Accounting and Finance Services, Audio Visual Services, Legal Services, Communication Services, Construction and Related Engineering Services, Environmental Services,

Financial Services and Education Services (Press Information Bureau, 2024, September 25).

5. Tough Stand Against Corruption

The Prime Minister of India declared a war against corruption immediately after coming to power. The Prime Minister called for "zero tolerance" against corruption. In his speech at Vigyan Bhawan in New Delhi in 2022, he said, the corrupt should not escape "at any cost" and they should not get political or social protection (Gaurav, 2022). Again, while he attended the golden jubilee celebration of the Central Bureau of Investigation (CBI) in April 2023 (ANI, 2023), he reiterated that there is no dearth of political will in the government to fight against corruption. Addressing the CBI officers, police officers, and other senior officials, the Prime Minister said, "Corruption is not a common crime; it takes away the rights of the poor and gives birth to many crimes. It is the biggest obstacle in the way of democracy and justice." The responsibility of the CBI is to free the country from corruption. The people understand his tough stand when he said that the corrupt should not escape "at any cost," and they should not get political or social protection. He further warned, "No matter how powerful the corrupt may be, they should not be saved under any circumstances,...No corrupt person should get political and social support, every corrupt person should be put in the dock by society."

6. Electricity for All

In his Independence Day speech in 2015, PM Modi announced that all remaining villages shall be electrified within 1000 days. As a result, rural electrification was held at a rapid speed. In April 2018, the Central government declared that all villages in India are electrified. The Times of India in an article reported: "The goal was reached four years after the Narendra Modi-led government launched the *Deendayal Upadhyaya Gram Jyoti Yojana* (DDUGJY) in 2014 for electrification of all un-electrified villages as per Census 2011" (The Times of India, 2022). Initially, the Union government declared that all the villages were electrified, but later in March 2021, the government admitted that after March 31, 2021, nearly 11.84 lakh households were out of electric connections. Again, in October 2017, the government launched the *Pradhan Mantri Sahaj Bijli Har Ghar Yojana – Saubhagya* for the electrification of the remaining households. Under the scheme, the Central government provides 60 percent of the project finance to the States. As a result, a total of 18,374 villages were electrified under DDUGJY, and a total of 2.86 crore households were electrified under the aegis of *Saubhagya* (Sharma, 2023). The present Government's initiative has increased electricity production, including renewable sources, from 1,110.395 BU in 2014-15 to 1624.158 BU in 2022-23. "The electricity generation target for the year 2023-24 was fixed at 1750 BU comprising 1324.110 BU Thermal; 156.700 BU Hydro; 46.190 Nuclear, 8 BU Import from Bhutan and 215 BU RES (Excl. Large Hydro)" (Ministry of Power, https://powermin.gov.in/en/content /power-sector-glance-all-india).

7. Connecting India Program

Connectivity is the lifeline of a society. The development of a country depends much on its communication system. The Government of India increased its road connectivity. As per the report 'Basic Road Statistics in India 2018-19,' India has a network of over 63, 31,757 kilometers of road on 31.3.2019, which is the second largest in the world. The total road construction has increased to 63,32,757 km in 2019 from 62,15,797 km in 2018 and has registered a growth of 1.9 percent (Press Information Bureau, 2022). Under the Modi regime, numerous passenger-friendly amenities like Wi-fi at railway stations, passenger helplines, security helplines, paperless unreserved ticketing, e-ticketing, e-catering, and CCTV cameras for the safety of passengers, particularly for women, have been launched. New railway tracks have been set up. About 1,983 km of railways have been commissioned and 1,375 km of railway electrification has been completed this year (2022), which is the best-ever performance. A total of 6 new pilgrim trains have been launched, and the Katra line has been opened to travel to Vaishno Devi. India is also taking rapid strides in the shipping sector under the UDA Government. The Sagarmala Project seeks to ensure comprehensive port-led development through vibrant coastal communities. Rapid progress is happening in the civil aviation sector, too. The Modi Government stressed the improvement of infrastructure from the beginning in all sectors, from railways to roads and from shipping to airports.

8. Economic Policy of the Government

The economy is the main criterion for a country's recognition in the global field. The size of GDP and GDP per capita are the two major components of the economy of a country. The World Bank in its biannual flagship publication report pointed out that, "India's growth continues to be resilient despite some signs of moderation in growth. The overall growth remains robust and is estimated to be 6.9 percent for the full year, with real GDP growing 7.7 percent year-on-year during the first three quarters of fiscal year 2022-23. Growth was underpinned by strong investment actively bolstered by the government's capex push and buoyant private consumption, particularly among higher income earners" (The World Bank, 2023). Thus, we find the health of the Indian economy is full of prospects. The National Statistical Office estimated that the annual per capita (net national income) at current prices for 2022-2023 stands at Rs. 1,72,000. India Today (Das, 2023) indicates, "This marks a growth of around 99 percent from Rs. 86,647 in 2014-15." Hence, it is found that India's per capita income has doubled under the BJP government.

Further, IMF Deputy Managing Director Gita Gopinath recently noted that India's economic performance is good and it is projected to be the world's third-largest economy by 2027. India has risen from the 10th largest economy in 2014 to the 5th largest economy in 2024. Not only that, it is the fastest-growing major economy in the world. "This has not only put more money in the hands of people, but it has also drastically reduced the number of people living below the poverty line," said President Droupadi Murmu in her speech on the eve of 2024 Independence Day (Financial Express, 2024, August 18).

The NDA Government took some drastic steps in reforming the economy. In 2016, the Indian Government suddenly introduced demonetisation of the old Rs.500 and Rs.1,000 banknotes as a step against the accumulation and circulation of black money in the country. However, in November 2016, the Government of India introduced the Rs. 2000 currency notes to meet the currency requirement of the economy. The decision of the Modi Government created a furor in India from different political parties, such as the Indian National Congress and the All India Trinamool Congress. However, the Modi government embarked on a transformed journey in 2017 in its tax landscape with the implementation of Goods and Services Tax (GST). It was "a path-breaking legislation for New India." The "GST replaced a fragmented and complex indirect tax regime that burdened businesses and consumers alike. Before GST, the tax framework consisted of numerous levies such as excise duty, service tax, VAT, CST, and others" (Press Information Bureau, 2024, June 28). All these created problems for both the traders and consumers. What benefit did India get from this Act? India earned a total Gross GST revenue collection of Rs. 1.73 lakh crore in May 2024. The above two Acts have boosted the Indian economy.

9. **The Vision of *Savka Sath, Savka Vikaas* (with all, development of all)**

The broad principles behind the reforms were creating public goods, adopting trust-based governance, co-partnering with the private sector for development, and improving agricultural productivity. This approach reflects a paradigm shift in the growth and development strategy of the government, with the emphasis shifted towards building partnerships to reap the development benefits *(Sabka Sath, Sabka Vikaas)* (The Economic Survey, 2022-23, p. 28). India is now digital. Digital systems such as the Goods and Services Tax Network (GSTN) and e-Way Bill system have enabled the formalization of business transactions. India's gross FDI has increased from an average of 2.2 percent of GDP during 2005-2014 to 2.6 percent in 2015-2022. The highest-ever annual gross FDI inflow of USD 84.8 billion was recorded in the financial year 2022. These trends are an endorsement of India's status as a preferred investment destination amongst global investors (The Economic Survey, 2022-23, p. 35).

10. Labor Force Participation

The health of the Indian economy is a reflection of India's good domestic policy. As a result of the government's various economic activities, people have availed themselves of the opportunity to participate in the labor force. Growth is inclusive when it creates jobs. When we look at the overall labor force participation rate in the country, we find good hope in the labor market. The overall labor force participation rate increased to 47.9 percent in July-September 2022 from 46.9 percent a year ago, while the worker-population ratio strengthened from 42.3 percent to 44.5 percent in the same period. The unemployment rate declined from 9.8 percent in July-September 2021 to 7.2 percent in July-September 2022. This trend shows that labor markets have started recovering from the COVID-19 impact (The Economic Survey, 2022-23, p. 164). The periodic Labor Force Survey (PLFS) shows that the urban unemployment rate for people aged 15 years and above declined from 9.8 percent in the quarter ending September 2021 to 7.2 percent one year later (quarter ending September 2022). (The Economic Survey, 2022-23, p. 19). The rural Female Labor Force Participation Rate (FLFPR) has also increased from 19.7 percent in 2018-19 to 27.7 percent in 2020-21, which is a positive development. It is a fact that Self-Help Groups (SHGs) are mostly women-dominated. At present, there are 1.2 crore SHGs, comprising 88 percent of all women SHGs, who are catering to 14.2 crore households (The Economic Survey, 2022-23, p. 35).

11. Health Policy of the Present Government

An Indian proverb says, "Health is Wealth." Prime Minister Sri Narendra Modi once said: "India is a treasure trove of herbal plants, it is, in a way, our Green Gold" (Ministry of Ayush). It indicates the government's health policy.

The government emphasized traditional medicines and age-old treatment methods through the introduction of AYUSH (Ayurveda, Siddha, Unani, and Homeopathy). It does not mean that the Modi Government neglected the modern allopathic treatment system. The Government has, for the first time, introduced a completely new ministry called the Ministry of Ayush. The Ministry formulated a very interesting scheme named *Ayush Oushadhi Gunvatta Evam Uttpadan Samvardhan Yojana*. The scheme aims to regulate Ayurveda, Siddha, Unani, and Homeopathy (ASU & H) medicines in India, utilizing the framework provided by the Drugs and Cosmetics Act, 1940, and its associated rules. The main objective of the scheme is "To enhance India's manufacturing capabilities and exports of traditional medicines and health promotion products under the initiative of Atmanirbhar Bharat" (Ministry of Ayush, https:// ayush.gov.in/#!/).

Further, ensuring the quality of health facilities for citizens is an important priority of the Modi government. Under the National Health Mission, the Government has made concerted efforts to engage with all relevant sectors and stakeholders to move in the direction of achieving universal health coverage and delivering quality healthcare services to all at an affordable cost. Today, the Indian healthcare network is among the largest in the world. India has successfully achieved the major milestone of bringing the Maternal Mortality Ratio to below 100 per lakh live births by 2020. Infant Mortality Rate has also decreased to 34 per 1000 live births (Sample Registration System). The *Ayushman Bharat Pradhan Mantri –Jan Arogya Jojana* (AB PM-JAY) is the world's largest health insurance scheme that intends to minimize the medical expenses of the target beneficiaries. The scheme provides health cover of Rs.. 5.00 lakh per family per year for secondary and tertiary care hospitalization to over 10.7 crore poor and vulnerable families (approximately 50 crore beneficiaries) that form the bottom 40 percent of the Indian population (The Economic Survey, 2022-23, p. 192).

Women and girls are one of the top priorities of the present government. The Maternity Benefit Act, 1961, was amended in 2017 by the National Democratic Alliance (NDA) Government to provide for "paid maternity leave to women workers and creche facilities by establishments. Vide Section 5 of the Maternity Benefit Act, 1961, as amended in 2017, the Government has increased paid maternity leave from 12 weeks to 26 weeks, of which not more than eight weeks shall precede the date of expected delivery" (Press Information Bureau, 2023, February 13).

12. Education Policy of the Present Government

The importance of education for all cannot be underestimated as it is the foundation of every individual. Dr. A.P.J. Abdul Kalam said, "Learning gives creativity, creativity leads to thinking, thinking leads to knowledge, and knowledge makes you great." To build a 'knowledge society' and 'skill India', the former education policy of 1986 (modified in 1992) was not sufficient. Hence, a National Education Policy - 2020 was formulated by the Modi Government, which is up-to-date, scientific, and ambitious. It is the first Education Policy of the 21st century, formulated after a gap of 34 years. The NEP 2020 is prepared to fulfill the dream of transforming India into a developed country by 2024. It restructured the curricular and pedagogical structure of school education and is now guided by the 5+3=3+4 design. The government, through the implementation of the NEP 2020, seeks to develop students' skills such as collaboration, self-initiative, self-direction, self-discipline, teamwork, responsibility, citizenship, etc. These are the soft qualities needed for 21st-century youths to compete with global students. In addition to learning quality Indian languages, the students will have the opportunity to learn some foreign languages such as Korean, Japanese, Thai, French, German, Spanish, Portuguese, and Russian at the secondary level itself.

In addition to language skills, now our students will have the opportunity to improve other skills such as scientific temper and evidence-based thinking; creativity and innovativeness; a sense of aesthetics and art; oral and written communication; health and nutrition; physical education, fitness, wellness, and sports; collaboration and teamwork; problem solving and logical reasoning; vocational exposure and skills; digital literacy, coding, and computational thinking; ethical and moral reasoning; knowledge and practice of human and Constitutional values; gender sensitivity; Fundamental Duties; citizenship skills and values; knowledge of India; environmental awareness including water and resources conservation, sanitation and hygiene, and current affairs and knowledge of critical issues facing local communities, States and country and the world. To prepare the students through School Education, the NEP 2020 included curricular and pedagogical initiatives, including the introduction of contemporary subjects such as Artificial Intelligence, Design Thinking, Holistic Health, Organic Living, environmental education, Global Citizenship Education, etc. The NEP 2020 (p. 15) for the first time stressed the learning of vocational crafts such as carpentry, electrical work, etc.

The Higher Education system will play an extremely important role in promoting human as well as societal well-being and in transforming India into a Developed India. The Indian Higher Education system is the laboratory of change for the young population. The National Education Policy 2020 seeks to increase creativity and innovation, critical thinking and higher-order thinking capacities, problem-solving abilities, teamwork, communication skills, and more in-depth learning and mastery of curricula across fields. It will impart value education to the students. Research and collaboration have been highlighted in the NEP 2020. In a word, the government's education policy is a guiding force to turn India into a Viksit Bharat by 2047.

The implementation process has already been started in various states. In the year 2022, a total of 26.5 crore children were enrolled in schools and 19.4 lakh additional children were enrolled in Primary to Higher secondary levels. Not only that, the total enrolment of children with special needs (CWSN) has also increased substantially (22.7 lakh).

13. Skill Indian Mission

This is a dream project of PM Modi. The Skill Indian Mission focuses on skilling, re-skilling, and up-skilling through short-term training programs. Under the Mission, the government, through more than 20 Central Ministries or Departments, is implementing various skill development schemes across the country. These include *Deen Dayal Upadhyaya Grameen Kaushalya Yojana* (DDUGKY), Rural Self Employment Training Institutes (RSETI), *Deen Dayal Antyodaya Yojana* - National Urban Livelihood Mission (DAY-NULM) etc. There are some other similar schemes, such as *Pradhan Mantri Kaushal Vikas Yojana* (PMKVY), *Jan Shiksha Sansthan* (JSS), etc. As a result of these schemes, between 2017 and 2023 (as of 5 January 2023), under the PMKVY 2.0, about 1.1 crore persons have been trained: 83 percent certified and about 21.4 lakhs placed. Under PMKVY 3.0, from 2021 to 2023 (up to 5 January 2023), 7.4 lakh persons have been trained, 66 percent certified, and 41,437 placed.

India dreams of being the manufacturing hub and skill capital of the world. For this purpose, India has set up the National Skill Development Corporation (NSDC), which aims to create a network of institutions across India. Collaborations and networking have been made with 11 countries in the world, including Japan, Germany, China, Denmark, and the United Kingdom, in the fields of skill development and vocational education training. This indicates that the government of India is concerned with the development of the skills of Indian youths. There are many other schemes and policies that have been formulated to improve the ease and comfort of the lives of people, assist the income generation of citizens, and increase the productivity of food and agricultural products.

14. Prime Minister's Internship Scheme

In the Union Budget, the scheme was first announced. The program aims to offer internships to 10 million young people in India over the next five years, beginning in 2024. The young unemployed Indian people aged between 21 to 24 years having an educational qualification of Madhyamik pass, or Higher Secondary Certificate, or its equivalent, or a certificate from an Industrial Training Institute (ITI), a diploma from a Polytechnic Institute, or a graduation degree such as BA. B.Sc., B. Com., BCA, BBA, B.Pharma, etc., will get the opportunity to have practical experience in real-world business settings by matching them with 12-month internships with India's top 500 companies. This scheme will prepare young people to enjoy the work, learn real-life environments across sectors, and gain valuable skills and work experience that will help them get permanent jobs in the future. Besides, after joining the internship, each intern will receive a monthly assistance of Rs. 5,000 for the entire duration of the 12-month internship....Additionally, a one-time grant of Rs. 6000 will be provided by the Government of India to each intern after joining the internship" (The Economic Times, 2024, November 8).

15. Government's Management of the World's Worst Pandemic, COVID-19

On 30th January 2020, the World Health Organization (WHO) declared a 'Public Health Emergency of International Concern' (PHEIC) and advised that all countries should be prepared for 'containment, including active surveillance, early detection, isolation and case management, contact tracing and prevention of onward spread.' More than 10 crore people were infected globally. More than 200 countries across all continents were under the threat of the COVID-19 pandemic. The entire world was under lockdown for several months, the movements of people and vehicles were restricted, and the production of goods and service industries was at a standstill. This horrible shock was unconventional in size and extent to all the emerging market and developing economies, as well as advanced economies such as the United States of America and European Union countries, and uncertainty in life and jobs became widespread. The Gross Domestic Product growth and business, and trade were at a minus level. Despite this fact, India handled the situation very wisely, cautiously, and successfully on different fronts under the stout leadership of Narendra Modi. Within less than one year of the outbreak of the COVID-19 pandemic, India manufactured its indigenous vaccines, COVAXIN (by Bharat Biotech) and COVISHIELD (by the Serum Institute of India). PM Modi personally encouraged the manufacturers and visited their factories to boost their morale. So far, India has administered more than two billion Covid-19 vaccination doses, including the remotest areas, and has become the second country to hit the milestone after China. India supplied over 235 million doses of COVID-19 vaccines to 98 countries under the 'Vaccine *Maitri*' (Vaccine Friendship) initiative. This was possible because of PM Modi's inspiration and encouragement to research and invent indigenous vaccines to halt the spread of COVID-19. The Serum Institute upped its total Covishield vaccine manufacturing capacity from 50-60 million doses per month to over 100 million doses per month (Jayakumar & Vinaykumar, 2021).

The global economy experienced an unprecedented crisis in the year 2020. The government of India took all steps to ease movement, conduct business, and continue health-related restrictions. The government gave top priority to the saving of people's lives and helped the citizens to survive in the middle of financial and health crises. Fiscal stimuli were provided by the Government of India to boost up economy. The government of India and the RBI together announced a total stimulus worth Rs. 29.87 lakh crore, which is 15% of the national GDP, for facilitating a resilient recovery of the economy from the impact of the COVID-19 pandemic and the following lockdown. Out of this total amount, stimulus worth 9% of GDP has been provided by the Government under *the Atma Nirbhar Bharat* Package. The Fiscal Stimulus under the *Atma Nirbhar Bharat Package,* as declared by the Government of India, was Rs. 1,71,6441 crore, which was actually 8.8 percent of total GDP. In March 2020, the government of India declared the *Pradhan Mantri Garib Kalyan Package* of Rs.1,70,000 (0.87%), and the PM himself announced health measures amounting to Rs.15000 crore (0.08%). Consequently, the Indian economy started to recover and rebound at the end of 2020 as the monthly gross Goods and Services Tax (GST) collection crossed the Rupees one lakh crore mark, which was a good jump in GST revenue collections since its introduction. India recovered and survived the century's worst pandemic only because of the government's affirmative action and the wholehearted cooperation of doctors and others.

16. Agriculture Policy of the Government

In addition to the above policies, schemes, and strategies, the Government of India has increased the budgetary allocation for the welfare of our farmers. The farmers are our food producers and feeders. The present Government introduced "The PM-Kisan scheme in 2019, which is an income support scheme it aims to provide Rs. 6000 per year in 3 equal installments. More than Rs. 2.24 lakh crore has been released so far to more than 11 crore farmers" (Ministry of Agriculture and Farmers Welfare, 2023, March 21). The present government has also increased the budgetary allocations for the welfare of our farmers. In the year 2013-24 the budget allocation of the Ministry of Agriculture (including DARE) and the Ministry of Fisheries, Animal Husbandry & Dairying was only 30223.88 crore. This has increased by more than 4.35 times to Rs. 131,612.41 crore in 2023-24. Apart from the above scheme, the government of India launched the Pradhan Mantri Fasal Bima Yojana in 2016 to address the problems of high premium rates for farmers and reduction in sum insured due to capping. "In the past 6 years of implementation, 37.66 crore farmer applications have been enrolled, and over 12.38 crore (provisional) farmer applicants have received claims. During this period, nearly Rs. 25,174 crore were paid by farmers as their share of premium against which claims of over Rs. 1,30,185 crore (provisional) have been paid to them. Thus, for every 100 rupees of premium paid by farmers, they have received about Rs. 517 as claims" (Ministry of Agriculture and Farmers Welfare, 2023, March 21).

The Pradhan Mantri Fasal Bima Yojana (PMFBY) is basically a voluntary Scheme. According to the Indian School of Public Policy, "The Pradhan Mantri Fasal Bima Yojana is a crop insurance scheme launched by the Indian Government in 2016. The scheme aims to provide financial support to farmers in the event of crop failure due to natural calamities, pests, or diseases. The policy was formulated to mitigate the risks faced by farmers and to encourage them to adopt modern agricultural practices" (Indian School of Public Policy, 2023, March 28). However, "The premium under the scheme is determined through biding however, farmers have to pay a maximum of 2% for Kharif, 1.5% for Rabi food and oilseed crops and 5% for commercial/horticultural crops and the balance of actuarial/bidded premium is shared by the Central and State Government on 50:50 basis and 90:10 in case of North Eastern States from Kharif 2020 season as per provisions of the scheme" (Press Information Bureau, 2021, 30 November). The Government has not only formulated the policy and provided financial support to the farmers, but the Union Ministry of Agriculture and Farmers Welfare has opened a window with a WhatsApp chatbot Number. Moreover, there are Farmer Corner, Insurance Premium Calculator, Application Status, Krishi Rakshak Portal & Help Desk. Even the Government of India has created an App for Farmers. The farmers are benefiting, and India's agricultural production is increasing year after year.

17. Trade and Commerce Policy

Without the production and export of goods and services, how can India earn foreign money? The Modi government is very enthusiastic about the exports of Indian goods. India launched the Foreign Trade Policy in 2023. "The Key Approach to the policy is based on the 4 pillars: (1) Incentive to Remission, (ii) Export promotion through collaboration – Exporters, States, Districts, Indian Missions, (iii) Ease of doing business, reduction in transaction cost and e-initiatives and (v) Emerging Areas – E-commerce Developing Districts as Export Hubs and streamlining SCOMET policy" (Press Information Bureau, 2023, March 31). The policy is based on the principles of 'trust' and 'partnership' with exporters. This has increased India's exports of electronic goods, engineering goods, rice, marine products, textiles, etc. However, India's total exports (Merchandise and Services combined) for November 2024 are estimated at US$ 67.79 billion, registering a positive growth of 9.59 percent vis-à-vis November 2023. Total imports (Merchandise and Services combined) for November 2024 are estimated at US$ 87.63 billion, registering a positive growth of 27.47 percent vis-à-vis November 2023" (Press Information Bureau, 2024, December 16).

18. Science and Technology Policy

The government of India launched its Science and Technology Policy in 2020. "The aspirations of STIP are to fulfill multifarious responsibilities to function collaboratively with all stakeholders; to promote holistic growth and development by developing scientific temperament, quality, access, equity, incorporating citizenship education; to promote linkages between higher education and industry to revamp economic systems; and to build R&D infrastructure, its effective usage with easy and equitable access, is another aspect of strengthening the STI ecosystem" (Department of Science and Technology, December 2020, p.14). The said policy aims to leverage the engagement of higher educational institutions with the economy and community. All universities are encouraged now to be responsive and respectful to the needs of the community by conducting interdisciplinary projects involving scientific, technological, and social science-based interventions. The institutions of higher learning are urged to build collaboration with other institutions to the mutual benefit of individuals as well as institutions. The Science and Technology Policy 2020 puts stress on quality research and academic achievement as well as social impact. The government also aims to create an enabling ecosystem for the seeding, sustenance, and growth of science and technology-enabled entrepreneurship. Through the policy, the Government of India seeks to make India an independent, research-oriented country. India mostly depends on the import of technologies in the priority sectors. The Policy, hence, aims to be recognized as a technologically self-sufficient country.

19. Space Research Policy

The Indian Space Program is conducted by the Department of Space, which is a Government of India body. The Department of Space aims to promote and develop space science and space technology. Indian Space Research Organization (ISRO) is the government agency that accomplishes space missions to fulfill its vision, mission, and objectives. ISRO was founded in 1969 to exemplify India's ambitious journey into space science and technology. So far, the ISRO has launched 127 Spacecraft Missions, while 18 Satellites realized by private players or students, and a total of 432 foreign satellites were launched by ISRO. Out of a total of 98 mission launches, 56 missions were launched between June 2014 and 5 December 2024. However, among the remarkable achievements of ISRO is the Mars Obriber Mission (Mangalayaan), which made India the first Asian nation to reach Mars' orbit. Additionally, ISRO's cost-effective launches, particularly through the Polar Satellite Launch Vehicle (PSLV), have successfully deployed numerous satellites for India and international clients" (The Times of India, 2024, August 23). Out of a total of 23 space missions right from the Aryabhatta in 1975, a total of 11 space missions were conducted during the Modi era. In the NDA 03 Government, the Prime Minister retained the Department of Space and the Department of Atomic Energy under his charge with a view to observing more closely the happenings and advancements in the space program. "PM Modi's second term, ISRO basked in the glory with milestone missions to the Moon and the Sun. India made history by successfully landing the Chandrayaan-3 lander-rover near the Moon's South Pole, a groundbreaking first for any country on Earth" (Tripathi, 2020). Another achievement of India in its space sector is opening up the aerospace sector to private companies. ISRO supported these private companies, such as Skyroot Aerospace, testing new rockets that could potentially make India a hub for launching small satellites. The Modi government aims to expand its presence in the global space. However, India's budgetary allocation for space programs is nominal in comparison with the USA. In the last decade, the Government of India invested nearly $13 billion, while the USA alone spent $117 billion in 2023. Hence, India needs to increase its investment in the space program.

20. Research and Development Policy

In India, research and development expenditure is mostly incurred by the public sector, while the global R&D trend speaks a different story. However, the Union Government is very much concerned about India's development through skill development, scientific research, education, and training. The "Union Budget 2024 allocated one trillion Indian rupees for research and innovation in emerging fields"(Rathore, 2024, September 24). The government also introduced loan guarantee programs to lower financial risks linked to high-cost innovation projects. The Indian corporate sector, unlike its counterparts in the US, Germany, and South Korea, spends an insignificant amount on R&D. "The private sector accounts for merely 36 percent of gross expenditure on R&D (gerd) in India" (Rathore, 2024, September 24). Finally, India needs to expedite collaboration between academia and industry. India has recently stressed research and development to increase production, discoveries, and patents.

From the above discussions, it can be safely concluded that all the governments have made necessary attempts to ensure GDP growth and the standard of living of people. Some have achieved success, while others have failed to achieve the same. Prime Minister Jawaharlal Nehru did a lot of development in the initial period of Independence. Prime Minister Indira Gandhi followed in the footsteps of her father, while PV Narasimha Rao initiated many bold measures to liberate the Indian economy for global investors. Dr. Manmohan Singh also took many policies for the transformation of India, but he had to face much internal political heat from coalition partners and even from Rahul Gandhi. Indian democracy is very strong and the Opposition plays a tough role in obstructing the welfare measures of the Government at every step. Despite many challenges – both from India and outside- the present Prime Minister, Narendra Modi excelled all his predecessors in formulating bold policies, implementing the same, and visualizing India as a developed country by 2047. Modi has unparalleled leadership qualities, a towering personality, problem-solving competence, and an unbiased outlook. India now feels proud of Narendra Modi.

In addition to the above, Narendra Modi is unique in his style of functioning and innovation in actions. He is an honest, hard-working, and visionary Prime Minister. Under his leadership, India has become the 5th largest economy within just 10 years. PM Modi is a heartthrob for both the young and old, in India and Western countries. He has taken unprecedented steps to take India to such a height that none of his predecessors in the recent past had ever thought of or had the caliber to perform, except P. V. Narasimha Rao in the nineties of the previous century. The developmental policies that were taken by the Modi Government made the majority of Indian people feel delighted and safe. Through the policies, it is hoped that the vision of a Viksit Bharat will be achieved if implemented properly and holistically by all the stakeholders. India's borders are now safe, India's economy is robust, India's agriculture is self-sufficient, Indian social security is inclusive, its space research and development in Science, Technology, Engineering, and Mathematics (STEM), etc., are envious to many Europeans and Americans. His sincere efforts, devotion to national service, clarity of vision, and hard work have made Indian citizens think and act in a more scientific way. His clarion call to work hard has inspired millions of Indians to work day and night for national development through personal skill development. The policies taken by the Modi Government have aroused self-respect, motivation, and self-development among Indian citizens. He has inculcated faith in the people through his words and actions. Hence, we can safely conclude that the policies, schemes, and programs formulated by the Modi Government will play an instrumental role in transforming India into a Viksit Bharat by 2047. If Pundit Jawaharlal Nehru is called the 'maker of modern India,' PM Modi may be called the 'maker of self-reliant India.' However, the following chapter will deal with the foreign policy of India from Jawaharlal Nehru to Narendra Modi. Let us turn the page to observe how the foreign policy of Modi shifted India's prestige and dignity in the global arena.

References:

1. The Formulation And Development of Public Policies in India. (2023, March 28). Indian School of Public Policy.

2. Birkland, Thomas A. (2011). *An Introduction to the Policy Process: Theories, Concepts and Methods of Public Policy Making. Third Edition*, Routledge.

3. Birkland, Thomas A. (2011). *An Introduction to the Policy Process: Theories, Concepts and Methods of Public Policy Making. Third Edition*, Routledge, p. 7.

4. Cochran, et al. (1999). *American Public Policy: An Introduction.* 6th ed. St. Martin's Press.

5. Dye, Thomas R. (1992). *Understanding Public Policy.* 7th ed. Prentice-Hall.

6. Peters, B. Guy (1999). *American Public Policy: Promise and Performance.* Chappaqua.

7. Birkland, Thomas A. (2011). *An Introduction to the Policy Process: Theories, Concepts and Methods of Public Policy Making. Third Edition*, Routledge, p. 8.

8. Birkland, Thomas A. (2011). *An Introduction to the Policy Process: Theories, Concepts and Methods of Public Policy Making. Third Edition*, Routledge, pp. 8-9.

9. Merchant, Minhaz. (2013, November 9). Congress: Why 2004 was a false dawn. *The Economic Times.*

10. The Factories (Amendment) Act, 2016.

11. Chikermane, G. (2018, July 27). Policies that Shaped India, 1947-2017: Independence to $2.5 Trillion. Observer Research Foundation, p. 27.

12. *Vivekananda: His Call to the Nation. A Compilation.* (2013) Advaita Ashrama.

13. Goldberg, Philip (2020, October 22). Countless Americans have been influenced by Swami Vivekananda, even if many don't know who he is. *Hindu American Foundation.*

14. (2014, August 15). Narendra Modi Calls Himself Pradhan Sevak in his Maiden Independence Day Speech. *The Indian Express.*

15. Ministry of Petroleum and Natural Gas. (N/D) Government of India, https://pmuy.gov.in/ accessed on 18.12.2024.

16. Ministry of Finance. (2023). *The Economic Survey, 2022-23.* Government of India.

17. Department of Financial Services. (N/D). Government of India, Pradhan Mantri Jan-Dhan Yojana.

18. Ministry of Commerce and Industry. (2022, September 22). *Make in India completes 8 years: annual FDI doubles to USD 83 billion.* Government of India.

19. Ministry of Commerce and Industry. (2024, February 7). Government of India, https://pib.gov.in/Press ReleaseIframePage.aspx?PRID=2003540 accessed on 18.12.2024).

20. Department of Commerce. (2023, April 13). *India's Foreign Trade.* Ministry of Commerce and Industry, Government of India.... https://commerce.gov.in/trade-statistics/latest-trade-figures/.

21. 10 Years of Make in India. (2024, September 25). Ministry of Commerce & Industry, Press Information Bureau.

22. Gaurav, K. (2022, November 3). No matter how powerful...' PM Modi's firm message on corruption. *The Hindustan Times.*

23. (2022, August 13). India at 75: all Villages Electrified. *The Times of India.*

24. Sharma, Ashutosh. (2023, February 10). Electrification still a challenge in rural India, *Frontline.*

25. Power Sector at a Glance. (N/D). Ministry of Power, Government of India, https://powermin.gov.in/ en/content/power-sector-glance-all-india, accessed on 19.12.2024.

26. Press Information Bureau. (2022, July 20). *Year End Review-2022: Ministry of Road Transport and Highways.* Government of India.

27. The World Bank. (2023, April 4). *Indian Economy Continues to Show Resilience Amid Global Uncertainties.*

28. Das, K. (2023, March 6). India's per capita income doubles, but does not mean you are richer. *India Today.*

29. India's GDP sees sharp growth trajectory; a look at the progress from 1947 to 2023. (2024, August 18). *The Financial Express.*

30. Celebrating GST Day: A Milestone in Economic Reform. (2024, June 28). Press Information Bureau, Government of India.

31. *The Economic Survey 2022-23.* (2023). Ministry of Finance. Government of India.

32. Ministry of Ayush. (N/D). Government of India, https://ayush.gov.in/#!/, accessed on 19.12.2024.

33. *The Economic Survey 2022-23.* (2023). Ministry of Finance. Government of India.

34. Ministry of Labor and Employment. (2023, February 13). Government of India, Press Information Bureau.

35. National Education Policy 2020. (2020).Government of India.

36. Prime Minister Internship Scheme 2024: Who is eligible, last date to register, how to enrol for PM Internship Scheme (PMIS) online. (2024, November 8). *The Economic Times.*

37. Jayakumar, PB, & Vinaykumar, Ravi. (2021, April 14). How much vaccines can India make? *India Today.*

38. Ministry of Agriculture and Farmers Welfare. (2023, March 21). *Government of India.*

39. The Formulation and Development of Public Policies in India. (2023, March 28). *Indian School of Public Policy.*

40. Press Information Bureau. (2021, November 30). Government of India, Ministry of Agriculture and Farmers Welfare.

41. Ministry of Commerce and Industry. (2023, March 31). Government of India, Press Information Bureau.

42. Ministry of Commerce and Industry (2024, December 16). Department of Commerce, Government of India, Press Information Bureau.

43. Science, Technology, and Innovation Policy (STIP). (2020, December). Government of India, Ministry of Science & Technology, Department of Science and Technology, p.14.

44. List of ISRO's space missions: From Aryabhatta to Chandrayan. (2024, August 23). *The Times of India*.

45. Tripathi, S. (2020, June 11). PM Modi to steer India's space dreams: What lies ahead in Modi 3.0?, *India Today*.

46. Rathore, M. (2024, September 24). Research and Development in India. *Statista*, https://www.statista. com/topics/12602/research-and-development-in-india/#topicOverview.

IV
India's Foreign Policy

- Henry Kissinger

After discussing India's public policies, this chapter will focus on the foreign policy from India's first Prime Minister Pundit Jawaharlal Nehru to present Prime Minister Narendra Modi. The foreign policy of India is so vast and complex that it is difficult to include them all in a small chapter like this one. However, the policies of Pundit Jawaharlal Nehru, Smt. Indira Gandhi, Rajiv Gandhi, and Dr. Manmohan Singh will be discussed briefly here followed by Modi's foreign policy. This chapter aims to examine if there is any paradigm shift in Modi's policy from his predecessors. Also, it is intended to investigate how far Modi's policies have impacted the lives of the Indian people and its economy, business and trade, international relations, and global politics that propelled the world leaders to consider India as a "global savior" and "global problem solver."

An Overview of India's Foreign Policy

What is the foreign policy of a country, why it is important, and what are the salient features of foreign policy? How far India's foreign policy is instrumental in making it a global superpower? This part seeks to analyze all these issues. Dinesh Kumar Jain indicates that "Foreign policies are developed by governments of diverse countries utilizing high-level decision-making procedures because national interests are paramount. It matters a lot how the rest of the world regards a country. Foreign policies that are harsh include dealing with the issues of other nations may lead to military action or economic embargoes being used often" (Jain, 2014). Indian foreign policy is largely concerned with maintaining cordial ties with all countries, especially with the neighboring countries, and it has been built on the principles of 'Non-Alignment' and *Panchsheel.*' The sole aim of a country's foreign policy is to "promote its national interests in international affairs"(Goyal, 2022, pp. 219-235).

In this regard, Johnson, David E Johnson, DP Jennifer, Roger Cliff Moroney, and others recently in a book chapter: "According to Stephen Philip Cohen, there is an idealistic tone to India's foreign policy that stems from Gandhian idealism. This idealism is one of the reasons that India is one of the largest supporters of UN peacekeeping operations. Indian strategists are also keenly aware that their international status, especially within the developing world, depends on their idealistic behavior. Successive Indian governments have aspired to great-power status in one form or another, an ambition based on India's sense of their history, on their ideology, and their emerging economic power" (Johnson, Moroney, Cliff et. al., 2009, p. 179). However, it seems that India's foreign policy was influenced by Gandhi's thoughts. In the *Young India* (20.10.2023) he wrote that a correspondence from Ludhina asked him some questions, and in reply to them, he gave answers. From that question and answer, his thought on India's foreign policy in the pre-independence era is reflected. The question and answer were like this: "(1) Shall India's foreign policy be governed by any other consideration but that of its population? Naturally the interest of India must be given preference over all others" (Gandhi, 1942, p. 22).

Further, "A country's foreign policy encompasses more than just its international policies; it also includes its commitment, present interests and ambitions, and the values of proper conduct that it espouses" (Malone et al., 2015). Through foreign policy, like any country, India also seeks to promote its national interest, establish its dignity in foreign lands, exhibit its strength and power, and attempt to regulate other's behavior to attain its own goals and objectives. According to Professor Mahendra Kumar, "The aim of foreign policy should be to regulate and not merely to change the behavior of other states. Regulation means adjusting the behavior of other states to suit one's own interest as best as possible" (Kumar, 1969, pp. 385-387). Indian foreign policy changed from time to time as per the need and outlook of respective governments.

In the pre-independence period, India's foreign policy was guided by the interest of the British Government. India adopted an independent foreign policy as soon as it attained freedom. The root of India's foreign policy was formed in the Resolution Regarding Aims and Objects of the Assembly, 13 December 1946, where we find Jawaharlal Nehru to move a resolution, therein paragraph 8 reads: "This ancient land attains the rightful and honored place in the world and makes its full and willing contribution to the promotion of world peace and the welfare of mankind." Further, Article 51 of the Constitution is a pledge that says "India will work for the promotion of world peace and security, enhancement of International Law and treaty obligations and settlement of its differences with other countries by peaceful means" (Verma, 1989, p. 304). Now, we will discuss briefly about the Non-Alignment Movement and *Panchsheel* in the following part.

Non-Alignment and *Panchsheel*

In the aftermath of the Second World War, when the world was bifurcated into two war groups, India joined none. The war-like situation is described as the Cold War. The Cold War has been described as "a situation in which each side continually envisages war with the acknowledged rival, it is a state of continuous preparation for war, a continuous war alert;... compatible with all forms of organized violence short of direct encounters between the armed forces of the two superpowers" (Lyon, 1963, p. 18). The world was divided into two belligerent blocs. It was "An implicit arrangement in any military alliance is that the weaker power surrenders some part of its freedom of action to the stronger power in return for a guarantee of security. Due to military weakness, the non-aligned countries had to rely upon the international system and the balance of power to provide their security in the short run." P.R. Chari illustrates "...the strategy of non-alignment, also implied buying time, through maintaining maximum independence of policy by keeping aloof from the cold war politics of two blocs, during which they could develop themselves first in the economic field and then in the military field" (Chari, 1976, p.70) Thus, it is seen as being an essentially anti-status quo movement with the characteristic of a dynamic policy. One of the major characteristics of non-align policy is its ability to judge international issues on merit. "Military alliances, on the contrary, are now becoming outmoded conceptions, SEATO has ceased to exist as a defense arrangement; the détente between the United States and China destroyed a security arrangement designed primarily to contain the Chinese Communist threat. The NATO is under strain..." (Chari, 1976, p. 72). Despite some constraints, NATO is standing and still active in countering threats to democracy and global peace and stability.

In the post-World War II era, when the world was bifurcated into two blocs namely the Western Bloc (led by the USA) and the Eastern Bloc (essentially by the Soviet Union). The developing countries and newly independent countries were drawn into any of the two blocs. But India being a proud and dignified country for thousands of years decided under the first Prime Minister Pundit Nehru that India would not join any bloc. Hence, NAM originated from a meeting in 1955 of several Asian and African countries in Bandung, Indonesia. The "Non-Alignment" was coined by Indian Prime Minister Pundit Jawaharlal Nehru in his famous speech in 1954 in Colombo, Sri Lanka. The founding fathers of the movement were Josip Bros Tito of Yugoslavia, Sukarno of Indonesia, Gamal Abdel Nasser of Egypt, Kwame Nkrumah of Ghana, and Jawaharlal Nehru from India. "NAM's main principles are what are popularly known as 'panchsheel" (five principles), though these were originally formulated by Chinese premier Zhou Enlai in the context of Sino-Indian relations. The five principles are: mutual respect for each other's territorial integrity and sovereignty; mutual non-aggression; non-interference in each other's internal affairs; equality and mutual benefit; and peaceful co-existence" (The Times of India, 2006).

Objectives of Foreign Policy

There are five main objectives of a foreign policy. (i) The primary goal of a foreign policy is to safeguard the country's territorial integrity and people's interests from both within and beyond the country. (ii) The second goal is to maintain ties with other countries of the international community and to pursue a policy of confrontation or collaboration with them in order to further its national interests such as economic development, environmental sustainability, military strength, safety, and security of its citizens anywhere in the world. (iii) The third goal of a country's foreign policy is to promote and advance its national interest. (iv) The fourth purpose of a foreign policy is to promote the country's indigenous literature and culture throughout the world. (v) The fifth purpose is to increase the state's influence either by expanding its sphere of influence or by putting other countries in a position of reliance. Apart from the above, two other cardinal objectives of India's foreign policy are "to live and let live," and "to grow and let grow." In this matter, the principle of *Basudhaiva Kutumbkam* is adopted. Now let us examine in brief about India's foreign policy under PM Modi. Before that, we need to discuss in short the foreign policy actions of Pundit Jawaharlal Nehru. In this part, the foreign policy of Indira Gandhi, P.V. Narasimha Rao, and Dr. Manmohan Singh will also be examined in short.

Foreign Policy of Pundit Nehru, Indira Gandhi, P.V. Narasimha Rao and Dr. Manmohan Singh

India's foreign policy was shaped by Pundit Nehru (1947-64). India's tough stand can be well understood from the speech of Nehru in the United States Congress, when he said, "Where freedom is menaced, justice threatened or where aggression takes place, we cannot be and shall not be neutral. On another occasion, he said, "Our policy is not to commit ourselves previously to follow a certain line. Our policy is the independence of action if we say. We are permanently neutral; it has no means except permanent retirement from public affairs in the national sense, "*Sanyas.*" No country can do that and certainly, we have no desire to retire from world affairs." A. Appadorai in one of his works has rightly commented, "Thus independent foreign policy is not the same thing as neutrality, it may demand, if and when war comes, that India should join the free nations to realize her objective of freedom and peace. It is not a negative policy, it is a positive one, designed to realize the objectives of peace, freedom, and friendliness with like-minded nations, and the economic development of herself and other under-developed nations, this independent foreign policy only means that India refuses to commit herself in advance to either bloc utilizing a pact or otherwise to surrender her freedom to judge each issue as it arises on its merits" (Appadorai quoted in Batria, pp. 8-9).

Deepak Lal discussed India's foreign policy from 1947 to 1964 under Jawaharlal Nehru. He pointed out that "As with any foreign policy, the claims of national security were very important in Nehru's model." There were two basic value assumptions in the model that required a two-pronged general strategy. On the one hand preserving national security in the world as it is, with its imperfect human beings and power-politicking amongst States, whilst at the same time trying to move towards the notional ideal of a "new" society, both at home and abroad" (Lal, 1967, p. 881). "For Nehru national security implied not merely physical security but also freedom from political and economic domination. The latter was almost as important for him as were physical security." In terms of sources of strength the author cited Nehru's statement: "Whether it is a problem of defence or trade or industry or economic policy, India cannot be ignored.... She cannot be ignored, because... her geographical position is a compelling reason. She cannot be ignored also, because of her potential power and resources" (Lal, 1967, p. 882).

Indira Gandhi (1966-77 & 1980-84) was a pragmatic politician. She carried forward the legacy of her father. Through foreign policy, she tried to rebuild her own image in the global arena as it was mostly shattered by her ban on media and arrest of opposition party leaders during the emergency period. She dismantled every institution – judiciary, press, parliament, and even cabinet, which came her way during the emergency. Despite the fact, she was the 'de facto First Lady' of India. Foreign policy can never be discussed in isolation; it is very much related to the national interest, national security, and domestic aspirations. She might not have governing experience but learned International Relations, diplomacy, and world politics from the discussions his father had with world leaders during various international meetings as a companion of her father. This gave her practical experience in international affairs. Dr. Ajay Kumar Sharma and Dr. Jitendra Kumar in an article (Sharma & Kumar, 2015, p. 20.) pointed out: "Nevertheless, she was open-minded with every other country but still the Western criticism and her growing resentment steered her towards the Soviet camp...Indira's mindset of resentment towards the West was not applicable to France, because she had a soft corner for it. For Mrs. Gandhi, 'West' to a large extent meant 'America', whose insincerity in the 1971 war, is explicitly condemned. She obviously points out that her amity with a country is a part of worldwide affairs and it doesn't mean that she should relinquish her sovereign outlook on any key issue; it is all stuff of bewilderment." Shashi Tharoor in an interview with Mrs. Gandhi asked some questions regarding her vision of the world and India's place and role in world affairs. From the conversation, her views on foreign policy can be well understood. Tharoor wrote in one of his books (Reasons of State, p. 89): "...Five considerations emerge for Mrs. Gandhi's statements" the value of independence and self-reliance; an assertive "Indianness"; and awareness of the use of foreign political policy and domestic economic ends, with both involving the concept of "strength"; a rejection of traditional international power politics; and finally almost surprisingly, a quest for international influence in the direction of peace and of the "eminence" resulting therefrom." She used to interact personally with the major powers such as the UK, USA, and Soviet Union, and the rest of the countries were dealt with by her foreign minister.

Indira Gandhi restructured some committees related to foreign affairs. In 1970, she abolished the Committees on Foreign Affairs, broke the Defence and Internal Affairs, and formed the Political Affairs Committee (PAC). During her tenure, she appointed four foreign ministers including Sardar

Swarn Singh, Mohammed Currim Chagla, Dinesh Singh, and Y.B. Chavan. Further, Sharma and Kumar mentioned that "Indians failed to recognize foreign policy as one of the fundamental pillars of governance" (Sharma & Kumar, 2015, p. 23). Foreign policy and public policies cannot be discussed separately; rather they are interdependent. Mrs. Gandhi in an interview once said: "A country's foreign policy cannot be divorced from its internal policy. Any country, any government, any political party must decide what it believes in, and all its policies must then flow from this basic conviction or belief" (Emmanuel, 1981, p. 132). To describe her image and personality Aruna Asaf Ali said, "She brought India back to the center of the international stage from the periphery. I watched with joy as the daughter of India, as Chairperson of the Non-Align Movement, recaptured the spirit of the fifties when her father initiated the Movement along with other political giants of that time such as Marshal Tito and President Nasser...She was fully aware that certain Western powers were alarmed at her growing strength, her forthright condemnation of imperialism, [and] her refusal to be pressurized by any big power" (Sawkar, 2022). She also gave primary importance to maintaining good relations with her neighbors such as Bangladesh. When she felt that the people in East Pakistan were being tortured and exploited by the Pakistani Army, she extended her support through diplomacy. Ultimately she bravely fought the India-Pakistan war of 1971 and decisively won the battle, and by splitting Pakistan into two she created a new country Bangladesh. She also wrote several letters to global leaders for almost six months from March to October 1971 to sensitize the merciless butchering of the Pakistani Army on the civilian population in East Pakistan. She also visited Moscow, France, Germany, Britain, Belgium, and the USA to arouse the world's consciousness and seek their support. Ultimately her relation with the then USSR came into use to win her battle against Pakistan. She was a sagacious and far-sighted global leader in a true sense.

P.V. Narasimha Rao (1991-96), a polyglot lawyer and experienced statesman from Telangana, became the Prime Minister of India outside the Nehru-Gandhi family in 1991. It was a crucial time in international politics too as the then Union of Soviet Socialist Republics (USSR) was disintegrated ushering in the end of the Cold War. "The then structure of the international system reflected the changing power dynamics with the United States (US) asserting its dominance in the international community. In the changed circumstances, Rao took a vital decision to deviate from the conventional approach to foreign policy by establishing diplomatic relations with countries having strategic significance for India" (Joseph & Mucheli, 2024).

Prime Minister Rao himself served as the foreign minister in the 1980s under the premiership of both Indira Gandhi and Rajiv Gandhi. He himself was an expert in international affairs. But being the Prime Minister of India he appointed Dr. Manmohan Singh, a renowned economist, as finance minister and a young lawyer P. Chidambaram, the commerce Minister; similarly, he appointed J.N. Dixit, a South Asia expert, as foreign secretary to demonstrate his authority in Indian politics as well as international affairs. He, like the present Prime Minister Narendra Modi, had the vision of making India a developed country. Mr. Chengappa in an article in *India Today* (1991) said: "Rao's first overseas visit, in late 1991, was to Germany. During his visit to Germany, his speech extolling the virtues of investing in India showed the acumen of a corporate chief executive and indeed, six months of rigorous study of the briefs given to him." He developed relations with the Middle East. Also, he decided to develop relation with Israel. "In 1991 itself, he invited the Chairman of the Palestine Liberation Organization (PLO), Yasser Arafat, for the state visit" (Kumar, 2022). During his tenure, India's diplomatic relations with Israel developed fully. He equally paid importance to Iranians and Arabs. His one of greatest contributions to Indo-China diplomatic relations is when he signed the 'Agreement on the Maintenance of Peace and Tranquillity along the ...India-China Border Areas. It was a landmark agreement in terms of the Indo-China relationship. Further, his Look East Policy is also a very significant foreign policy initiative that sought to strengthen India's ties with Southeast Asia, counter the influence of China in the region, and increase strategic and security cooperation.

He also intended to develop bilateral relations as well as India's image in the international domain. Hence, Rao paid a visit to South Korea, Indonesia, Thailand, Singapore, and Malaysia. During his time, Indo-Pak relation was improved. His period is characterized by six meetings between him and his Pakistani counterparts in his first 2 years in office. He tried to normalize relations with the United States of America and invited Bill Clinton to be the chief guest for the Republic Day parade in Delhi, but it was declined by the Clinton administration. Under Rao's leadership, India signed a new defense agreement with Moscow in 1994. India under PM Rao prepared ingredients for the nuclear bomb but could afford to explode in 1991. However, he gave a note to his successor Atal Behari Bajpayee to explode the same. He was an ambassador of Indian tradition and culture too. "Rao's foreign travels were notable for the cultivation of both businessmen and Indologists. In that sense, he was a pioneer in economic as well as cultural diplomacy" (Kumar, 2022).

Unlike Narasimha Rao, Dr. Manmohan Singh (2004-14) was a unanimous pick of the Congress Party. Being a sober economist, an academician in heart, and a loyal to Congress supremo, Singh could not make independent decisions in either domestic or international affairs. Indian people had a lot of expectations from him in relation to India's national growth and development as well as the growth of diplomatic relations with the globally powerful leaders. He was successful to a large extent. Dr. Singh started his foreign policy innings when his predecessor Atal Bihari Vajpayee left. "There was no shake-up in India's foreign policy. He chose not to deviate from the stand that Vajpayee pursued – a policy of greater engagement – with regard to the US, China, and Pakistan, the three countries critical in India's foreign relations" (Roy Chaudhury, 2014). Dr. Manmohan Singh successfully expanded relations with each of these countries. Indo-US bilateral relations during his tenure took a new shape when they signed a landmark civil nuclear deal, which liberated India from the Nuclear Suppliers Group. International experts consider it as recognition of India as a de facto nuclear power by the US Administration. He left no stone unturned to improve relations with Pakistan. Dr. Singh engaged with three successive governments and made several peace overtures. "The Samjhauta Express and Delhi-Lahore Bus Service are the two main initiatives made by both countries to create healthy contact between the countries" (Sarkar, 2013, p. 514).

Japan is another country that has invested in India in several automobile companies and it has contributed to setting up India's infrastructure, especially New Delhi's metro subway system. Indo-Japan Relation is an age-old affair. Dr. Singh visited Japan and signed a treaty in 2006 named "Joint Statement Towards Japan-India Strategic and Global Partnership." India improved ties with Japan to such a level that Japan granted a low-interest loan of $4.5 billion to construct a high-speed rail line between Delhi and Mumbai. Also, both countries were concerned with the problem of international terrorism and signed a security cooperation agreement in which both will hold military exercises on fighting terrorism. "Prime Minister Dr. Manmohan Singh signed at the 3rd ASEAN-Inddia summit in November 2004 on India-ASEAN for peace, progress and shared prosperity" and set up Entrepreneurship Development Centres in ASEAN member states like - Cambodia, Burda, Laos and Vietnam"(Sarkar, 2013, p. 514).

Barack Obama had great respect for Dr. Manmohan Singh. On 24 November 2009, Dr. Manmohan Singh was invited as the guest of honor at the first state dinner. In return, from 6-9 November 2010 Obama also paid a visit to India and signed numerous trade and defence agreements with India. He addressed the Joint Parliamentary session of the Indian Parliamentary and announced his support for India's claim for permanent membership in the UN Security Council. India's relationship with France is always good. During the regime of Dr. Manmohan Singh French President Nicolas Sarkozy visited India in 2008 as the chief guest at the Republic Day parade. Dr. Singh also visited on 14 July 2008 during the Bastille Day as the chief guest of honor. India's relationship with Russia was also tightened. He made an official visit to the Russian Federation in 2013 at the invitation of President Vladimir Putin, and the same relationship continues to this day with Narendra Modi. Mr. Putin and Dr. Singh "agreed to work towards the creation of a Joint Study Group to study the possibility of signing a comprehensive Economic Cooperation Agreement (CEDA) between India and Customs Union of Belarus, Kazakhstan, and the Russian Federation. Both countries agreed to cooperation in science and technology, educational and cultural cooperation, inter-regional cooperation, cooperation in the field of Disarmament and Non-proliferation, enhancing security cooperation in Asia and Asia Pacific, and cooperation among BRICS countries. Both Russia and India believe that the crisis of Syria should be settled only through political means" (Sarkar, 2013, p. 515). Now, we will examine the foreign policy in contemporary India under the leadership of Prime Minister Narendra Modi.

Foreign Policy under PM Modi

Prime Ministers come and go but the basic structure of foreign policy of a country remains almost unchanged. When Narendra Modi came to power in 2014, the world was curious to know if there would be any shift in India's foreign policy. The curiosity of the people was genuine, because he was the first Prime Minister who belonged to the Hindu nationalist party and had neither prior experience of any foreign office, nor he had any time before becoming a Member of Parliament. Hence, quite naturally many policy strategists and foreign policy experts were confused about the future course of India's foreign policy under his leadership. In this regard, SD Pradhan states that "In July 2014, at an international conference in Vietnam, a group of foreign policy experts from the Western countries desired to know what the nature of India's foreign policy under PM Modi would be. It was a difficult question for me to answer; hence I decided to go by the manifesto of the BJP. I told them that 'the Indian policy would strive to improve ties with key states to aid economic development and enhance its global standing while bolstering its security interests" (Pradhan, 2022).

There came many situations when India had to take a wise stand. Recently India caught between historic ties with old friend Russia and a burgeoning partnership with the United States. But India deftly navigated relations with great global powers following the invasion of Ukraine, while staying true to its position of strategic autonomy (Mishra, 2023). This paradigm shift in India's foreign policy began its journey with Prime Minister Narendra Modi which encompassed the "Neighborhood First Policy" embodied by SAARC as well as the 'Look East Policy' to forge more extensive economic and strategic relationships with other East Asian countries. In his first oath-taking ceremony in 2014, the Prime Minister invited "all the leaders of the SAARC countries, including Pakistan Prime Minister Nawaz Sharif. Outside the SAARC the invitation had gone to Mauritius PM Navin Ramgoolam also (The Times of India, 2014). This ushered in a new era of India's foreign policy under the Modi Government. In the second swearing-in-ceremony of PM Modi, leaders of all BIMSTEC nations (BIMSTEC or the Bay of Bengal Initiative for Multi-Sectoral Technical and Economic Cooperation regional group of countries including Bangladesh, India, Myanmar, Sri Lanka, Thailand, Nepal, and Bhutan) were invited to attend along with Mauritius and Kyrgyz Republic.

India's foreign policy has taken a new turn under PM Modi. Today the global situation has changed; the strength of the Indian government has become stronger; and the attitude and perception of the Prime Minister has been renewed many-fold. India has shunned the policy of "Non-Alignment," instead it has adopted the policy of "Multi-Alignment." India's strategic orientations are now guided by the Quadrilateral Security Dialogue (Quad) partnership including the United States, Japan, and Australia in the Indo-Pacific. The world politics has transformed from bi-polarism to multi-polarism. India's Foreign Minister S. Jaishankar while speaking recently (March, 2022) at the *Institut Francais Des Relations Internationales* (IFRI) in Paris, contended that the world was undergoing "profound geopolitical, geo-economic and technological changes" (Tourangbam, 2022). The world politics is always volatile. It has become more uncertain in recent years.

In such a stormy geopolitical situation, India has a very clear and firm objective, i.e. to set up autonomy to protect and promote its national interests and exert its supremacy in the global sphere. The Prime Minister is wise enough to comprehend the geopolitics of the world, and at the same time, he realizes India's current socio-economic, political, and military strengths. He properly hits the iron when it is red. Monish Tourangbam in a recent article (Tourangbam, 2022) writes, "Today's India is materially more endowed and overtly more aspirational in the search for its rightful place in the international system....at a time when Delhi's military, diplomatic, and economic resources provide it more latitude than ever before, its positions on matters of international concern are watched with more scrutiny."

How did India Emerge as a Global Leader During the Modi Regime?

The far-sighted Prime Minister of India took stock of the ongoing global challenges particularly the tensions that arose between Russia and US-led Western powers. After the attack of Russian troops on Ukraine last year (2022) the relations between Russia and the Western powers in general and the United States, in particular, have reached a nadir. When the Western powers began to show their red eyes on Russia, China did not waste time extending goodwill gestures and helping hands to its Communist friend. The second most powerful economy China when coming closer to Russia, the USA felt insecurity in the international arena; though it continued to get cooperation and solidarity from European countries, especially from Germany and the U.K. But their combined strength was not enough that defeat the Chinese, Russian, and some other erstwhile Communist states. Moreover, all are economically and militarily powerful with nuclear powers.

In the wake of Russia-Ukraine tension, the global oil crisis reached a new height. Most of the European countries and the USA depended substantially on Russian crude oil. In an article, Reuters reports that "Outside the EU, Russia's top crude oil export markets are China, India, and Turkey" (Reuters, 2022). To punish Russia, the European Union and the USA imposed the world's toughest economic sanctions and sought to politically isolate Russia. In such a situation, India faced international pressure to halt Russian oil imports. But India listened to its inner call and in the true spirit of strategic autonomy; it carefully balanced buying Russian oil while sustaining relations with the West regardless of the political pressure. As the war progressed and India showed little intention of cutting ties with Russia or curtailing its energy dependence, the United States though dissatisfied with the government of India showed maturity in its decision to accommodate

India. India remained tough and stuck to its commitment to forging its independent foreign policy.

This tough stand of India with its US counterpart became a boon, and it opened additional avenues for India to engage with the countries of the European Union. Narendra Modi used the opportunity to travel to three European countries viz. Germany, Denmark, and France in early May of 2022 cemented India's resolve to expand relations with its European partners. This visit brought many new avenues for India. In a blog article (My Gov., 2022) of the Government of India it was revealed that "During his visit to Germany, Denmark, and France, he met leaders and various entrepreneurs. The Prime Minister held bilateral talks with the Nordic leaders. Looking at the political, strategic, and economic significance of this visit, it was highly important and successful. Given India's good relations with both Russia and Ukraine and the ongoing Ukraine-Russia conflict, Modi's role in restoring stability and peace in the region is highly anticipated. India is not in favor of any one party as it has a neutral stand taking inspiration from the principle of Non-Alignment. India being a neutral country is a friend of both sides and holds a crucial global presence as a part of Quad and as a special invitee to the G-7 grouping." For economic prosperity, India has joined another Quad for West Asia with the US, UAE, and Israel. India's meeting with the European leaders created a global perception regarding India that the country is changing and they recognized India's power and importance in international trade and security. In every country where he visited PM Modi was accorded an overwhelming and most effusive welcome by the Indian diaspora. These visits engaged more and better strategic partnerships with European countries in the fields of defense, space, civil nuclear cooperation, and people-to-people relations. However, Modi's travels followed the visit of Ursula von der Leyen, president of the European Commission, to India in April 2022 for the Raisina Dialogue. "These efforts lay the path for ongoing European countries despite impediments that have long hindered closer ties" (Mishra, 2023).

India-Russia Friendship

India defied the US ban on Russia's oil, and it continued good relations with both Russia and Ukraine without supporting or condemning publicly any one of the rivals. India had its own national interest and it had to fulfil it. India had to ensure the life and security of students and other people stranded after the conflict grew in Ukraine, and it was a massive challenge for the Government of India to safely bring its people back from war-torn Ukraine. India deeply maintains its allies with the USA and others in the Indo-Pacific, because India never forgets the challenges that might be posed at any time by China. India's defense partnership with Russia is a primary ingredient of India's military preparedness. India respects and adores the long-standing friendship with Russia since the Indo-Pak war of 1971. History suggests that, on 8 December 1971 Washington dispatched a ten-ship naval task force, the US Task Force 74, from the Seventh Fleet off South Vietnam in the Bay of Bengal in support of Pakistan during the Indo-Pak war. Consequently, the Soviet Union backed India politically and militarily and even responded to India's call by deploying two groups of cruisers and destroyers as well as a submarine armed with nuclear warheads in response to the American military presence in the area. Moreover, Russia has been a strategic partner since the independence of India. In this regard, the Indo-Soviet Treaty of Peace, Friendship, and Cooperation of 1971 is apt to be mentioned here. In contemporary world politics, India might invest time and energy in Quad, and its military may carry out sophisticated interoperability exercises and sign foundational agreements with the US, defense purchases and co-production with Moscow remain the backbone of India's foreign policy.

The Roots of Indo-Russia Relationship

India's relationship with Russia dates back to one and a quarter-century old. Under the British colonial period, Russia opened its first consulate in Mumbai in 1900. India found friendship in Russia in her struggle against anti-colonial and anti-imperial movements. With the growing of the Cold War in the post-World War II period, "it became more anti-West,' and both countries shared anti-U.S. sentiments. In November 2022 when the top foreign diplomat Dr. S. Jaishankar traveled to Moscow, he stood alongside his Russian counterpart Sergei Lavrov and called their relationship "steady and time-tested." The Indo-Russian relations grew substantially over the years with defence and strategic dimensions as key elements of the relationship. "Since 1947, India and Russia have diplomatic relations. In 2017, the two countries celebrated 70 years of establishment of diplomatic relations, which on the whole remained warm and cordial and are still so" (Pradhan, 2021). Russia always stands by India in crises and extends its solidarity and support, may it be Indian national sovereignty over Kashmir or Goa.

At present India is the fastest-growing economy in the world. By 2023, India is going to be the third-largest economy in the world. Without fuel, no real growth is possible in the 21st century. All the industries and individual citizens are dependent on fuel and energy. India has not sufficient oil and gas reserves of its own, and most of the oil it needs is required to be imported. India, though buys more oil from Middle Eastern countries than Russia, but the price of their oil has skyrocketed. Hence, to meet the domestic energy needs India had to import 1.2 million barrels of Russian crude, which was a whopping 33 times more than a year earlier. The reason behind this decision was the "deep discount" of Russian oil.

The USA and the Western powers imposed a tough embargo on Russian fuel. However, India undertook a very sturdy and uncompromising decision to import oil. The decision of India to purchase crude from Russia was ultimately accepted by Washington and "Earlier this month U.S. Assistant Secretary of State for Energy Resources Geoffery Pyatt said Washington is "comfortable" with India's approach on Russian oil. And Karen Donfried, the assistant secretary of state for European and Eurasian Affairs, said the U.S. is not looking at sanctioning India for this" (Frayer, 2023).

India has a venerable relationship with Russia. India has been buying arms and ammunition from Russia for many decades now and it can be traced back to the Cold War period. Today India is Russia's biggest arms dealer and Indian arsenal is mostly Soviet-made. Recently, India has started procuring aircraft and artillery from France, Israel, and America. Despite that, Russia has reportedly supplied India with around $13 billion in weapons in the past 5 years alone. Not only that, The Economic Times in a report highlighted that "...and New Delhi has orders placed with Moscow for weapons and military equipment...India is the world's biggest buyer of Russian arms, accounting for around 20% of Moscow's current order book" (The Economic Times, 2023). India cannot but help buy weapons from Russia and keep good relations with her. It is a well-known fact that India's biggest foreign policy challenge is not the Russian invasion of Ukraine; rather it is China. Historically and geographically India and China share more than 2,000 miles of disputed border. In the wake of Russia's attack on Ukraine, the world is witnessing a very close tie emerging between Russia and China. So, the current Indian approach is "we don't want Russia to go completely into the Chinese fold. Because for India, China has become the No. 1 national security threat" (Frayer, 2023). It is a matter of concern for India when a Russian aircraft engine is reaching Pakistan via China.

Russia was, on the other hand, equally concerned about India's increasing engagement with the USA (Pradhan, 2021).

Modi-Putin Friendship: an Extraordinary Chemistry

Despite all the facts, Russia also shows its keenness to strengthen relations with India. Considering India's thriving power and global influence under the Modi regime, the Russian President invited PM Modi as the chief guest at the September 2019 Eastern Economic Forum, which reflected its willingness to integrate India and its Far Eastern economic strategy. Even Putin's visit to India in 2020 was an overall "satisfaction at the sustained progress" as the two leaders pointed out in a joint statement.

Indo-Russian friendship has taken the best shape under Prime Minister Narendra Modi. The diplomatic relations between the two leaders - President Vladimir Putin and Prime Minister Narendra Modi - have turned into friendship, one can call it an informal friendship too. On 22nd October, 2024 when Prime Minister Modi went to Russia's Kazan to attend the 16th BRICS summit, in their first meeting they at first shook hands and then hugged each other warmly before beginning the talks. During the meeting, Mr. Putin highlighted his friendship with Modi by saying "Our relationship is so strong that you will understand me without any translation" (Chakraborty, 2024). He further said, "In Kazan, we must make a number of important decisions aimed at further improving the activities of the association and strengthening multifaceted cooperation within its framework. And we greatly value our cooperation in this area, I mean that our states stood at the origins of the association's creation" (Chakraborty, 2024). Once again upheld that India and Russia have a "Privileged strategic partnership."

Indo-US Relations

India's relations with the USA were never as good and cordial as is now seen during the Modi Administration. Besides, US foreign policy has also evolved in the last seven decades. John Hemmings writes, "The development of the U.S. alliance system at the tail end of the 20th century in the post-Cold War era has significance compared to the era that came before it. From the inception of the system in the 1950s, it was characterized by its "hub-and-spokes" relationship between each U.S. ally and Washington" (Hemmings, 2020, p. 145). Since the nineties of the previous century, the USA had started to put more importance on China.

Indo-US Relations in the Present International Context

Despite all the international tensions and crises, India and the USA continue to develop their relations warm and cordial to safeguard and promote each other's interests in the global canvas. This is a contemporary phenomenon. This relationship has never existed earlier. "In the first few years of the twenty-first century, New Delhi and Washington overcame decades of suspicion to forge a "strategic partnership." In return for a reversal of U.S. nuclear non-proliferation policies, Washington bet "that a more powerful India will help the United States directly oppose worrisome Chinese policies, indirectly balance China by drawing away Beijing's attention and resources, and provide net security benefits in South and beyond" (Gilboy & Heginbotham, 2013, p. 7). Narendra Modi has developed an unprecedented relationship with the former presidents Barack Obama and Donald Trump, and the present president Joe Biden. History barely could forget the syndrome of the close relationship between PM Modi and Barack Obama during the latter's official tour to India during his second term in office. Today India and the United States cooperate closely with multilateral organizations, including the United Nations, G-20, Association of Southeast Asian Nations (ASEAN) Regional Forum, International Monetary Fund, World Bank, and World Trade Organization. Together with Australia, Japan, and United States India is a member of Quad that seeks to promote a free and open Indo-Pacific and provide tangible benefits to the region. India is also one of twelve countries partnering with the United States on the Indo-Pacific Economic Framework for Prosperity (IPEF) to make US economies more connected, resilient, clean, and fair. At present, India is a member of the Indian Ocean Rim Association (IORA), at which the United States is a dialogue partner. Considering India's growing power and influence in the International forums, the USA advocates India's permanent membership in the reformed Security Council, and it welcomed India's joining the Security Council for two years in 2021 (U.S. Department of State, 2022).

The USA understands well, that if India, China, and Russia once bonded together, there would be a disaster for the Western world, particularly the USA, and their dominance in the world economy, trade, and military exercise might be at stake. China can never be a good and faithful ally to the Western powers particularly the USA due to their ideological as well as strategic differences. On the contrary, India was never inclined to any bloc; it has maintained a Non-Alignment policy since its independence. India proved herself as a non-violent and non-aggressive country for a long. India is recognized as a peaceful and truthful country. Hence, India is adorable, acceptable, and reliable to any country in the world. For all these reasons, India has emerged as a "global leader," "global savior" and "global problem solver."

Why India Maintains an Independent Foreign Policy?

Since the Cold War period, India has maintained a Non-Alignment policy. Besides, India's geographical position compels it to practice strategic autonomy in making its foreign policy. India is no doubt now a predominant country in the world, but it cannot afford to escape its two nuclear powerful neighbors – China and Pakistan. It is an undeniable fact that, in the continental and maritime environment in South Asia, China has distinct footprints in the security and economic realms. India has a sweet-bitter relationship with Russia. India warns Mr. Putin "It is not a time to war" but at the same time remains absent from the UN General Assembly in time of censure and banning Russia. India is fully aware of the longstanding geopolitical roots of the Russia-Ukraine war. It (the conflict) was a result of the faceoff between NATO's eastward drive and Russia's gradual feeling of insecurity.

Prime Minister Narendra Modi knows how to keep a balance with the two rival camps of the Cold War era - Moscow and Washington. However, the Prime Minister paid a visit to respond to the invitations by Austria and Russia on 8-10 July 2024. Vladimir Putin, a very stern President of Russia, is a close friend of Mr. Modi. They have informal relations too. However, this historic visit saw the 22nd Annual India-Russia Summit. Indian Prime Minister's main aim was to negotiate with Mr. Putin to end the Russia-Ukraine conflict for the greater interest of the people of both countries as well as the whole world. Mr. Modi's visit to Russia also witnessed the signing of 9 Memorandum of Understanding including Indo-Russia cooperation in trade, economic, and investment spheres in the Russian Far East for the period from 2024 to 2027 as well as cooperation principles in the Arctic zone of the Russian Federation.

India is not only aligned and tilted with Russia. Indian foreign policy embraces all and talks about the holistic development of the world, and a world without war, fear of threats, and violations of human rights. Indian Prime Minister, after his visit to Russia, visited Ukraine in late August 2024 to build a bridge of confidence between the countries and give a strong signal to his Western counterparts that India is liberal and an envoy of peace and prosperity. Though a section of foreign policy experts claim that it was Modi's act of maintaining diplomatic balance. Because Kyiv did not see Modi's embrace of Mr. Putin in a good sense. However, Narendra Modi also hugged and embraced Ukrainian President Volodymyr Zelensky. Indian Prime Minister always wants to give a tight hug to his male counterparts to indicate his warm love and affection for them. It is Indian culture and courtesy. There in Kyiv, the Prime Minister emphasized "dialogue and diplomacy" for settling any International dispute. India showed support and solidarity with the people of Ukraine. He tried to settle the ongoing conflict between Kyiv and Moscow through negotiation and diplomacy.

Again, Indian Prime Minister Narendra Modi visited the USA in September 2024 to attend the UN General Assembly meeting in New York. There he held bilateral talks with other heads of states. During his visit to the USA, he met with the business community also. Narendra Modi addressed at an event on September 22 at the Nassau Veterans Memorial Coliseum, a multi-purpose indoor arena in Uniondale, New York. Modi's only aim is the well-being of his countrymen and the development of the world. The global leaders are also expected to meet and talk with him regarding their bilateral issues and international issues related to peace, war, progress, human rights, science, technology, space, energy, and infrastructure. The greatness of Modi lies in his success rate in international cooperation and the increase of foreign direct investment in India. It is not that India maintains relations with only the big brothers of the Western hemisphere. India's relations with Japan and other Asian countries are good and amiable, which helps India to progress and attain economic growth. Recently European leaders praised Narendra Modi's peace initiative in the Russia-Ukraine conflict. "President Biden had also praised India's prominent global role, including Prime Minister Modi's leadership in the G20 and Global South, as well as his efforts to strengthen the QUAD, ensuring a free, open, and prosperous Indo-Pacific" (Chakraborty, 2024). Not only that Mr. Modi and President Donald Trump are also good friends. During the election campaign in the USA, Mr. Trump praised Modi. On October 10, 2024, Donald Trump said, "He's great, he's a friend of mine," and he added "But on the outside he looks like your father, he's the nicest... total killer." Not only that, Mr. Trump also called Narendra Modi "a good person." (Lakshman, 2024). From all these words one can easily guess how strong the Indo-US relations are today under PM Modi.

Indo-Japan Relations

The relations between India and Japan are age-old. Tomoharu Kato in his book entitled *India Through Japanese Eyes* (1953) traces the Indian influence on Japan. In the Preface of the book, Shigeo Nagano, President of Fuji Iron & Steel Co., Ltd. wrote that "India stands out as the most important for the role she and her leaders are playing in world affairs today. For many centuries India has contributed towards an exchange of Eastern and Western civilizations. Now in less than a decade since her independence, India has established itself as a powerful Asian nation and as an important factor in achieving world peace and prosperity. As for Indo-Japanese relations, it is no secret that India's civilization has had a great deal of influence over the Japanese people. Trade relations between the two countries are rapidly growing in size and importance. There is every reason to believe that India and Japan will be closer and deeper in their relations with the passing of time" (Kato, 1953, pp. 1-2).

Mithilesh Kumar Singh in a recent book chapter (Roy Choudhury et al., 2020, p. 10) writes "India-Japan relations have been based on affinity since ancient times. This relationship has progressed almost seamlessly from the beginning until the twenty-first century. The two countries first came into contact through the exchange of Buddhism in the sixth century. Religious and cultural congruence has brought them closer. India and Japan also share several similar ideas, such as promoting democratic values and respecting regional and global peace and security. In the 21st century, the religious and cultural ties have evolved into a strategic partnership at the bilateral and multilateral levels. In this regard, the two countries have made remarkable progress in politics, economy, peace, security, and defense. Further, this bilateral relationship has enabled the development of science and technology, the forging the digital partnerships, and people-to-people ties. Both countries have also increased their participation at the global and multilateral levels to address concerns such as climate change, environmental protection, clean and renewal energy promotion, regional and global peace along security and prosperity. After 2000, Indo-Japan's strategic and global partnership expanded steadily and it witnessed an expansion in the economic sphere, foreign policy, education, science, and technology. The visit of Dr. Manmohan Singh to Japan in 2006 was important because the status of the bilateral partnership was updated to 'India-Japan Strategic and Global Partnership." Apart from this a combined exercise and anti-piracy measures were also presented between Japan's Maritime Self-Defence Force and the Indian Navy since 2007.

The Modi-Abe Era – Special Partnership

Since 2014, the two countries have given different structures to their relationship. In 2014, P.M. Narendra Modi visited Japan. The two countries gave a new name to their relationship by declaring it a 'Special Strategic and Global Partnership.' During the Modi-Abe period, components such as close economic agreement, free and open Indo-Pacific Strategy, rule-based order infrastructure, and connectivity, civil nuclear cooperation, maritime security, and defense cooperation, regional issues and universal challenges and cooperation, etc., occupy an entirely new place in India-Japan relation. As economic cooperation, the year 2016 saw the highest FDI from Japan i.e. 564 billion Yen (as per MOFA, 2021).

Under infrastructure connectivity since 2014, the PMs of both countries are committed to supporting each other for infrastructure connectivity within India's North-East Region (NER), further extending connectivity with the neighboring states. Japan has provided an ODA loan of $845 million for the road being constructed (Tura-Dalu Road (NH 51) in Meghalaya and Aizwal – Tuipang and road (JH 54) in Mizoram. Not only that, PM Modi and Abe in May 2017 created a free and open Indo-Pacific region through the AAGC (Asia-Africa Growth Corridor), connecting South Asia and South East Asia with the African continent by building the sea corridor and providing quality infrastructure, institutional connectivity, capacity building, and people to people exchange. India and Japan signed the 'Peaceful Use of Nuclear Energy' agreement in 2016 in the field of nuclear energy, which is called a milestone in Japan-India relations (Singh, 2020, p. 26).

Indo-British Relations in the Last Decade

The maxim "History repeats itself" proves true. Indian Prime Minister Narendra Modi became a global leader and his presence anywhere in the world creates an enigma among the leaders. Narendra Modi, from the very day of his oath-taking, undertook an initiative to make and mend India's relations with both the neighboring and Western powers. Wherever he goes people shout Modi Modi. They want to see Modi, shake hands with Modi, and talk with Modi. Modi madness is found everywhere in the world including the United Kingdom, our erstwhile colonial master. In 2015 Narendra Modi roared onto the stage of Wembley Stadium in London by a crowd of 60,000 people. On the occasion at *Namastey Wembley* Modi said, "India is full of diversity. This diversity is our pride and it is our strength. Diversity is the specialty of India. Seeing the people's continuous chants - "Modi! Modi! Modi, the then British Prime Minister David Cameron wondered aloud if he could have attracted such a crowd by himself. He later commented, "This is the most spectacular celebration of British-India relations we have ever seen" (The Times of India, 2015). Further, when Rishi Sunak became the Prime Minister of Britain, PM Modi tweeted "Special Diwali wishes to the 'living bridge' of UK Indians, as we transform our historic ties into a modern partnership" (Basak, 2022). This ushered in a new era of international relations with the U.K.

Further on the sidelines of the G-20 summit in India Narendra Modi and Rishi Sunak met in November last year (2022). After his talks with Sunak, Modi said India attaches great importance to the robust India-UK ties while the Ministry of External Affairs said the discussions touched upon important sectors of collaboration such as trade, mobility, defense, and security. Under the 'UK-India Young Professionals Scheme,' the UK promised to offer 3,000 young professionals annually between the ages of 18-30 years to go and work there for up to two years. This scheme would grow and promote a bilateral relationship with India and its wider commitment to foreign stronger links with the Indo-Pacific region. The British Prime Minister asserted that the UK will be a firm friend to the Indo-Pacific region (The Economic Times, 2022).

As per the Department of Business and Trade of the Government of the United Kingdom, total trade in goods and services (exports plus imports) between the U.K. and India was £34.0 billion in the four quarters to the end of Q3 2022, an increase of 51.7% or £11.06 billion in current prices from the four quarters to the end of Q3 2021. India was the UK's 12th largest trading partner in the four quarters to the end of Q3 2022 accounting for 2.1% of total UK trade. In 2021, the outward stock of foreign direct investment (FDI) from the UK in India was £19.1 billion accounting for 1.1% of the total UK outward FDI stock. Similarly, in 2021 the inward stock of foreign direct investment (FDI) in the UK from India was £9.3 billion accounting for 0.5% of the total UK inward FDI stock. Trade and commerce are gradually increasing between the two countries.

PM Modi and Sir Keir Starmer

Prime Minister Narendra Modi is such a person who meets with global leaders with open arms with his signature smile, which is full of simplicity, and Indianized etiquette. On the occasion of the G-20 summit in Rio de Janeiro, Brazil the two leaders met and both of them greeted each other. Prime Minister Modi congratulated H.E. Sir Keir Starmer on his assumption of office, while Prime Minister Starmer also extended warm wishes to Prime

Minister Modi on his historic third term in office. The "two Prime Ministers reaffirmed their commitment to strengthen the India-UK Comprehensive Strategic Partnership with a focus on the economy, trade, new and emerging technologies, research and innovation, green finance and people-to-people contacts...Both leaders underlined the importance of resuming the Free Trade Agreement negotiations at an early date and expressed confidence in the ability of the negotiating teams, to address the remaining issues to mutual satisfaction, leading to a balanced, mutually beneficial, and forward-looking Free Trade Agreement" (Ministry of External Affairs, 2024). Prime Minister Modi also announced the establishment of two new Consulate General of India in the United States in Belfast and Manchester.

India's Position in the Contemporary World Affairs

To understand India's foreign policy under Narendra Modi, we need to keep an eye on his Foreign Minister Dr. Subrahmanyam Jayshankar. He said, "We want to maintain a friendship with the whole world, but we will not compromise with the security of the country and its citizens." Further, in a lecture given by Ambassador (Redt.) Achal Malhotra in Central University of Rajasthan on July 22, 2019, stated, "The main and first and foremost objective of India's Foreign Policy - like that of any other country - is to secure its national interests. The scope of "national interests" is fairly wide. In our case, it includes for instance: securing our borders to protect territorial integrity, countering cross-border terrorism, energy security, food security, cyber security, creation of world-class infrastructure, non-discriminatory global trade practices, equitable global responsibility for the protection of the environment, reform of institutions of global governance to reflect the contemporary realities, disarmament, regional stability, international peace and so on."

India has left no stone unturned to expand its economic interest, security, and international trade through multilateral cooperation with world leaders. To achieve sustainable economic growth in the Indo-Pacific, India initiated diplomatic discussions within the Indo-Pacific Economic Framework (IPEF) and the Indo-Pacific Oceans Initiative (IPOI). It was reported by Vivek Mishra in the *South Asian Voices* (Mishra, 2023) that, "During 2022, India showed a greater embrace of its role as a net-security provider role in the Indo-Pacific." India's "No fear" strong attitude was reflected in different occasions. Recently India took an "elder brotherly" role in resolving some tensions and political instability in its neighboring countries such as Afghanistan, Nepal, Sri Lanka, and Bangladesh. Amid regional and international political turmoil, India took the courage to test its BrahMos missile into Pakistani territory in March 2022 to give a strong signal to the world, particularly to its errant neighbor. India's tough stand and hard action in Pakistan and China and her keenness to play an important role in shaping the international environment, while managing conflicting interests in India's favor. To quote Morgenthau we can say, "International politics, like all politics, is a struggle for power and one who has that experience in politics can easily deal with international affairs" (Pradhan, 2022).

Indo-China Relations

India and China are the two great economies of Asia. Presently India and China are "more rivals than partners" (The Economist, 2010). Indian views on China are ambivalent. Bilateral relations with China are "shot through with suspicions and expectations of an inevitable clash of interests...but China receives only episodic attention from the Indian government" (Pervical, 2013, p. 8). However, "After some progress in the early years of the century, relations have stalled. India's armed forces remain warily focused on China's military capabilities. Interpretations of the landmark 2005 agreement on the Sino-Indian border continue to differ; no progress is expected in the foreseeable future" (Pervical, 2013, p. 8). "India's civilian leadership was initially attracted by the commercial possibilities involved in expanding trade, but the hoped-for exchange of Indian service for Chinese manufactures has not taken place. India exports primarily raw materials in exchange for Chinese manufactures. Unable to compete effectively, New Delhi has deliberately slowed the penetration of the Indian domestic market by Chinese goods..." However, "Beijing tends to see India more as a difficult neighbor rather than as a direct strategic rival. It is less concerned with Indian diplomatic and commercial initiatives in East and Southeast Asia than it is with Indian ambitions for predominance in South Asia and the Indian Ocean littoral" (Pervical, 2013, p. 8).

Foreign Policy Shift under PM Modi

Keeping the main principles intact, India's foreign policy has been modified under the Modi Government. India's foreign policy has several key aspects now. The first one is that PM Modi treats foreign policy as an instrument of protecting and promoting the national interest of India and his approach to the rival nations is soft in peacetime but strong in times of wilful disturbance of internal peace and security. Secondly, earlier India would hesitate to take any retaliatory action against an errant country, particularly Pakistan and China; but now the situation has completely shifted. India's earlier standpoint of unwillingness to hurt the sentiments of her rivals has been replaced by boldness with a clear objective that relations with India are for mutual benefit.

Narendra Modi gave foremost importance to (re)building India's relations with her neighboring countries. He, as a result, revamped the 'Look East Policy' into the 'Act East Policy.' The objective of "Act East Policy' is to promote economic cooperation, and cultural ties and develop strategic relationships with countries in the Asia-Pacific region through continuous engagement at bilateral, regional, and multilateral levels thereby providing enhanced connectivity to the States of North Eastern Region including Arunachal Pradesh with other countries in our neighborhood. The North East of India has been a priority in our Act East Policy (AEP). The AEP provides an interface between North East India including the state of Arunachal Pradesh and the ASEAN region. Various plans at bilateral and regional levels include steady efforts to develop and strengthen the connectivity of the Northeast with the ASEAN region through trade, culture, people-to-people contacts, and physical infrastructure such as roads, airports, telecommunication, power, etc. (Press Information Bureau, 2015). The Modi government further added 'Act Far East' and 'Act West Asia' policies. His management of the complex relationships with Saudi Arabia, Israel, the UAE, and Iran marks him out as a master diplomat.

Modi undertook a policy of 'effective multilateralism' that fostered the growth of many nations and he believes that not only the voices of a few, but the voices and views of many can shape the global agenda. This might be termed as global inclusive growth. With this basic concept in mind, India began to develop relations with less developed and less voiced countries. He was the first Prime Minister to visit Mongolia and upgrade a comprehensive partnership to a strategic partnership in 2015 and in the following year PM Modi endeavored to elevate the relationship with Vietnam. Modi's historic visit to Israel in 2017 marked a strategic partnership. Narendra Modi is the first Prime Minister since 1986 who visit Canada and UAE to strengthen bilateral relations.

He revitalized and renewed relationships with neighboring countries through his policy of "Neighborhood First." He ratified the Land Border Agreement with Bangladesh and resolved the lingering issues of adverse enclaves. With our neighboring country Bangladesh, India shares a long 4,096-kilometer (2,545 miles) international border, the fifth-longest land border in the world. Hence, strategically Bangladesh is very important for India. Infiltration of illegal goods, animals, and people through the border is a common phenomenon that often impacts the economy and politics as well as Indo-Bangladesh relations.

Prime Minister Modi strongly believed in the growth and development of self and others through bilateral and multilateral trade and commerce. He has given a greater push to invite Foreign Direct Investment into India. He used foreign agreements to support 'Make in India' and *Atmanirbhar Bharat Abhiyan* (Self-reliant India Campaign).' Modi launched the 'Make in India' program globally in September 2014 as a part of India's renewed focus on Manufacturing. The objective of this initiative is to promote India as the most preferred global manufacturing destination. He realized the actual growth and development of India is impossible without the manufacturing and skill development of the youths. Globally PM Modi has managed to transform the 'distrust of China' into 'trust in India.' At present, India shares preferential market access and economic cooperation through trade agreements with over 50 countries and is in the process of having FTA with Australia, UAE, and EU. As a result of Modi's drive on commerce and industry today (up to 13th April, 2023) India's overall foreign trade has reached $66.14 billion in exports and $72.18 billion in imports including merchandise and services (Department of Commerce, 2023).

Border Security Issues Under Modi

Prime Minister Modi is now well recognized for his toughness in national border security. In the last few years, after PM Modi came to power, there has been a radical shift in India's border security policy. It carried out Surgical Strikes across the border, both in the east and west, to demonstrate its willingness to go beyond the conventional methods to deal with the scourge of terrorism. With Balakot Airstrikes, it has shown the world that it is no longer the yesteryear's India that will sit back and lick its wound, but it will mount a swift offensive and exact revenge on its adversaries. He believes in the principle of speaking less and doing more. His toughness is found in his approach to zero tolerance for terrorism emanating from neighboring countries, especially from Pakistan and China. Unlike his predecessor in the UPA-II government Dr. Manmohan Singh, who exhibited shocking pusillanimity in refraining from taking Pakistan to task after the dastardly Mumbai 26/11 attacks, PM Modi authorized an audacious surgical strike against the terror launch-pads responsible for sending terrorists that carried out the Uri terror attack in 2016. Days after the terror attack, the

Indian Armed Forces launched a counter-operation, inside Pakistan-occupied Kashmir, and destroyed the terror launch pads, signaling the fundamental shift in its policy on tackling terror attacks in India. In 2019, the Modi government sanctioned an unprecedented airstrike in Balakot, deep inside Pakistan, to annihilate a terror camp operated by Jaish-e-Muhammad in response to the Pulwama terror attack (Jain, 2022). These acts of Modi have established his tough personality in global politics.

India has a long 3,488 km border with China. In the last decade, China emerged as India's most consequential national security challenge, a reality that has become more pronounced since a deadly skirmish at the countries' disputed border nearly three years ago. In June 2020, Indian and Chinese troops clashed along the Line of Actual Control (LAC) in Galwan Valley – the worst such incident in decades (Jacob, 2023). In the face-off between India and China in eastern Ladakh in June 2020, India lost 20 soldiers, while Chinese casualties were over 40. India further retaliated by blocking over 200 Chinese Mobile Applications. Also, India was blocked in the country over its association with Chinese multinational technology conglomerate Tencent. Initially, the Chinese Army had occupied the heights near the Finger 4 but the Indian Army later occupied the heights which overlook the Chinese positions at heights including the Green Top. India deployed T-72, and T-90 Tanks along the LAC to counter China. India retaliated by canceling tender for 44 semi-high-speed *Vande Bharat* trains, which was a jolt to the Chinese economy. The Haryana Government also canceled the Rs.780 crore Power Sector Contract with the Chinese firm after the Galwan clash (ABP News Bureau, 2020).

Recent Indo-Canada Relations

Recently the diplomatic relationship between India and Canada has soured in relation to the murder of Hardeep Singh Nijjar, a Khalistanti 'Terrorist." Recently, "Canada and India each expelled their top diplomats due to the fallout from Canadian Prime Minister Justin Trudeau's allegation last year that there were possible links of Indian intelligence with the killing of a Canadian citizen, Hardeep Singh Nijjar. India categorized Nijjar as a Khalistani terrorist (he had faced no criminal charges in Canada but was put on a no-fly list and his bank accounts were frozen). This issue also froze India's relationship with Canada, once a very good friend of India, where millions of Indians would go to study, work, and stay. Many people accuse that Mr. Trudeau has an obligation towards the Canadian Sikh community, who "constitute only 2% of Canada's population, but their political clout is far disproportionate because of geographical concentration" (Mannathukkaren, 2024). It has been observed by the world that the Sikhs in Canada disregard the Indian National Flag, but the Canadian Government remained silent. The Khalistani supporters held their referendum also. Even they glorify the assassination of Mrs. Indira Gandhi, which is completely intolerable to Indians.

Why Justine Trudeau is supporting the Sikhs there in Canada? Is it because of the fact that he has failed to counter the Chinese interference in Canadian elections? Is it because he badly needs the support of his existing Sikh MLAs, or he is puzzled by the report of his declining popularity? Whatever it may be, he has already been warned by US President Donald Trump to impose a 25% tax on Canadian imports.

Indo-Bangladesh Relations

Since its creation in 1971 India and Bangladesh have always had very good relations. Unfortunately, after a political uprising in the month of August 2024, the longest-serving Prime Minister Sheikh Hasina left her country and took shelter in India. Thousands of protesters ransacked the house of the Prime Minister and destroyed the metro rail, airport, and important museums and buildings. They even broke the jail and released the prisoners. Thereafter, a caretaker government has been set up with the Nobel Peace Prize winner Dr. Mohammad Yunus as its Chief Advisor. However, the government of Dr. Yunus has completely failed to protect the safety and security of the minority Hindus there. After the downfall of Sheikh Hasina almost regularly the Hindus are being asked to resign from Schools, Colleges, and Universities and many top officials have been threatened to resign. There is a total *matsanaya* in Bangladesh in the post-Hasina era. "India-Bangladesh ties have been frosty since former Prime Minister Sheikh Hasina fled to India after her removal in a student-led mass uprising in August, but diplomatic tensions have soared in recent days after the two South Asian neighbors traded accusations of alleged ill-treatment of the Hindu minority. The war of words escalated after Bangladeshi authorities arrested Hindu religious leader Chinmoy Krishna Das last week on sedition charges, setting off protests across several places in India" (Sarkar, 2024). Hot talks and threats against the two religious communities and political parties have already been hurled from inside the borders. The situation has been gradually worsening, and a war-like situation has emerged between India and Bangladesh. However, it is a matter of happiness that diplomatic-level talks have begun, and it is expected that the tension will be normalized soon.

Modi Receives Highest Popularity in the World

The Modi madness was not only found in the U.K., the same madness was found among the Indian diaspora in all the countries of the West, which was never witnessed earlier at any time in history. Wherever he travels from America to Denmark and from the United Kingdom to Bangladesh everywhere he rocks the minds of immigrant Indians and their countrymen. The grand success of the 2019 'Howdy, Modi!' event carried an important message: Narendra Modi was the first prime minister to recognize the power and strength of the Indian diaspora in spreading the 'Swaraj Spirit.' Ever since Narendra Modi came to power as the head of the National Democratic Alliance (NDA) in 2014, he has perfected the art of filling up huge stadiums and grounds abroad with patriotic jingles and he is quite popular among large sections of the Indian diaspora in countries like the U.S. and U.K. (Basak, 2022). The "Howdy, Modi!" event in Texas in 2019 could be seen as a prime example of his popularity in the USA. This same Modi was denied a US visa in 2005 following the 2002 Godhra riots in Gujarat when he was the chief minister there. But nobody's time remains the same always; it revolves. He did not have popularity in the US just 15 years back, and now the "Howdy, Modi" was a landmark event that was never seen by the USA before. According to the official website of the event, "Over 50,000 people attended the event which quickly sold out, making it the largest gathering for an invited foreign leader visiting the United States other than the Pope. For the first time, Modi and Trump shared the stage to address the 50,000-strong Indian diaspora during the September 2022 event titled "Shared Dreams, Bright Future" that had it focused on the success of Indian-Americans as well as the "strength of the US-India relationship." Describing the joint appearance of the two leaders as "unconventional and unique," Harsh Vardhan Shringla, the then-Indian Ambassador to the US has said that the event was a reflection of the strong bipartisan support there has been for US-India relations. He said Indian Americans are an "organic bridge" between the world's two largest democracies" (Basak, 2022). During his recent visits to France, Germany, and Denmark Narendra Modi received equal overwhelming welcome from the Indian diaspora and the people of those countries including top leadership.

From the above discussions, it can be safely concluded that our Prime Minister is 'a global leader' for his larger role in promoting and protecting international peace and prosperity, security, and human dignity. For his towering personality, problem-solving capacity, and unbiased outlook, he is praised, liked, and respected by the majority of world leaders and their citizens. India has occupied a special position under Prime Minister Narendra Modi. India's foreign policy objectives may remain the same, but the process of handling world affairs has made global leaders change their perceptions of India. Now India is more assertive in striving to achieve its goals while remaining away from the rivalry of powers as far as possible. Its international stature has been heightened a lot. Now, people of India living in India or any part of the world feel one kind of self-esteem and pride regarding India and its Prime Minister. Modi has radically transformed India and its status in the global sphere.

Thus we find that India has achieved a milestone in different fields from the economy to women's empowerment. The editor of the *LSE IDEAS Reports* 2012 Nicholas Kitchen considers that "India's rise has certainly been impressive, and warrants the attention that it has commanded. India has been one of the world's best-performing economies for a quarter of a century, lifting millions out of poverty and becoming the world's third-largest economy in PPP terms. India has tripled its defense expenditure over the last decade to become one of the top military spenders. And in stark contrast to Asia's other billion-person emerging power, India has simultaneously cultivated an attractive global image of social and cultural dynamism" (Kitchen, 2012, p. 4). Now every Indian either living within its territory or elsewhere in the world feels secure and proud of India. What Thomas A. Birkland wrote (2011, p. xiv) about America applies to India also. He said, "...the Internet boom seemed, to some, an unlimited engine of growth and innovation, and Americans felt reasonably secure at home and abroad." The same is appropriate in India too. Food security, economic security, and border security give the Indian government the luxury to bring about necessary reforms through the legislature to strengthen Indian federal democracy, people's empowerment, ecosystem, space research, trade & commerce, agriculture, etc., and further focus on various international issues such as global conflicts, monetary reforms, climate change, cybercrime, international peace, and security, etc. In recent years, India has taken up many tough decisions in terms of border security, the Russia-Ukraine war, importing oil from Russia, and defying US sanctions. India's Act East policy, national security policy, and prioritization of the neighboring countries have established her position in the international arena. All these indicate that India is emerging as a potential power. Now let us discuss the concept of power in international relations.

Can India be Called a Global Power?

To answer the question if India can be called a 'global power'; it is a prerequisite to understanding the concept of power in international relations. Hans J. Morgenthau (Morgenthau, 1948, p.13) considers that "International politics, like all politics, is a power struggle. Whatever the ultimate aims of international politics, power is always the immediate aim." India is striving to gain international recognition and attain power. Morgenthau further said, "When we speak of power, we mean man's control over the minds and actions of other men. By political power, we refer to the mutual relations of control among the holders of public authority and between the latter and the people at large" (Morgenthau, 1948, p.13). In the words of Morgenthau, we can say: "Political power is a psychological relation between those who exercise it and those over whom it is exercised. It gives the former control over certain actions of the latter through the influence that the former exerts over the latter's minds. That influence may be exerted through orders, threats, persuasion, or a combination of any of these" (Morgenthau, 1948, p.14).

The concept of power is the most important component in international relations. Manez Faris Rasheed referred to Morgenthau to elucidate the concept of power: "Hans J. Morgenthau defines international politics as a struggle for power and uses the theory of realism to explain it. Realist theory holds that politics, like society, is governed by objective laws rooted in human nature and that the national interest, defined in power terms, is the major objective of a nation's foreign policy. One goal of a nation is to maintain and increase its power and to reduce other nations' power" (Rasheed, 1995, p. 95). Further, the concept of power is defined by Michael Barnett and Raymond Duvall (Barnett and Duvall, 2005, p. 45). The authors consider that "Power is the production, in and through social relations, of effects on actors that shape their capacity to control their fate. This concept has two dimensions at its core: (I) the kinds of social relations through which actors' capacities are affected (and effected); and (2) the specificity of those social relations."

Stefano Guzzine (2009, p. 5) in an article elaborated the concept of Measurement of Power. He referred to Prof. Daniel Frei's lecture delivered at the University of Zurich in 1969, where he said, "If there were a consensus on the concept of power and its measurement, peace would cease to be a problem." Frei had insisted that power is all a matter of perception and not objectively measurable. According to him, the best we could hope for is to find proxies for power, some form of power status symbols, on which world actors could agree" (Guzzine, p. 5). Guzzine, further, considers that "Power does not reside in a resource but stems from the particular relation in which abilities are actualized... Power is relation and situation-specific" (Guzzine, p. 7). Guzzine referred to Robert Dahl's definition mentioned in Who Governs? where he said, power is "getting someone else to do what he/ she would not have otherwise done." On the other hand, K.J. Holsti (1964, p. 180), a professor at the University of British Columbia, points out that, "Statesmen, they claim, have a choice between practicing "power politics" and conducting foreign relations by some other means. Wilson and others made the further assumption that there is a correlation between a nation's social and political institutions and the way it conducts its foreign relations."

There is a distinction between the "great power" and the "small powers" which is usually based on some rough estimation of tangible and intangible factors which we have called capabilities. In domestic politics, it is possible to construct a lengthy list of those capabilities and attributes that seemingly permit some to wield influence over large numbers of people and important public decisions. Robert A. Dahl (1961) lists such tangibles as money, wealth, information, time, political allies, official position, and control over jobs, and such intangibles as personality and leadership qualities.

The same propositions also hold in international politics. "Capabilities may also be tangible or intangible. We can predict that a country in possession of a high Gross National Product, a high level of industrial development, sophisticated weapons systems, and a large population will have more influence and prestige in the system than a state with a primitive economy, small population, and old-fashioned armaments. And yet, the intangibles are also important. In addition to the physical resources of a state, such factors as leadership and national morale have to be assessed. We could not, for example, arrive at an estimation of India's influence in world politics unless we regarded the prestige and stature of its leadership abroad" (Holsti, 1964, p. 180). In 2006, Joseph Nye elaborated on the concept of power. According to him, "Power is the ability to alter the behavior of others to get what you want, and there are basically three ways to do that: coercion (sticks), payment (carrots), and attraction (soft power) (Nye, 1990, p. 35).

How Power is Manifested?

Does power work through interactions and social constitution? To unfold the conception we can take the help of Michael Barnett and Raymond Duval, who wrote, "One position on this dimension treats social relations as comprised of the actions of preconstituted social actors toward one another. Here, power works through behavioral relations or interactions, which, in turn, affect the ability of others to control the circumstances of their existence. In these conceptions, power nearly becomes an attribute that an actor possesses and may use knowingly as a resource to shape the actions or conditions of action of others" (Barnett and Duvall, 2005, p. 45). There is another aspect that consists of social relations of the constitution. "Here, power works through social relations that analytically precede the social beings with their respective capacities and interests. Constitutive relations cannot be reduced to the attributes, actions, or interactions of pregiven actors. Power, accordingly, is irreducibly social" (Barnett and Duvall, 2005, p. 46).

Indicators of Power

There is a controversy regarding the concept of power. Also, social analysts like "Holsti, who asserts that the concept of power is not useful for the study of world politics. Power conceptualization does not account for the determination of national goals nor international relations." On the other hand, some analysts stress that power should be dealt with as the central theme of the study of politics and given principal importance. The quest for power becomes an end in itself. Here, power becomes absolute and the social environment presents a totalitarian character, e.g. Hitler in Germany and Stalin in Russia" (Rasheed, 1995, p. 99). There are certain components of power in international relations. Morgenthau enumerates nine elements of power. "These include geography, natural resources, industrial capacity, the state of military preparedness, population, national character, national morale, equality of diplomacy, and the quality of government. Good government is an independent requirement of national power and means three things: balance between the material and human resources and the foreign policy to be pursued; balance among these resources; and popular (public) support for the foreign policies to be pursued; balance among these resources; and popular public support for the foreign policies to be pursued" (Rasheed, 1995, p. 95). Rasheed further indicates that the earliest writers such as Morgenthau, Aron, and Keohane and Nye, believe that power rests with man. Aron defines "political power as a human relationship. This definition derives from Hobbes' state of nature that each man is at war with all other men. The other view taken by writers such as Claude, Gilpin, and the second and third images of Waltz is that power is defined in terms of military, economic, and technological capabilities of the state" (Rasheed, 1995, p. 98).

Then, how to measure the capabilities of power of a state? This has been studied for many years by students and scholars of international politics. They have made meticulous comparisons of the mobilized and potential capabilities of various nations. K.J. Holsti alludes that, "Comparative data relating to the production of iron ore, coal, hydroelectricity, economic growth rates, educational levels, population growth rates, military resources, transportation systems, and sources of raw materials are presented as indicators of a nation's power" (Holsti, 1964, p. 186).

A very interesting example has been given by Holsti regarding "great essentials". He pointed out that, "In the period 1925 to 1930, it (the United States) was the only major country in the world that produced from its own resources supplies of food, power, iron, machinery, chemicals, coal, iron ore, and petroleum. If actual influence had been deduced from the quantities of "great essentials" possessed by the major actors the following ranking of states would have resulted: (I) United States, (2) Germany, (3) Great Britain, (4) France, (5) Russia, (6) Italy, (7) Japan. However, the diplomatic history of the world from 1925 to 1930 would suggest that there was little correlation between the capabilities of these countries and their actual influence. If we measure influence by the impact these actors made on the system and by the responses they could invoke when they sought to change the behavior of other states, we would find for this period quite a different ranking, such as the following: 1) France, (2) Great Britain, (3) Italy, (4) Germany, (5) Russia, (6) Japan, (7) United States" (Holsti (p. 187). Further Holsti indicates that, "In wielding of influence in modern international politics is, however, seldom a bilateral process. In a system where all states perceive some involvement and relationship with all other actors, governments seek to use the capabilities and diplomatic influence of other actors by forming diplomatic or military coalitions. Indeed, modern diplomacy is largely concerned with eliciting the support of friends and neutrals, presumably because widespread diplomatic support for an actor's policies increases the legitimacy of those objections, thereby increasing the influence of the actor. "Small" states, in particular, can increase their influence if they can gain commitments of support from other members of the system" (Holsti, pp. 187-188). On the other hand, Jeffrey Hart (1976, p. 290) considers that, "Military expenditures, the size of armed forces, gross national product, and population are frequently used as indicators of national power in empirical studies."

India's Soft Power

The concept of soft power was first introduced by American Scholar and frequent policy maker, Joseph S. Nye Jr., who defined it as "when one country gets other countries to do what it wants" and as "co-optive power" (1990, 2011, p. 35). He, further, noted: "Today... the definition of power is losing its emphasis on military force... The factors of technology, education, and economic growth are becoming more significant in international power" (Nye, 1990, p. 154). The year 2011 has been declared "the year of India in Canada" and offered by New Delhi to provide an opportunity for the Canadian people to have a taste of Indian classical and contemporary music, even rock bands. There were trade shows and cultural performances from one coast to another coast. Even the International Film Awards extravaganza was held in Toronto, which touched the people of the city and created a frenzy among the people in the city. These are the soft powers of India.

On the other hand, C Raja Mohan argued as early as 2003 that, "India could always count itself among the few nations with strong cards in the arena of soft power," asserting that India's biggest "instrument" of soft power was its diaspora. India's diaspora is certainly an asset, but far from the only one. Beyond its cultural and civilizational riches, its vibrant (if at times chaotic) democracy, its free media, its mostly independent judiciary, its dynamic civil society, and the impressive struggle for human rights since independence all make it attractive to the public in much of the world where these characteristics of its national experience are known. In addition, India's largely non-violent defeat of colonialism served as an important beacon for freedom movements and newly independent countries elsewhere in the 1950s and 1960s" (Malone, 2011, p. 35).

Shashi Tharoor also in one of his articles *India as a Soft Power* quoted Joseph Nye to expand the concept of soft power. Tharoor considers that "The soft power of a country rests primarily on three resources: its culture in places where it is attractive to others; its political value when it lives up to them at home and abroad; and its foreign policies when they are seen as legitimate and having moral authority" (Tharoor, 2012, p. 330). Tharoor, further quoted from a book by Nye, The Paradox of American Power, where he analyzed the concept of soft power beyond the American borders. He felt that other nations could acquire it. Quoting Nye Tharoor said in the contemporary age of information, three types of countries are likely to gain soft power and to succeed such as "Those whose dominant cultures and ideals are closer to prevailing global norms which now emphasize liberalism, pluralism, autonomy; those with the most accessed multiple channels of communication and thus more influence over how issues are framed, and those whose credibility is enhanced by their domestic and international performance."

India has many things including rich culture, art, music, philosophy, fabric, architecture, yoga, non-violence tradition, spirituality, and heritage that can be exported to the countries of the Western world. Shashi Tharoor pointed out the British historian E.P. Thompson to elucidate the Indian heritage of diversity what makes India: "...perhaps the most important country for the future of the world. All the convergent influences of the world run through this society. There is not a thought that is being thought in the west or the east that is not active in some Indian mind" (Tharoor, 2012, p. 337).

Contrary to soft power there is hard power, which is the ability to coerce and grow out of a country's military and economic might. Amit Gupta (2006, p. 50) considers that Indian "secular values and its parliamentary system remain a powerful and visible force that the elites of some of the other countries in the region have to contend with." He further said, "Broadly speaking, however, Indian soft power comes from the following sources: its democratic traditions, its educational and intellectual power, its media capability, its expanding biotechnology capability, and of course the existence of a 20 million-strong diaspora."

All these indicate that India has the world's most powerful soft power, which is enviable to the rest of the world. Moreover, India's present strength of the military, its economy, its GDP growth rate, its influence on neighboring countries, Africa, Europe, and America; its close relations with the top global leaders in world, its military ties and maritime relations with world's developed countries have been instrumental to become a strong global power. Today India and the United States cooperate closely with multilateral organizations, including the United Nations, G-20, Association of Southeast Asian Nations (ASEAN) Regional Forum, International Monetary Fund, World Bank, and World Trade Organization. Together with Australia, Japan, and United States India is a member of Quad that seeks to promote a free and open Indo-Pacific and provide tangible benefits to the region. India is also one of twelve countries partnering with the United

States on the Indo-Pacific Economic Framework for Prosperity (IPEF) to make US economies more connected, resilient, clean, and fair. At present, India is a member of the Indian Ocean Rim Association (IORA), at which the United States is a dialogue partner. Considering India's growing power and influence in the International forums, the USA advocates India's permanent membership in the reformed Security Council, and it welcomed India's joining the Security Council for two years in 2021 (U.S. Department of State, 2022). Celebration of International Yoga Day by the Indian Prime Minister on the grassy North Lawn outside of the United Nations Headquarters set a Guinness World Record as most nationalities – 135 – practiced a yoga session. Standing ovation to Modi by the Congress Members during his joint session speech proves India's closeness, power, and influence to the Western world. Also, "Standing next to Modi on the White House South Lawn, Biden said he has long believed that the relationship between the United States and India will be "one of the defining relationships of the 21st century" (Collins, 2023). Can anybody deny today India is a global superpower? We will now shift our attention from global to national. Hereunder, we will focus on some important government schemes, policies, and Acts that have brought about revolutionary change in the lives of people in India. In this regard, I must apologize at first, because hundreds of schemes and policies were formulated by the existing NDA Government in the last 9 years, and many of the schemes and laws were either merged or abolished according to relevance and necessity. However, it is quite impossible to discuss all of them in this small chapter. Therefore, a few major public policies that have transformed the economic, social, and political image of India will be highlighted here.

Conclusions

From the above discussions we can say that, unlike his predecessors, Narendra Modi is unique in his style of work, method of functions, and innovative actions. He is an upright, hard-working, and visionary Prime Minister. PM Modi is a heartthrob for both the young and old and men and women – in both India and Western countries. He has taken unprecedented steps to take India to such a height that none of his predecessors had ever thought of or had the caliber to perform. His relations with SAARC leaders (except Pakistan), and Western, African, and Middle-East leaders are warm and cordial, and the relationship is based on mutual respect, cooperation, mutual growth, and mutual security. The development policies, security measures, and foreign policies that were adopted by the Modi government made the majority of Indian people delighted, secure, and satisfied. At present, India's borders are safe, the Indian economy is robust, Indian social security is inclusive, and space research and development in Science Technology Engineering, and Mathematics (STEM) is unprecedented. PM Modi's sincere efforts, devotion to national service, clarity of vision, and unselfish patriotism have made him lovable and respectable to the Indian citizens. His mild speaking art is inimitable. But his tough stand in cases of border security or corruption is fearful of the intruders and culprits. He has faith in himself; he has thus inculcated faith in the people through his words and actions. He has been able to establish peace, feeling, security, and integrity between and among people within and outside India. By crossing the national border, he has played a larger role in resolving international disputes; extending monetary, medical, and military services; and spreading India's classical culture and art of living to the people in the world. He strongly advocates for India's permanent membership in the Security Council of the United Nations. He is truly a noble statesman; a foreseer diplomat and an advocate of international peace and security. From his activities and achievements, we can safely conclude that his policies, schemes, and Acts have been instrumental in transforming India's image in the global arena. If Pundit Jawaharlal Nehru is called the 'maker of modern India,' PM Modi may be called the 'maker of self-reliant India.'

References:

1. Jain, D.K. (2014). India's Foreign Policy, Ministry of External Affairs (GOI). In Goyal, A. (2022). *An Insight into India's Foreign Policy. Indian Journal of Law and Legal Research,* 4(2), pp. 219-235. https://mea.gov.in/indian-foreign-policy.htm.

2. Goyel, A. (2022). An Insight into India's Foreign Policy. *Indian Journal of Law and Legal Research,* 4(2).

3. Johnson, D.E., Jennifer, D.P., Moroney, R. C., Markel, M. W., Smallman, L. and Spirtas, M. (2019). Preparing and Training for the Full Spectrum of Military Challenges: Insights from the Experiences of China, France, the United Kingdom, India, and Israel, Rand Corporation. (2009). In *Preparing and Training for the Full Spectrum of Military Challenges* (1st ed.), p. 179.

4. Gandhi, M. (1942). *Non Violence in Peace and War.* Navajivan Publishing House.

5. Malone, D.M., Mohan, R.C., and Raghavan, S. (2015). *India and World, The Oxford Handbook of Indian Foreign Policy.*

6. Kumar, M. (1969). Theoretical Aspects of International Politics. *JSTOR*, 25(4).

7. Verma, D.P. (1989). Jawaharlal Nehru: Panchsheel and India's Constitutional Vision of International Order. *India Quarterly*, 45(4), 304.

8. Lyon, P. (1963). *Neutralism*. Oxford University Press.

9. Chari, P.R. (1976). Non-Alignment and International Security. *India International Centre Quarterly*, 3(3), p. 70.

10. Chari, P.R. (1976). Non-Alignment and International Security. *India International Centre Quarterly*, 3(3), p. 72.

11. Non-alignment' was coined by Nehru in 1954. (2006, September, 18). *The Times of India*.

12. A. Appadorai quoted in Batria, P. (n.d.). *India's Foreign Policy*. Nath Publishing House.

13. Lal, D. (1967). Indian Foreign Policy, 1947-64. *Economic and Political Weekly*, 2(19), p. 881.

14. Lal, D. (1967). Indian Foreign Policy, 1947-64. *Economic and Political Weekly*, 2(19), p. 882.

15. Sharma, AK, and Kumar, J. (2015 Dec.). Shashi Tharoor's Reasons of State: A Study of Indira Gandhi's Foreign Policy." *The Literary Herald*, Vol. 1, Issue 3, p. 20.

16. Pouchpadass, E. *My Truth: Indira Gandhi*. New Delhi: Vision Books, 1981, p. 132.

17. Quoted by Smriti Sawkar. (2022). "Champion of the Third World: Indira Gandhi and the Spectacle of the 1983 NAM summit." In Commonwealth and Comparative Politics, Vol. 60, Issue 4, 23 Nov. https://doi.org/10.1080/14662043.2022.2142400.

18. Joseph, S.V. & Mucheli, R.D. *Economic and Political Weekly*. Vol. 59, Issue No. 9, 02 March, 2024.

19. Chengappa R. (1991, September, 30). PM in Germany: Striking the right note. *India Today*. http://indiatoday.in/magazine/diplomacy/story/19910930-narasimha-rao-candid-approach-makes-an-impact-in-germany-814896-1991-09-30 accessed on 7.12.2024.

20. Kumar, S.B. (2022). P.V. Narasimha Rao: A Strategist and Commanding Contributor to Governance. *Indian Journal of Public Administration*, Vol. 69, Issue 1, https://doi.org/10.1177/00195561221109086.

21. Roy Chaudhury, D. (2014, February, 23). India's foreign policy: With landmark deals, Manmohan Singh government promised much, delivered little. *The Economic Times*.

22. Sarkar, B. (2013, December). India's Foreign Policy Under the Prime Minister of Dr. Manmohan Singh. *International Journal of Scientific Research*, Vol. 2, Issue 12, p. 514.

23. Sarkar, B. (2013, December). India's Foreign Policy Under the Prime Minister of Dr. Manmohan Singh. *International Journal of Scientific Research*, Vol. 2, Issue 12, p. 515.

24. Pradhan, S.D. (2022, January 9). Key features of Indian Foreign policy under PM Modi. *Times of India*.

25. Mishra, V. (2023, January 13). India's Foreign Policy in 2022: A Year in Review. *South Asian Voices*.

26. 8 World Leaders who got Narendra Modi's invitation in swearing-in. (2014, May 23). *The Times of India*.

27. Tourangbam, M. (2022, March 14).The New Geometry of India's Foreign Policy. *The Diplomat*.

28. Factsheets: How much crude oil does the EU still import from Russia? (2022, September 20). *Reuters*.

29. My Gov. (2022). *PM's 3 Day Visit to Europe – Part I.* https://blog.mygov.in/editorial/pms-3-days-visit-to-europe/# Government of India.

30. Mishra, V. (2023, January 13). India's Foreign Policy in 2022: A Year in Review. *South Asian Voices*.

31. Pradhan, S.D. (2021, November 27). India and Russia add another pillar to their strategic relations. *The Times of India*.

32. Frayer, L. (2023, February 23). A year into the Ukraine war, the world's biggest democracy still won't condemn Russia. *NPR*.

33. Russian arms supplies to India amounts to $13 bln in past 5 years. (2023, February 13). *The Economic Times*.

34. Frayer, L. (2023, February 23). A year into the Ukraine war, the world's biggest democracy still won't condemn Russia. *NPR*.

35. Pradhan, S.D. (2021, November 27). India and Russia add another pillar to their strategic relations. *The Times of India*.

36. Chakraborty, A. (2024, October 22). "Even Without A Translator": Putin On How Well PM Modi Understands Him. *NDTV World News*, Kazan, Russia.

37. Hemmings, J. (2020, September 1). The Evolution of the U.S. Alliance System in The Indo-Pacific Since the Cold War's End. In *Hindsight, Insight, Foresight: Thinking About Security in the Indo-Pacific*, p. 145.

38. Gilboy, G.J. & Heginbotham, E. (Summer 2013). Quoted by Bronson Pervical (2013). *China, India and the United States: Tempered Rivalries in Asia.*

S. Rajaram School of International Studies.

39. *U.S. Relations with India*. (2022, July 18). U.S. Department of State. https://www.state.gov/u-s-relations-with-india/.

40. Chakraborty, A. (2024, October 22). "Even Without A Translator": Putin On How Well PM Modi Understands Him. *NDTV World News*, Kazan, Russia.

41. Lakshman, S. (2024, October 10). Donald Trump praises PM Modi, says he is the 'nicest human being' but can also be a 'total killer.' *The Hindu.*

42. Kato, T. (1953). *India Through Japanese Eyes*. The Indo-Japanese Association.

43. Roy Choudhury, S., Thankachan, S., and Bakshi, P. (eds). *Indio-Japan Relations@ 70: Building Beyond Bilateral*. K.W. Publishers Pvt. Lte.

44. Ministry of Foreign Affairs. (2021). MOFA.

45. Singh, M.K. (2020). From Civilizational to Strategic Partnership: Waling the Road. In Roy Choudhury, S., Thankachan, S., & Bakshi, P. (eds). *Indio-Japan Relations@ 70: Building Beyond Bilateral*. (p. 26). K.W. Publishers Pvt. Lte.

46. British Prime Minister David Cameron's Top Quotes at Wembley Stadium. (2015, November 13). *The Times of India.*

47. Basak, S. (2022, October 31). Modi Madness Among Indian Diaspora In The West Puts Spotlight On India Too. *Outlook.*

48. PM Modi and his British counterpart Rishi Sunak agreed on 'enduring importance' of UK-India relationship. (2022, November 16). *The Economic Times.*

49. Ministry of External Affairs, Government of India. (2024, November, 18). Rio de Janeiro.

50. Mishra, V. (2023). India's Foreign Policy in 2022: A Year in Review. *South Asian Voices.*

51. Pradhan, S.D. (2022). Key features of Indian Foreign policy under PM Modi. *The Times of India.*

52. "Pass Impasse," *The Economist*, February 4, 2010. Quoted in Lyod, R. (2010, May 20). The India-China Relationship: a tempered rivalry? Policy Analysis 61. *Australian Strategic Policy Institute.*

53. Pervical, B. (2013). *China, India and the United States: Tempered Rivalries in Asia*. S. Rajaram School of International Studies.

54. Pervical, B. (2013). *China, India and the United States: Tempered Rivalries in Asia*. S. Rajaram School of International Studies.

55. Pervical, B. (2013). *China, India and the United States: Tempered Rivalries in Asia*. S. Rajaram School of International Studies.

56. *Act East Policy 2015.* (2015, December 23). Press Information Bureau. https://pib.gov.in/newsite/printrelease.aspx?relid=133837.

57. *India's Foreign Trade.* (2023, April 13). Department of Commerce. Ministry of Commerce and Industry, Government of India. https://commerce.gov.in/trade-statistics/latest-trade-figures/

58. Jain, J. (2022, May 26). 8 years of Modi government: How PM Modi radically transformed India's foreign policy. *OpIndia.* https://www.opindia.com/2022/05/8-yrs-of-pm-modi-the-radical-shift-in-india-foreign-policy/

59. Jacob, Happymon. (2323, April 4). Why India downplays China's Border Threat. *FP.* ...https://foreignpolicy.com/2023/04/04/india-china-border-dispute-bjp-modi-consensus/.

60. Year Ender 2020: From Boycotting Brands to Apps: India's Response to China Post Galwan Valley Attack. (2020, December 25). *ABP News Bureau.*

61. Mannathukkaren, N. (2024, November 6). On India-Canada diplomatic relations Explained. *The Hindu.*

62. Sarkar, P. (2024, December 5). Bangladesh mission in India attacked: Why are ties in freefall? *Al Jazeera.*

63. Basak, S. (2022, October 31). Modi Madness Among Indian Diaspora In The West Puts Spotlight On India Too. *Outlook.*

64. Kitchen, N. (2012). India: Next Superpower? *LSE IDEAS SPECIAL REPORT.*

65. Birkland, T. A. (2011). *An Introduction to the Policy Process: Theories, Concepts and Methods of Public Policy Making.* Routledge.

66. Morgenthau, H. J. (1948). *Politics among Nations: the Struggle for Power and Peace.* Alfred A. Knopf.

67. Morgenthau, H. J. (1948). *Politics among Nations: the Struggle for Power and Peace.* Alfred A. Knopf.

68. Rasheed, M. F. (1995). The Concept of Power in International Relations. *Pakistan Horizon, 48*(1), p. 95. https://www.jstor.org/stable/41371577

69. Barnett, B. & Duvall, R. (2005). Power in International Politics. International Organization, 59(1), p. 45.

70. Guzzine, S. (2009). On the measure of power and the power of measure in International Relations. Danish Institute for International Studies, DIIS. Working Paper January.

71. Holsti, K.J. (1964). The Concept of Power in the Study of International Relations, Background, 7(4), p. 180.

72. Nye, J. (1990). cited by David M Malone (2011). Soft Power in Indian Foreign Policy. *Economic and Political Weekly, 46*(36), p. 35.

73. Barnett, B. & Duvall, R. (2005). Power in International Politics. International Organization, *59*(1), p. 45.

74. Barnett, B. & Duvall, R. (2005). Power in International Politics. International Organization, *59*(1), p. 46.

75. Rasheed, M. F. (1995). The Concept of Power in International Relations. *Pakistan Horizon, 48*(1), p. 99. https://www.jstor.org/stable/41371577

76. Rasheed, M. F. (1995). The Concept of Power in International Relations. *Pakistan Horizon, 48*(1), p. 95. https://www.jstor.org/stable/41371577

77. Holsti, K.J. (1964). The Concept of Power in the Study of International Relations. *Background, 7*(4), 9. 186.

78. Holsti, K.J. (1964). The Concept of Power in the Study of International Relations. *Background, 7*(4), 9. 187-88.

79. Hart, J. (1976). Three approaches to the measurement of power in international relations. *International Organization, 30*(2), p. 290.

80. Nye, J. (1990). cited by David M. Malone. (2011). Soft Power in Indian Foreign Policy, *46*(36), p. 35. *Economic and Political Weekly.*

81. Nye, J. (1990). cited by David M. Malone. (2011). Soft Power in Indian Foreign Policy, *46*(36), p. 154. *Economic and Political Weekly.*

82. Malone, D.M. (2011). Soft Power in Indian Foreign Policy. *Economic and Political Weekly, 46*(36), p. 35.

83. Tharoor, S. (2012). India as a Soft Power. India International Centre Quarterly, *38*(3/4), p. 330.

84. Tharoor, S. (2012). India as a Soft Power. India International Centre Quarterly, *38*(3/4), p. 337.

85. Gupta, A. (2006). India's Soft Power. *Indian Foreign Affairs Journal, 1*(1), p. 50.

86. Collins, M. (2023). Red carpets and yellow yoga mats: Five moments from Indian PM Modi's state visit. *USA Today.*

V

Keys for Turning India into a Superpower

We have already discussed in the previous chapters the present strength of India, what more India can learn from the world's most powerful countries, India's responsive action through the formulation of public policies and foreign policy, etc. This chapter seeks to deal with the vision of the Prime Minister of India that aims to turn India from a developing to a developed country i.e. Viksit Bharat by 2047. People might have visions, people might have dreams, and people might set goals, but the main issue is there must be a roadmap to achieve the goal. The Government of India has a large pool of higher academic Institutions, Organizations and think tanks, who are getting lakhs of rupees as salary and other facilities from the Government of India. But where is the roadmap? Have the policymakers been able to prepare a blueprint for attaining the goal? The Prime Minister also declared merely the idea of Viksit Bharat before the 2024 Elections, maybe to win the hearts of the voters, but where is the blueprint, and where are the bold initiatives to date? Even today when I am writing this part (11th day of December, 2024) there is not a proper plan and road map with the Government as is evident from the following words of the Prime Minister. In a virtual speech (December 8, 2024) on the occasion of Karyakar Suvarna Mahotsav of the Bochasanwasi Akshar Purushottam Swaminarayan (BAPS) Sanstha, the Prime Minister "...Urged citizens to become the force behind the country's march towards the target of "Viksit Bharat 2047" and announced that next month a "Viksit Bharat Young Leaders' Dialogue" would be held to give the youth a platform to exchange ideas" (The Tribune, 2024). This indicates that the government of India is still grappling with formulating a detailed plan to achieve the goal.

Further, we find that on 11 December 2023, the Prime Minister launched 'Viksit Bharat@2047: Voice of Youth' where he said "This is the period in the history of India when the country is going to take a quantum leap." He also pointed out: "Idea starts with an 'I' just like 'India' begins with an 'I', development efforts begin from self" and "Youth power is both the agent of change and also the beneficiaries of change" (PIB, 2023). In that workshop, the Prime Minister addressed the Vice Chancellors of Universities, Heads of Institutes, and faculty members across the country to mark the beginning of the initiative. But to date, very scanty numbers of reports and books have been published in this regard. All these indicate the policy crisis of the Government of India. My question is: then, what did the University wits do in the last year? What the social science research institutions are doing in this regard? And what affirmative steps have been taken by policymakers for the general public? What the great Indian-origin Nobel Laureate economists are doing in fulfilling the dream of the Prime Minister? What role is being played by the NITI Aayog, the apex public policy think tank of the Government of India? However, in any of the workshops at Raj Bhawans across the country, I was neither invited nor attended. Despite that, being an independent researcher and a thoroughly patriotic Indian, out of my duty toward my motherland and love for the country, I have prepared a roadmap for the attainment of a $30 trillion economy by 2047, when India will celebrate its 100 years of Independence.

It seems to me that it is the duty of the Government's top policymakers to prepare a road map that should be widely popularized and sensitized among all the citizens so that they can work accordingly. There is a maxim in Management: plan your work and work according to your plan. However, the urge of the Prime Minster for the participation of the youths is good and praiseworthy, because without people's whole-hearted participation, no policy can be properly implemented successfully. The word 'country' is an abstract idea; its main component is the population. Hence, without the participation of the population, no vision can be achieved by a country. Considering this tangible fact in mind, I have embarked on drawing up a roadmap for achieving the vision of a Viksit Bharat initiated by our Prime

Minister. Here, I shall divide my discussion into three sections such as the concept of Viksit Bharat; a few lessons from other developed countries; and some important directions for the successful attainment of the vision Viksit Bharat. However, before going to delineate the roadmap, we may explore the concepts of 'development,' 'Sustainable Development,' and 'Viksit Bharat.'

What is a Viksit Bharat?

The term 'Viksit Bharat' is the Hindi translation of the English word 'Developed India.' In this terminology, the focus is given to India's development. Now the concept of 'development' should be examined first. Generally, the term "development" is very often used by economists, politicians, social scientists, and policymakers. The term is simply used to describe an improvement in the quality of human life. However, different social scientists and international organizations have defined the terminology from different perspectives. There are hundreds of definitions of 'development.' Only a few important and relevant concepts will be highlighted here to comprehend the terminology. Wanninayake (2020, p. 52) considers that "Development is an all-encompassing word, which is frequently invoked in every discipline, policy dialogue, as well as day-to-day happenings." The term "development" is actually a polysemic, i.e. it has many meanings. Basically, human development indicates affirmative changes in people's standard of living, increase in income through decent jobs, enjoyment of freedom of choice, and democratic rights. The concept of development has nicely been elaborated in the first paragraph of the UN Agenda for Development (A/RES/51/240): "Development is one of the main priorities of the United Nations. Development is a multidimensional undertaking to achieve a higher quality of life for all people. Economic development, social development, and environmental protection are interdependent and mutually reinforcing components of sustainable development" (UN Document: Development, 1997).

In the earlier stage of development economics, development was measured by the Gross Domestic Product of a country, Gross National Product, and GDP Per Capita Income. In this regard, Wanninayake in one of his recent works pointed out that "Until the 1970s, development was understood purely in economic terms when it was assumed that increasing the production capacity of a nation would automatically improve the quality of life of the people through trickle-down effect" (Semasinghe, 2020, pp. 53-54). Further, Lord Robbins (1966) was quoted by Wanninayake regarding the method of measuring development: "Development was measured in relation to the income per head and as the ready availability of goods and services as distinct from the experiences of satisfaction felt by the people" (Robbins, 1966). But the concept of development was entirely shifted by Professor Amartya Sen. According to Professor Sen "Human Development, as an approach, is concerned with what I take to the basic development idea: namely advancing the richness of human life, rather than the richness of the economy in which human beings live, which is only a part of it. That is, I think, the basic focus of the human development approach" (Sen, 2004). Thus we find there is a shift in the idea of development – from economic growth of a country to human-centric development. This view was first brought to light by Mahbub-ul-Haq, a close friend of Amartya Sen, in the first Human Development Report published in 1990. Recently the United Nations has given importance to human capacity building. According to the United Nations, "Capacity-building is defined as the process of developing and strengthening the skills, instincts, abilities, processes, and resources that organizations and communities need to survive, adapt, and thrive in a fast-changing world. An essential ingredient in capacity-building is the transformation that is generated and sustained over time from within, transformation of this kind goes beyond performing tasks to changing mindsets and attitudes (United Nations, https://www.un.org/en/academic-impact/capacity-building).

Whatever may be said, it cannot be denied that the size of the economy is the main indicator of a country's richness. Further, the GDP per capita income also cannot be ignored. Norman Hicks and Paul Streeten in a work in the 1970s (Hicks & Streeten, 1979, p. 567) asserted that "The use of national accounting was inspired by the attention of Western economists to the broad aggregates of Keynesian economics, which was itself of major influence on economic thought at the time (1950s) when attention was being increasingly paid to the less developed countries." The attention of the world's economists is still focused on third-world countries. However, "National accounting served to integrate, through a weighting system based on market prices or factor costs, such disparate items as agriculture and industrial production, investment, consumption, and government services. In fact, national income accounting was a tool for analysis that other social scientists sometimes viewed with considerable envy" (Hicks & Streeten, 1979, p. 567).

However, these assumptions have almost turned out to be invalid at present. Hence, an alternative and better approach was evolved with the indicators of human, social, and economic development which cover areas and aspects that cannot be reflected in most income-based measures. "These so-called "social indicators' attempt to measure the development of health, nutrition, housing, income distribution, as well as other aspects of cultural and social development" (Hicks & Streeten, 1979, p. 567). Again, according to The World Bank (The World Bank, IBRD-IDA) "Economic indicators include measures of macroeconomic performance (gross domestic product [GDP], consumption, investment, and international trade) and stability (central government budgets, prices, the money supply, and the balance of payments). It also includes broader measures of income and savings adjusted for pollution, depreciation, and depletion of resources." Finally, the present concept of Sustainable Development is as follows: "Sustainable development is how we must live today if we want a better tomorrow, by meeting present needs without compromising the chances of future generations to meet their needs" (United Nations).

The concept of development has now been changed into sustainable development. In September 2015, after the conclusion of the Millennium Development Goals (2001), all the members of the United Nations adopted 17 Sustainable Development Goals as a universal call to action to end poverty and hunger; ensure good health and well-being; quality education; gender equality; clean water and sanitation; affordable and clean energy; decent work and economic growth; industry, innovation, and infrastructure; reduced inequalities; sustainable cities and communities; responsible consumption and production; climate action; life below water and life above water; peace, justice and strong institutions; and partnerships for attainment of the Sustainable Development Goals. The Agenda 2030 can be called the first step in attaining the goal of *Viksit Bharat*. Let us now discuss the concept of *Viksit Bharat* in the following part.

The Viksit Bharat Concept of the Prime Minister

'Viksit Bharat 2047' is the current government's vision to turn India into a completely developed nation by 2047. Before the 18th Lok Sabha elections held between April and June 2024, the Prime Minister concluded a meeting with his Council of Ministers to discuss the new government's action plan in the next 100 days after the formation of the government. This type of hype has become a trend in Indian politics in recent times. Before winning the elections, political leaders of any Party burst crackers, say big words, give absurd promises to the electorate, and show firm confidence to weaken the mental strength of the Opposition Parties. This declaration (of Viksit

Bharat) may be taken up as such a plan. However, the plan was good, and like many patriots, I also liked this plan of the Prime Minister. However, the plan lacked proper guidelines or Standard Operating Procedures. I also started doing research in 2020 on a related subject and published a book in June 2024 with the title *How Can India Become a Superpower by 2047: A Vision*. This volume is an abridged but precise and revised version of the said book, where a lot more new and innovative ideas have been incorporated to fulfill the dream of making India a superpower by 2047. However, in the said declaration, the Prime Minister stated that "...The core objective of the Viksit Bharat vision is to foster inclusive economic participation among all citizens. A key component of this initiative is the ambitious goal of elevating India to the rank of the world's third-largest economy within the next five years, contingent upon the NDA assuming power once more. Goals set under the mission is to turn India into a $30 trillion developed economy in about two decades for a projected 1.65 billion population. The document envisions economic growth, sustainable development goals, improvements in the ease of living and doing business, enhanced infrastructure, and bolstered social welfare initiatives" (Deccan Herald, 2024).

How to Transform Present India Into a Viksit Bharat?

From the above discussions, we have already learned the concept of development from various perspectives; sustainable development goals, and various indicators of development. Now, we will try to explore the means and methods of turning the present India into a Viksit Bharat.

How to achieve a $30 trillion economy and turn India into a Viksit Bharat is the most significant chapter of this book, as it shows the paths of how to fulfill the national goal through the achievements of personal skill development, income growth, foreign direct investment, exploration and utilization of natural resources, and export-oriented industrialization. Before going to achieve the goal, we need to see the calculation of what a $30 trillion economy meant for India. In today's (11.12.2024) rate US$300000,00000000 is equal to Indian Rs. 25441581,03000000.00 (@ Rs.84.79 per US$1) as of 11.12.2024. And today's population is 145 crore, and it is projected to be around 1.62 billion in 2047. If 60% of its population, i.e. 97.2 million people (adding more than 2.8 crores to make it 100 crore population) can earn Rs. 25,44,158 in a year (Rs.2,12,013 per month), this $30 trillion economy can be accomplished today itself. But it is not possible now. Moreover, we have to calculate in terms of 2047. Suppose in 2047, the value of each Indian Rupee will be reduced to Rs.100 per US$1. Then

US$300000,00000000 x Rs.100 = Indian Rs.30000000,00000000.00. Dividing this amount by 100 crore population, each individual's income should have to be Indian Rs.30000000,00000000.00 ÷ 100,0000000 population = Rs.30,00000 in a year. Further, if Rs. 30,00000 is divided by 12 months, it would be Rs. 2,50,000 per month. So, the target of each of the 100 lakh Indian people would be to earn Rs. 2,50,000 per month in 2047. At that time, India's GDP per capita would be US$ 30,000 from today's $2600.00 approximately.

But the point is how this big amount could be earned. For this purpose, a clear roadmap has been provided for all the stakeholders. These include the number of new micro small and medium-scale enterprises to be set up at least @100 numbers in every district in a year for the coming 23 years. More gazelles and start-ups are to be set up, manufacturing industries to be increased, foreign direct investments are to be attracted, India's exports to be increased, corruption must be dealt with an iron hand, communal harmony to be strengthened, and participation of women and backward communities to be ensured on an equal basis. More doctors and nurses, technocrats, scientists, and fundamental research are to be encouraged, and for that purpose, more funds should allocated to the health and education sectors. Population control and infiltration from neighboring countries require government attention. Government policy requires more full proof and implementing agencies should be responsible and accountable to the people not in merely black and white; but rather in a practical sense. The CBI and Enforcement Directorate staff require more professionalism and their success rates must have to be increased to bring acceptability and respect in the eyes of common citizens. Political reforms such as one-party rule or strong coalition to be formed for running a government; sabotaging by opposition parties and bad naming the existing government in foreign lands should be strictly dealt with by the Judiciary. Instead of the distribution of doles, the skill development of people especially students is to be emphasized in no time. Moreover, the National Education Policy 2020 has to be implemented in every state of India at the earliest. Skill development training must be imparted to the students from Class VI. There should not be any political interference in educational institutions and academic decisions of the Universities. Science & technology, information and communication technology, and STEM (Science Technology Engineering, and Mathematics) should be popularized among the existing students, and proper staff and infrastructure have to be provided to all the institutions.

At least 6 percent of the GDP has to be allocated for education and research purposes to attain a $30 trillion economy within the next two and a half decades. The following part shows more specifically how and by whom all these policies would be taken up and implemented. This is the most significant part of the book. It does not merely tell you about the policies, but it also says how to implement the same within our limited resources and existing infrastructure.

1. Arouse Your Respect for India

Without respect and love, one cannot give fully to his loved one. In the case of India, every Indian at first should love and respect the country. Why love and respect this country? Reminisce, for thousands of years, India has been a vast and rich country with abundant natural resources, fertile land, maritime trade, and above all, spirituality. Indian sub-continent was a commercial zone as well as a knowledge hub of vital importance in ancient times. Indian trade and commerce pervaded Africa, Asia, Arabs, Greece, Rome, and many other European countries. Considering India's plentiful minerals and spices, the richness of art, culture, literature, architecture, and flourishing spirituality, hundreds of foreign pilgrims, knowledge-seekers, traders, and explorers embarked on the Indian shores. Most of them returned to their countries with at least some assets from India, while some greedy European merchants and trading companies engaged themselves in trade rivalry and subsequently, they turned into political rivalry on Indian soil, and ultimately the British merchants succeeded in capturing India's political powers. They robbed Indians for centuries and converted us from rich to poor. Their exploitation and oppression continued for hundreds of years. After a continuous struggle against the British Rulers for almost two hundred years, India attained Independence in 1947. Since then, the journey of India as a sovereign democratic country has become a challenging one with poverty, illiteracy, malnutrition, lower income, gender disparity, border conflicts, internal turmoil, and other democratic deficits. Despite various problems, the Indian government has endeavored to uplift the socio-economic condition of people. But the government alone can never develop a vast country like ours. Therefore, we all have to participate in the development work as per our individual capacity and scope considering the ideology of our country first, and family and self-interest next. Always love and praise for India.

Mark Twain, a renowned American novelist once said, "India is the cradle of the human race, the birthplace of human speech, the mother of history, the grandmother of legend, and the great-grandmother of tradition. Our most valuable, and most constructive materials in the history of man, are treasured up in India only" (Mandal, 2024, p. 51). This proves that India is a great country with rich culture, tradition, and scientific discoveries for centuries. India was such a glorious country in the past that many great people of the world eulogized its greatness, vastness, and richness. Raman Singh writes in a recent article that Albert Einstein went one step ahead in acknowledging India's contribution to world civilization wherein he remarked: "…we owe a lot to the Indians, who taught us how to count, without which no worthwhile scientific discovery could have been made" (Singh, 27 Jan. 2023). Similarly, the great Indologist Max Muller once said, "If I were asked under what sky the human mind has most fully developed some of its choicest gifts, has most deeply pondered on the greatest problems of life, and has found solutions, I should point to India" (Singh, 27 Jan. 2023). Further, Henry Beveridge (1867, Preface) in his famous book *A Comprehensive History of India, Civil, Military and Social from the First Landing of the English, to the Suppression of Sepoy Revolt; including An Outline of the Early History of Hindoostan, Vol. 1* wrote: "India, the most valuable dependency of the British crown, is also one of the most interesting portions of the globe. Even some of its physical features are on a scale of unparalleled grandeur. The stupendous mountain chain along its northern frontier rising gradually from a plain of inexhaustible fertility has snowy summits that tower nearly six thousand feet above the loftiest of any other country in either hemisphere; while over the vast expanse of its magnificently diversified surface, almost every product possessed of economical value grows indigenously, or having been introduced is cultivated with success."

2. Set a Big Goal and Work Wisely to Increase Your Income

If growth refers to a country's population, national income, per capita income, level of consumption, savings, investment, and foreign trade over a period of time; we have to focus on all these components. Equally, we need to increase exploration of our natural resources and open up the door to foreign direct investment in defense, aviation, infrastructure, education, tourism, manufacturing industries, etc. At first, we have to learn the art of increasing our personal income. Skill development and capacity building are the two most important attributes for every Indian youth nowadays. Let us first learn some lessons from the examples of three countries such as the USA, China, and Japan that miraculously increased their Gross National Income, GDP per capita income, foreign trade, savings, and investment.

How American Rich Became Richer?

We can learn from the story of America about how to increase income and how Indian people can be billionaires. In the USA, billionaires control the lives and politics of that country. This is true for India too. Do you like to become an influencer or a billionaire? I am sure you will say 'Yes,' as everybody wants to do so. But how it can be accomplished? Here, I am sharing ideas with you, especially the youths of India, regarding how to make and increase money. In the year 2019, out of the 400 billionaires of the USA, 93 billionaires, or 23.5% of the members of the Forbes 400, made their money through investing, like Warren Buffett and Carl Icahn. People have wide social networks, software products, or revolutionary technological knowledge that can make billions of dollars. With 69 tech billionaires, including Bill Gates, Mark Zuckerberg, Snapchat's Bobby Murphy, and Evan Spiegel, you also can earn big money in India. Online marketing, selling, and trading can also be a big source of earnings. Amazon's founder Jeff Bezos has a $114 billion fortune by selling almost everything online. Further, "Harvesting, processing, manufacturing, selling, and marketing food and drinks is another good way to gain admission to the elite club of the ultrarich. The logic behind this is simple: People gotta eat, and there's money to be made by feeding them. About 10% of the list, 41 billionaires, created their wealth by feeding the masses...Howard Schultz, the former CEO of Starbucks, made his $4.7 billion fortune by turning the Seattle beanery into a global top brand" (Forbes, 2019). Real estate is another tried and true way to make a buck. President Donald Trump himself is a billionaire with a net worth of $3.1 billion. He is a real estate businessman. The 10 topmost industries where people can make money quickly are (i)Finance and investment, (ii) Technology, (iii) Food & Beverage, (iv) Real Estate, (v) Fashion and Retail, (vi) Media & entertainment, (vii) Energy, (viii) Service, (ix) Sports, and (x) Manufacturing. Therefore, I recommend that Indian people adopt these professions and become billionaires. America is the country that produces the most Nobel Laureates and, the most gold medal achievers in the Olympics and controls the global economy, trade, military, financial, and social organizations. In a word, at present, they control global politics, global trade and commerce, economy, land power, airpower, seas, and space. However, China is rising as a rival power to the USA. Let's learn about China.

Take a Lesson from China

In this regard, we can highlight the assertions of Robert E. Wright, who wrote in a recent article: "Undoubtedly, Americans made many other improvements in 1802 that escaped the author's notice. But the real story behind America's 19th-century growth miracle lay not in the details of corporation formation, particular inventions, or the proliferation of innovative practices or better breeds, breads, or meds...they believed their lives and property were their own, to do with as they wanted and not exposed to expropriation by their neighbors, foreign politics, or their own governments" (The Daily Economy, 2020). It seems to me that as they have the highest GDP, liberal economy, free democracy, strong institutions, robust military, skilled citizens, hard-working mentality of the people, and very modern infrastructure, hence, they can perform better than most other countries in the world whatever goal they want to achieve. India must follow the US system of governance, and similar economic activities to grow its GDP and Per Capita Income and excel in other fields.

I have discussed in detail what the Indian government, students, and various professionals can learn from China in Chapter 2. China is the second-largest economy in the world. And both China and India got independence almost simultaneously. So, we cannot ignore China, a big economic giant. Here, I would say only a few words to my Indian brethren in regard to the astonishing development of China, and our take away from China. Every Indian student who is studying in any educational institution must keep "Competitiveness" in mind. First with your classmates, then with the students of your district, in the third stage with the students of your state, in the fourth stage compete with the students of India, and finally compete with the students of the world. Do not let any other student to excel you. Consider yourself as "the best boy/girl in the world," and study, behave, and perform accordingly. Secondly, the District Magistrate of every district should dictate the SDOs and BDOs to bring foreign direct investment in their individual district, and urge the people to be entrepreneurs and invest money and provide necessary loans and training to invest in manufacturing industries and enterprises. At least 100 small-scale, and Micro Small and Medium Scale Enterprises must have to be set up in each district in a year. This would be continued for the next 23 years. Let us become the 'World's Factory' replacing China by 2047. The promotion, salary increment, and other financial benefits of the DMs, SDOs, and BDOs might be linked with the performance they show during their tenure as the heads of a district, sub-division, and block. Thirdly, the government should improve its tax policy, license policy, and *dadagiri* policy of local political leaders in relation to setting up factories and enterprises. Like China, the Indian government should formulate all such policies such as the acquirement of land, providing licenses, infrastructure, water, electricity, etc. that will smoothen the foreign direct investment in India. Through further policy reforms, India can attract more Foreign Direct Investment in education, defense, insurance, infrastructure, and even space research & development. Otherwise, how will our educated youth get the earning opportunity? How India's GDP per capita income will be hiked and how India's GDP will grow? Fourthly, like the Communist Party of China, India should have a strong national party like that of the Bharatiya Janata Party or Indian National Congress which will have the majority of MLAs in most of the state legislatures and will function in line with the policies formulated by the Union Government. For more details, read the chapter 7 again.

Japan is a Master of Resilience

Also, India should follow Japan to increase its GDP and per capita income quickly. In the Second World War Japan was devastated completely. But how Japan turned back within a few decades is a lesson for all the aspiring countries in the world. In Japan also, the new Constitution of 1947 adopted a Unitary form of Government. Japan basically adopted a unitary parliamentary constitutional monarchy with a bicameral legislature, the National Diet. Japan, instead of changing others, focused on changing themselves. After World War II, they realized the consequences of their attack on Pearl Harbor in Honolulu in the United States of America in 1941. So, they atoned for their misdeeds by concentrating on the improvement of technology, working more hours than the people of the United States, taking lesser salaries than the workers of the USA, and developing automotive and electronic manufacturing industries. In a word, they gave up militarism and concentrated on economic development for the development of their country and the people. They follow traditional culture, respect family values, and adopt a sober work culture. Can Indian youths and workers not follow the same ethos to increase income and self-development for furthering the income of the nation as a whole? Like Japanese people, the Indian population should take up the habit of personal saving. Investment in trading and business is another way India should follow. Japanese people give the topmost priority to their country. American President-elect Donald Trump also gives top priority to his motherland and openly says "America First." Similarly, India must not compromise with its national and international interests, and the Indian Prime Minister should distinctly say - "India First."

How Japan's Economy Grew?

Japan's economic growth is miraculous. In this regard, Masahiro Takada writes: "The rapid economic growth in Japan from the beginning of the 1950s to the early 1970s did not only result from special government policies and revolutionary events but were also achieved by the cumulative effort and hard work by the people. The unique characteristic and ability of the Japanese people to imitate and improve the skills learned, and then apply them to their own system was the most important factor for their successes." I too suggest the government of India send our students to Japan, Germany, the USA, and Israel to learn technology and take a bond from them they will return back to India and work for the development of India with the same technology that they have learned there...One of the factors that the Japanese made use of their unique characteristic to expand the economy was to improve and make practical use of technologies and technological know-how imported from foreign countries" (Takada, 1999, p. 12).

3. Indian Scientists and Technologists Must Invent Low-Cost Mass Production Systems

Indian scientists and technologists will have to invent low-cost mass-production systems. You see Japanese cars, electronic gadgets, printing machines, Japanese bullet trains, household goods like kitchen knives, Kinome ceramic coffee filters, Hario Cha Cha Dripper, Mamenoko Tawashi scrubbers, and so on. "Japan has created new technology, such as the low-cost mass production systems, by combining numerous technologies imported from abroad. The most important point to recognize about Japan's import of technology was that it was translated into industrial strength only because it was combined with domestic innovation" (Takada, 1999, pp. 12-13). Let Indian scientists and technologists follow the same method to Indianize the goods with the combination of various mixed items.

Continuous technological research and development is sine qua non for all business and manufacturing companies in India. A good example can be taken from Japan's steel industry. It is learned that "Japan's steel industry successfully improved the quality of the special steels used in automobiles and as a result of technological progress in the casing of parts, the automobile industry, too, grew into an industry to be able to compete in international markets for the first time. Similar progress occurred in the shipbuilding industry also, and numerous industries were growing almost at a proportionate rate" (Takada, 1999, p. 13). India also needs to follow China in this regard.

4. The Union Leaders Must Vow to Protect, Assist, and Increase Industrial Production

In Japan, a very cordial labor and management relationship has been built. This improves production as well as employee-employer relations. The unity between labor and management was established from the active role taken by the unions. But in India, the disruptive and destructive role is mostly played by the labor unions led by the Communist Party of India. Like Japan, Indian union leaders should show loyalty to the management and assist the company in improving the relations between the laborers and managers and thus grow the production of goods, which brings more profit for the organization and benefits the employees. Indian labor unions should follow the principle of joint management from their Japanese counterparts. Indian industrialists should also safeguard the interests of the laborers and all tier workers with rightful pay, timely pay, adequate opportunity for promotion, and life-long membership of the workers.

5. The Government Must Formulate Stronger and Better Policies

Behind the development and growth of every country, there remains strong government policies. It is the core ingredient of the development mantra. In India, at present, the BJP-led NDA-III government is not as strong as the previous two terms, where the BJP could take up many bold decisions unilaterally because it had a complete two-thirds majority in Parliament. But the present NDA-III government is dependent on BJP's allies, who are not very reliable. They can break the government at any moment if they get some better bait from the Opposition Alliance. Moreover, the Congress-led Opposition I.N.D.I.A. alliance is creating obstacles in Parliament at almost every step of the policy-making process. That is why I urge the electors that India should form such a government that could perform without any obstruction from any internal obstruction. But I never support the government should act like a dictator. I only recommend a stable government in the Centre. In this regard Professor Md Zafar Alam Bhuniyan (Bhuniyan, 2019) in a recent article indicates: "During the miracle years, the voters continued to elect members of one political party, the Liberal Democratic Party, thereby, avoiding the political unrest that hurt the economies of other nations during this time." Indian electors may consider such a strategy for the welfare of the country and its people.

As the Narendra Modi Government is doing miraculously well in reforming the policy and economic development of India, he must be given some more time to continue making India a developed nation. The policies and strategies are very important in shaping the future of a country. What happened in Japan? In Japan "The policies and strategies were set forth carefully by the policy-making authorities to protect and sustain the growth, and therefore the Japanese political system had a major role in its development as well" (Takada, 1999, p. 15). Like the Yoshida Doctrine in Japan, Prime Minister P.V. Narasimha Rao's economic liberalization policy can be regarded as the turning point of the modern Indian economy. Prime Minister Narendra Modi, like Ideda, has gotten inspiration from Rao's policies and he is making his own way to fulfill the dream of a Viksit Bharat. Policy formulation is not a big deal; policy implementation is the main issue. Hence, the Government must develop a work ethic as well as a more improved control mechanism to implement the policies for the successful accomplishment of the goal of Viksit Bharat.

6. The Government Must Continue Its GDP Growth @10.00 Per Cent

It is not that India's economy will automatically increase in its own way. Besides, the making and growing of a few hundred billionaires will not make India a developed nation. For that reason, the income growth of the majority of its population should be ensured. We do not need lopsided growth; rather we require holistic and inclusive development. All the Ministries of the Union Government as well as State Governments have to work hand in hand and shoulder to shoulder to achieve the goal of Viksit Bharat. India's GDP should have to be continued at the average growth rate of 10.00 or 11.00 percent. If you look at Japan in the 1960s, you will find that "Although a few problems arose from heavy industrialization, this plan has contributed greatly to the later half of Japan's rapid growth with an average growth rate of 10.8 percent in the late 1960s and drove the economy to become the second largest in the world by the year 1968" (Takada, 1999, p. 15). Indian policymakers should also focus in a similar way on the GDP growth rate. The Union Government can never alone do this herculean task. All the State Governments and Union Territories should act positively. There might be political differences, there might be ideological differences, and there might be differences of opinion and perceptions between the leaders of the Union Government and State Governments, but neither of them should cherish parochial attitude in terms of National Growth and increase of GDP Per Capita Income. There might be healthy competition among the states and Union Territories regarding the growth of the economy, scientific innovation, research, educational and infrastructural development. The best states should be encouraged by the Union Government and praised openly in a special function, and a special allocation of funds for the successful states must be done. Like Teachers' Day, Republic Day, Independence Day, and Gandhi Birth Day, every year there should be a celebration of 'Most Prosperous State Day' in New Delhi on a particular day. May be third day of January be selected for this purpose. Prize can be given on some important criteria such as most foreign direct investment attracted by a state, total poverty alleviation, decent job allocation to the youths, numbers of start-ups and gazelles have been set up, a participation rate of women and minorities in economic and political activities, setting up the numbers of MSMEs and heavy industries, reduction of gender and minority violence in states, etc.

7. Triple the Numbers of MSMEs in the Next 23 Years

As per the information of the Ministry of Micro, Small, and Medium Scale Industries, at present India has "1,05,21,190 number units in the total small scale industry sector" (Ministry of Micro, Small and Medium Enterprises, 31 July 2023). This number will have to be increased by at least three-fold i.e. at least 3 crore small-scale industries should be there in India in the year 2047. The Ministry of Micro Small and Medium-Scale Enterprises should give a target to the District Magistrates and Sub Divisional Magistrates to set up MSMEs proportionately under their jurisdiction. Make a plan to set up at least 20 new MSMEs in every subdivision every year. The aim of Viksit Bharat will be accomplished easily. India's economy will then shine.

8. The Government Must Set a Target to Grow GDP and Per Capita Income at least 8 Times

The latest Forbes India reports show that at present, the size of India's GDP is merely $3.9 trillion and GDP Per Capita (Nominal) is only $2.7 thousand. So, it is very nominal in comparison with the USA ($28.78 trillion) and China ($18.53 trillion) (Forbes India, 2024). When compared with the GDP Per Capita Income of India with that of USA and China, a grim picture comes before us. The per Capita Income of the US population is $86.6 thousand, while it is $12.97 for China. Where do you stand today?

How to grow GDP and Per Capita Income? Presently, India has some of the highest numbers of unicorns (this term is used in the venture capital industry to describe a startup company with a value of over $1), and gazelles (A gazelle company is a high-growth company that has been increasing its revenue by at least 20% annually for four years or more). It is revealed by Forbes India that, "As of May 2024, the Indian Startup Ecosystem, ranking third globally in terms of unicorn count, collectively valued at $349.67 Bn. In today's fast-paced and dynamic economy, Indian Unicorns are thriving. These startups are not only creating groundbreaking solutions and technologies but also fueling significant job growth" (Forbes India, 22 Aug. 2024). Every year at least 25 new unicorns have to be developed. The government of India and the state governments must take the initiative to encourage startups and increase their trade and commerce. All logistical and financial support must be extended to the startup companies. With the encouragement of the Government, more numbers of startups will be set up. India's youth will get better and decent jobs, and India's GDP and Per Capita Income will increase.

Further, in India, the Ministry of Heavy Industries should be more active and bold like that of the Japanese Ministry of International Trade and Industry (MITI). In Japan, "...another political factor that greatly influenced the growth was the role taken by the Ministry of International Trade and Industry (MITI). MITI, which was regarded as the most powerful government organization during the time of rapid expansion, was mostly responsible for the industrial growth in Japan. The Ministry's approach was one of providing encouragement and guidance to the initiatives of private business: creating a suitable un-level playing field which would give that critical advantage to industries identified by the government as having potential for long-term success" (Suzuki). Not only that, MITI also focused on the growth of industries such as steel, shipbuilding, chemicals, and machinery. "These industries were thought of as having large and rapidly growly world markets and that expanding these industries was key to entering into the international markets and helping the economy to grow quicker" (Takada, 1999, p. 15). The fulfillment of India's dream of a Viksit Bharat depends to a large extent on the policy and strategy of the Ministry of Heavy Industries. So, I call upon Minister Sri H.D. Kumaraswamy to act fast and wisely. Don't waste time and give all of your energy and expertise to setting up more and more heavy industries in every district of India. Micro Small and Medium Scale industries should be set up in every block of India. The Governments - both the States and the Union - should provide financial help with low or nil interest, give management training, accounting training, and extend other assistance to the entrepreneurs to encourage them to perform to the best of their caliber. The concerned minister should seek foreign direct investment in heavy industries too. But one thing must be kept in mind, and that is the pollution of the country.

9. The Government Must Keep Up its Promise to Feed the Indians and Others Around the Globe

If industry is our one heart, then agriculture is our soul. Hence, the agriculture sector should be encouraged to produce export-quality rice, wheat, milk, eggs, meat, and other edible products. Similarly, India's horticulture should be encouraged to produce more export-quality fruits, plants, ornamental trees, etc. Training and funding from the block development offices must be provided to the farmers. We must remember, acknowledge, and remunerate our feeders and backbone of society. We are happy that India has the world's largest cattle herd (buffaloes), the largest area planted for wheat, rice, and cotton, and is the largest producer of milk, pulses, and spices in the world. It is the second-largest producer of fruit, vegetables, tea, farmed fish, cotton, sugarcane, wheat, rice, and sugar. The agriculture sector in India holds the record for the second-largest agricultural land in the world, generating employment for about half of the country's population. We must respect our farmer friends. More technology and instruments need to be used to increase the production of agricultural goods and horticulture. The quality of seeds must be improved, and electricity and water supply should be continuous with controlled prices. The fair price of crops must be given to the farmers. Indian unutilized land must be utilized to increase agricultural production.

10. The Automobile Industry Has to be Expanded in More States

The automobile industry in India is growing rapidly. The export of our two-wheelers and four-wheelers should be increased. India's annual production of automobiles in FY22 was 22.93 million vehicles. In FY23, total passenger vehicle sales reached $3.89 million. In FY23, total automobile exports from India stood at 47,61,487. This sector's share of the national GDP increased from 2.77% in 1992-1993 to around 7.1% presently. The number of production and the number of vehicles have to be tripled by 2047. There must be small cars for Indian villages, and big cars for the metropolitan cities. The availability of car loans in easy installments should be extended by banks and financial companies. The vehicles should be all-weather, and all roads should be friendly. Automobile companies may consider manufacturing amphibious cars and environment-friendly electric vehicles. More electric charge centers by the roadside should be set up. There is a huge demand for those in coastal as well as regular flood-affected areas. To control air pollution, electric vehicles should be produced and sold in India. Export-quality four-wheelers should be manufactured.

11. India's Defense Exports should be increased

The Indian Defence Ministry must act more aggressively to produce export-quality defense products. There must be innovation in defense technologies in India. India must learn from Israel, Japan, Germany, China, and South Korea about defense manufacturing technology, or initially production may be done in collaboration with these countries. Our dependency on Russia and France in regard to the import of missiles, rifles, combat aircraft, submarines, etc., should be reduced quickly. Instead, Defence Research and Development Organization (DRDO), Bharat Heavy Electricals, Bharat Dynamics Limited, Larsen & Toubro Shipbuilding, Mazagon Dock Shipbuilders Limited, and others must work more diligently to manufacture longer-range missiles, night vision rifles, combat aircraft, fighter planes, nuclear submarines, tanks, bullets, etc. Gradually, we should set up indigenous manufacturing units and then export defense equipment to the world. The target of India is US$26 billion to be achieved by 2026, but it will have to be increased to $200 billion by 2047. Digital India and Make in India programs are to be expedited. Digital currency should also be popularized. You cannot escape from this, as now it is the trend of the world market.

12. India should take the Initiative to Popularize the Indian Rupee in the International Market

The US Dollar is not only concentrated within the territory of America. Why should Indian rupees be confined within India only? India should endeavor to popularize the Indian rupee in the international market. India should also take the initiative in setting up International Banks like those of the IMF and World Bank in Delhi or Mumbai, or Kolkata. Monetary reforms, if required, must be considered. Let our Indian currency be spread in the global market. Hindi should be included in the list of official languages of the United Nations, as it is the third most popular language in the world. India should do more to become a permanent member of the Security Council of United Nations. India has all the capabilities and expertise to become the world's spiritual leader. There should be a World Peace Council under the UN system, where India should be a permanent Chair. India should be recognized internationally as the *Biswaguru* (World's master) for promoting and protecting democracy, global peace, spirituality, security, and prosperity. The world has already recognized India as a peace-loving country. Now, the government of India should collaborate with BRICS to make an alternative institution to the IMF and the World Bank.

13. Ministry of Electronics and Information Technology Must Chase a Big Target

At present, the Union Minister (from 11 June 2024) of Electronics and Information Technology is a former IAS from the Odisha Cadre. However, having his expertise and experience as a Managing Director of GE Transportation, and Vice President of Locomotives and Head of Urban Infrastructure Strategy, he was chosen by the far-sighted Prime Minister as the Minister of Railways, Minister of Electronics and Information Technology, and Minister of Information and Broadcasting. He must now take a leading role in taking India to the loftiest level through his policy formulation and implementation by the government and non-government machinery. India's current target in the electronics system design and manufacturing (ESDM) sector is to generate US$1 trillion worth of economic value from the digital economy by 2025. This target is to be framed at $10 trillion by 2047. The IT & BPM sector became one of the most significant growth catalysts for the Indian economy. In the financial year 2022, the IT sector contributed to 7.4% of India's GDP. It is projected to grow by 10 percent by 2025, and it would have to increase to 40 percent by 2047. India should take electronic goods, pharmaceutical products, consumer hardware, electronic components, and Android phones for exports. The Ministry should focus on the semiconductor manufacturing industry and the export of the same. Why India should import smartphones in the 2[nd] decade of the 21[st] century? Instead of importing smartphones and laptops, India should manufacture its own technology phones like Samsung Galaxy, Apple iPhone, Asus ROG, and laptops such as Lenovo, Dell, Apple, Acer, etc. According to the Press Information Bureau (Press Information Bureau, 2024) "The global electronics market, valued at US$ 4.3 trillion, is dominated by countries like China, Taiwan, USA, South Korea, Vietnam, and Malaysia. India currently exports approximately US$ 25 billion annually, representing less than 1% of the global share despite a 4% share in global demand. To enhance competitiveness, India needs to localize high-tech components, strengthen design capabilities through R&D investments, and forge strategic partnerships with global technology leaders." After electronics and information technology, we shall examine the status of the power sector, and how to provide more clean energy.

14. The Indian Power Sector Should Produce More Clean Energy

India's power sector needs more production of clean energy. At present, there is a shortage of electricity in India. The power cuts are often felt in the months from April to August in India. The power demand has already been increased, and it will be doubled in the next 25 years because production will continue to rise in quantity. More factories and business establishments will be set up in every district of India. Instead of using conventional fossil fuels, we have to focus more on the production and use of solar power, hydropower, and wind power. The target of 450 Gigawatt (GW) of renewable energy capacity from solar power by 2030 must be fulfilled. Let India produce more non-conventional power.

India has the opportunity to learn from Australia in regard to meeting the demands of fuel. Australia planned to ramp up its extraction and use of gas until 2050 and beyond as part of its Future Gas Strategy. Australian Minister for Resources Madeleine King recently said: "The strategy makes it clear that gas will remain an important source of energy through to 2050 and beyond, and its uses will change as we improve industrial energy efficiency, firm renewables, and reduce emissions. But it is clear we will need continued exploration, investment, and development in the sector to support the path to net zero for Australia and for our export partners and to avoid a shortfall in gas supplies" (World Economic Forum, 2024). Therefore, India should also expedite its exploration for natural gas and petroleum, and invest more money to support the path to net zero for India.

15. Foreign Investors Should to Incentivised to Come and Invest in India

India is the world's largest market. India is a peaceful country. The democratic setup of India is globally renowned. I urge all global investors to come to India, have a taste of India's hospitality, invest your money to make your profit, and give decent jobs to our skilled and English-speaking youths. The Government may incentivize foreign investors. India invites FDI inflows in drug manufacturing, infrastructure development, defense manufacturing, space research, the medical devices sector, robotics, and the energy sector. The education sector is also an open field of investment. The tourism and entertainment world is very lucrative in India. FDI in all these sectors is attractive. It is high time that India produces now more life-saving drugs, injections, tablets, and medical equipment and exports the same after fulfilling the needs of the Indian people. In 2022, India's export of medical devices was only $2.90 billion, and it is expected to rise $10 billion by 2025. The pharmaceutical industry and drug manufacturers should consider investment in additional sectors of medical devices. There is also heavy demand for good and cheap medical devices in India. Still, we are dependent on good-quality medical devices. Let us manufacture qualitative medical devices in India. "A majority of India's medical devices, ranging from a simple thermometer to cotton wool and electrocardiograph (ECD) machines to catheters, are imported, and up to 11 percent of them from China...In certain device categories, Chinese imports are as high as 87 percent of total imports" (Porecha, Businessline, 19 June 2020). The large medical equipment manufacturers of India, such as Medisure Inc., Johnson & Johnson, Poly Medicure, Novartis AG, Abbott, etc., may consider setting up medical device industries, and foreign investors also invest in manufacturing units in India. India has large tracts of open land, good quality of road and air service, cheap labor, skilled workers, an easy license system, and a stable Union government. What more does a company require? All are here in India. Every foreign investor is welcome to India.

16. All Indian States Should Attract and Invite Foreign Tourists

With a total area of 3,287,263 sq. km extending from the snow-covered Himalayan heights to the tropical rainforests of the south, India has a rich cultural and historical heritage, variety in ecology, terrains, and places of natural beauty spread across the country. This provides a significant opportunity to fully exploit the potential of the tourism sector. We welcome all foreign investors to invest in the Indian tourism and entertainment sectors. Also, foreign visitors must visit India's temples, sea beaches, forests, hills, caves, architecture, and works of art. India's taste of culture, hospitality, welcoming attitude, and service to our guests is unique in the world. India believes in *Atithi Devo Bhavo*, which means our guests are equivalent to God. Whenever the Prime Minister visits a foreign land, he often urges the Indian diaspora to discover our rich heritage and vibrant culture. Recently (23rd November, 2024), Shri Narendra Modi urged the Indian community abroad and friends from other countries to take part in *the Bharat Ko Janiye* (Know India) Quiz. His motto was to improve relations and 'strengthen the bond with our diaspora.' All the state governments should propagate and popularize whatever potential they have with good and lucrative advertisements to attract foreign tourists. It will bring foreign currency, improve the local economy, and strengthen people-to-people relations. Also, India will have the opportunity to showcase its culture, natural beauty, architecture, works of art, human values, and spirituality, as well as recent high-rise buildings and advancements in science and technology.

17. The Indian Government Must Respect Pluralism and Adopt Inclusionary Policies

Can a bird fly with one wing? Can a human being be born with one parent? If a bird cannot fly without two wings and a child cannot be born without the union of two opposite genders, then how can India grow and develop fully without the active participation of both men and women, and the Hindus and Muslims? Without the whole-hearted participation of the fifty percent population, i.e., women, India's dream of a Viksit Bharat is next to impossible. Similarly, without the participation of the minority communities such as the Muslims, Christians, and Buddhists, the dream of India to become a Viksit Bharat is impossible. As both women and girls are integral parts of the human population, both Hindus and Muslims are also equally important components of the Indian social fabric. Women and girls, as well as the Muslim and backward populations, are very important assets of society. They must not be ignored and excluded from the mainstream development agenda. The United Nations indicates that "The empowerment of women and their full participation on a basis of equality in all spheres of society is fundamental for development"(The United Nations General Assembly, 1997).

The 2030 Agenda for Sustainable Development Goals promises to take all measures so that 'No One is Left Out.' India's present BJP-led NDA government is biased toward the Hindu majoritarian population. But, the key leaders of the BJP fail to understand that they are the inhabitants of India. They have been living in this country for hundreds of years. They have a great role to play in national development. Also, many of them are playing an important role in making Viksit Bharat. I have a question for the top leadership of the BJP. Why is there not a single Member of Parliament from the Muslim Community in the BJP? Why is there not a single Muslim MLA in the West Bengal Legislative Assembly from the Bharatiya Janata Party? So, is it not a clear indication of exclusionist politics being played by the BJP, the present ruling party in the center? Aren't they (Ruling BJP) responsible for the lopsided growth of India as a whole?

Hence, I call upon the BJP's top leadership to consider the issue and bring as many Muslims in the Parliament as possible. Similarly, they should be allocated ministerial berths. If you cannot do this, the others who come to power will do, and must do it for the holistic growth and development of India. Do not underestimate the power of minorities. The BJP is setting a bad example of zero level of political participation of the Muslim minority in the highest decision-making body of India. It indicates their meanness, short-sightedness of political vision, and a non-prudential political decision-making body. It is expected that they (the BJP) will soon be wise to include more women, minorities, non-Brahmin, and backward community people in the governance and top decision-making bodies. The earlier they understand the truth that the goal of a Vikshit Bharat cannot be achieved by the Hindus only, the earlier the goal will be achieved. Whole-hearted participation of all people is necessary.

18. India Must Utilize the Skills of Talented Youths

The Wheebox India Skills Report 2023 suggests that in 2023, 50.3% of young people are found to be highly employable overall. The percentage of the employable women workforce has increased to 52.8%, compared to 47.2% for men. The report also points out that 89% of graduates were actively seeking internship opportunities. The survey indicates that candidates from Uttar Pradesh, Maharashtra, and Delhi had the highest employability. "Amongst B.Tech, MBA, and B.Com were found to be the most employable talent from amongst various domains. Mumbai, Lucknow, and Mangalore were the cities with the most employable talent, and the most preferred cities for work by graduates were Bangalore, Chennai, and Delhi/NCR. The world is rapidly aging, but India is still young. In the next few decades, India will be a talent powerhouse and one of the largest contributors to the global workforce" (The Economic Times, 29 December 2022). This means India does not have a shortage of skilled workforce. The government of India must take care of our skilled young people.

19. Students Should Develop Entrepreneurship Skills at the School Level

Average Indian families teach their kids from school days to study hard and after the completion of formal education, appear in competitive examinations to get a government job, so that life becomes secure and safe for their children. This takes at least 25 years for average students to get a job. And nowadays, government jobs are scarce. Look, India has 130 institutions of national importance, including the Indian Institute of Technology, Guwahati, Assam; All India Institute of Medical Sciences, Delhi; National Institute of Technology, Karnataka; Indian Institute of Technology, Kharagpur, etc. It is revealed in a survey report of the Higher Education Department, Government of India, that there are 1043 Universities, 42,343 Colleges, and 11,779 Stand Alone Institutions listed on the AISHE (All India Survey on Higher Education) web portal. Also, there are 522 General, 177

Technical, 63 Agriculture and Allied, 66 Medical, 23 Law, 12 Sanskrit, and 11 Language Universities, and the rest 145 Universities are of other categories. The report of the All India Survey on Higher Education 2019-2020 highlights that total enrolment in higher education has been estimated to be 38.5 million, with 19.6 million boys and 18.9 million females. Female students constitute 49 percent of the total enrolment. It is learned from the survey that 2,02,550 students are enrolled in Ph. D., which is about 0.5% of the total student enrolment.

I mention the above figures because it seems to me that India will never be able to provide government jobs to these vast enrolled or pass-out students of Universities, let alone millions of pass-out students from Schools. Therefore, I encourage our students to undertake more entrepreneurship education and skill development training to set up their own industries and enterprises. Instead of being workers, the better-educated students can improve their skills to become owners of workshops and factories. A government loan is available if you cannot afford your own financing. Entrepreneurship development is the means of enhancing the knowledge and skills of entrepreneurs through several classroom coaching programs and training. The entrepreneurship development process helps new firms or ventures to get better in achieving their goals better, improve their business, and the nation's economy. There is always risk in business and entrepreneurship, but it is also a fact that there is more profit and earnings in business than in government jobs. To make India the "Business Hub" and "Production Hub" or "Manufacturing Hub" of the world, replacing China, our meritorious, mediocre, or low-merit students, and skilled students both should come forward to set up industries, factories, and business enterprises on Indian soil only.

20. Students Should Be Sensitized to Studying the Need-Based Subjects

If the majority of our students are studying now in general streams, very few of them are getting government or private jobs nowadays. Many of them are frustrated and so also their parents. The world has changed and is changing rapidly. In place of traditional subjects, a lot of new subjects and areas of study have come up now. The new areas such as food and beverages, fashion technology, accounting, taxation, commerce, science, technology, digital payment systems, beauty parlor, gymnasium, health and hygiene, software, and hardware development training will become helpful for average students. The aviation industry, non-fossil fuel industries such as hydropower, wind power, solar power, etc. space technology, and travel industry are some sectors where intelligent and meritorious students can find their future. Learning different foreign languages such as German, English, Russian, and French; and training in business management, finance management, personnel management, international trade, business management, etc. will help our students to work in various fields. Opportunities in health consultancy, education consultancy, psychological consultancy, marriage consultancy, and divorce and family management will be widened in the future. Teaching through technology is going to be the norm in the coming days. Classroom teaching will gradually be less significant; and online teaching, online examination, online marriage, online divorce, online job, online engagement, online service, online banking, and online payments will be more popular in the days to come. Media, mass communication, computers, laptops, mobile phone manufacturing, and repair will be a huge demand in the coming days. Small car manufacturing, battery and electric vehicle manufacturing, and service industry are going to be more lucrative in the days to come. Cryptocurrency asset management might be a new area of income. The market for Artificial Intelligence in India is also very attractive at present. It is valued at $7.8 billion (August 2021), which represents a 22% increase in the size of the market over 2020. In a year 20% jump in personnel has been found, and the average salary is also Indian Rupees 14.3 lakh a year. Hence, I encourage our students to select subjects of study wisely in higher education.

A lot of things depend upon the selection of subjects. Two things are very important in selecting subjects in Class XI and XII or College and University. First, one should understand the necessity and utility of the subject in the present time, and Second, the demand of the industries and government organizations for the subject. The teachers and parents have a very important role in this matter. Remember, the good and rightful selection of a subject may help to prosper the career of a student; but bad and wrong selection may spoil the prosperity of a student. Moreover, students must be consulted by their parents and guardians before selecting subjects of study for their sons and daughters.

21. Take a Strategic Goal and Engage More Youths in the Development Process

If Beijing can firmly take an ambitious strategy to put its influence over the global economy, aim for global power, and perhaps global primacy over the next generation, why New Delhi should remain behind? I have already proposed a mixed form of government modeled on the combination of the

USA and China. The tenure of government should also be extended to a minimum of 10 years or there should be a single-party rule in our country. A corruption-less long-term strong Central government can only fulfill India's dream of becoming a superpower. I strongly advocate for *Ek Bharat Shrestha Bharat*, Ek Party Ek Government with federal structure and autonomy of State Governments. But, if our political masters cannot take any affirmative action by 2024, I may tell my fellow citizens to take a strategic goal to outperform our counterparts in the USA, China, Japan, Germany, and Israel individually. When many people join hands together to achieve a great goal, the strength of a million hands becomes so powerful that it can do whatever it likes.

At the same time, I suggest: if you are a student, read for more hours than the students of afore-mentioned countries; if you are a scientist, devote more time and energy to discovering better technology, better software, and better medicine and selling them at a lesser price; if you are an entrepreneur, produce things that are not even thought of by the western countries; if you are a researcher, out-sail your counterparts in the world research canvas. Similarly, all professionals such as farmers, teachers, administrators, judges, lawyers, and industrialists should give their best as an individual and as a collective force. All the works have to be performed keeping the only goal of our national interest in mind. Let us sacrifice all our personal ego, personal interest, and personal development and well-being. I am not advocating for sacrificing personal development completely. Rather, I tell you to work for personal development and growth, but it must be done without harming others' interests at present and in the future. So, can we take an oath to give our best from today? Just say with me regularly - "India is my birthplace, India is my mother, I love my mother, I love my India. I shall serve my mother, and I shall serve India." Sacrifice your life at the altar of Mother India. Be spiritual, respectful, honest, hard-working, and tolerant. Your success chance will be increased ten-fold.

22. The Government Must Expedite International Trade and Commerce

It is said that economic prosperity is inextricably linked with international trade and commerce. The local manufacturers with sound management skills and flow of money should set up more and more industries, and produce goods and services that have global requirements. I wish my brethren to be Global, i.e. living in local areas they must be thinking about the global needs and demands of people. Two things should be kept in mind – the quality should be better and the price should be competitive. How did China capture the Indian market or the global market? Similarly, we have to spread in the global market. Not only heavy and electronic goods, I encourage my brothers and sisters to produce every good and item required by both men and women, children and old people. Let people use our footwear, toothpaste, brush, comb, doormat, share, bed sheet, light, toys, medicine, vaccine, ship, airplane, missiles, rockets, books, theories, ideas, our plans - all from India. You can do it. I have full faith in your caliber, skill, dexterity, and mental faculty. I know very well that, our students are very intelligent, and they are very efficient people who can produce, market, and supply their products anywhere in the world. What now we have to do is - Live locally but think globally. The second industrial revolution must take birth in India with the expert knowledge, know-how, or collaborative finance of Indian and Western entrepreneurs. That industrial revolution will increase our productivity, our power, our dignity, and ultimately our image in the global market. Imports should be discouraged through tariffs. China recognizes that the global trade regime has been indispensable to the country's economic and military rise. I advocate free trade among the countries. The government of India declared a National Logistic Policy to transport goods from one state to another. Similarly, it is very important for international transportation. Many research studies have shown that free trade enhances the welfare of the people. Also, it is a fact that global economic growth and growth in global trade have moved in tandem in the past two centuries.

23. India Should Publish a National Vision Document

Like China, India should formulate a composite vision document. Chinese President Xi Jinping in his historic speech to the 19th Party Congress in October 2017 said that China would "become a global leader in terms of composite national strength and international influence" and would build a "stable international order" in which China's "national rejuvenation" could be fully achieved. India must come out of its traditional system of governance and take the necessary steps to set up a strong Union Government, maybe with necessary Constitutional Amendments at the earliest. The earlier the better. The making of a vision document describing a sector-wise 25-year plan will give dividends to both the government and citizens. India must mention its aims and objectives for both the domestic and international arena, and declare a detailed work to be performed by every individual, institution, and others to achieve the vision of Viksit

Bharat. It needs more precise and scientific study by expert researchers. Every District Magistrate may be given the responsibility to achieve the goal of Viksit Bharat. He/she may prepare a vision document with the help of the district's best researchers and university professors. Similarly, the Union Government may ask for the same from each State. The Chief Secretaries of all states and Union Territories may be told to make a State Vision Document for 2047. Then the plan documents may be compiled at the national level. The major political parties may be invited to participate in this endeavor. In addition to this, the Indian Human Development Report should be prepared either by Niti Aayog or the Home Ministry as is prepared by the United Nations Development Program every year.

India must highlight its strategic partnership in the world. For this purpose, there might be necessary bilateral and multi-lateral partnership treaties with our neighbors as well as other global partners. If China has "a yearning for partial hegemony," India should also express its willingness to lead the Asian countries initially to lead the world in the future. India has the potential to lead the world. Instead of arms race and war threats, India will lead through spirituality and ethics. Indian Panchsheel Policy can act as the foundation stone for international relations. To begin with, it should lead the Asian nations first through free trade, free travel, and free academic exchange. India can easily access to any country with the age-old strength of spirituality. Let India open its borders with all other 47 Asian countries through negotiation and multilateral agreements. Let everything be open and competitive. India can propose friendship and alliance with China, Japan, Turkey, Iran, South Korea, UAE, Israel, and Singapore. These are the leading countries in Asia. These countries might come together forgetting their economic, political, and geographical positions to bring about major changes in the US-led WTO, IMF, and UNO system. Even the partnership of India with China can be a great threat to the entire Western powers. If both China and India join hands together, they can create a new Indo-Chinese global economic and administrative order. India and China are the oldest friends even many years before the establishment of the USA and the UK, and once again they can revive the friendship based on Buddhist and other liberal Hindu spiritual principles. Both China and India, or an alliance of the above-mentioned nine countries can transform the existing global power equation. Not the Western economies, Asian economies would win and build the global system to dominate the world in the days to come. In that new global order, not China but India will lead because of its spirituality, non-violence, non-aggression, and love for all people in the world. People will happily accept India as a global leader in the future. I firmly do believe this.

24. India Must Become a Supplier, Instead of a Procurer

In 2019, India and the U.S. signed defense deals worth more than $3 billion. The previous United Progressive Alliance (UPA) governments (2004-14) had signed the landmark nuclear deal and established close military relations with Washington. Since then, the U.S. has sold more than $15 billion worth of sophisticated weaponry to India. According to reports published in Frontline (April 23, 2021), "India is on the verge of entering into a multibillion-dollar deal with the U.S. to buy 30 armed drones and more than 150 combat jets for the Indian Air Force and the Indian Navy" (Cherian. Frontline, 2021). This is shocking. Instead of procurement, India must produce sophisticated weaponry and other technology, supply the same to the world market, and earn billions of dollars. Initially, India should invite the world's largest and most developed technologically advanced countries such as Japan, China, USA, Israel, South Korea, Germany etc. Gradually learn the artifacts and technology, and then manufacture indigenously.

Indian defense researchers might devote more time and energy to discovering more sophisticated nuclear weapons, more powerful missiles, and larger battle tanks to meet the requirements of the world. Indian farmers will supply the needs of people by producing more high-quality rice, wheat, and vegetables. Similarly, Indian Scientists and researchers will manufacture more developed supersonic missiles, long-range surface-to-surface, and surface-to-air missiles. More powerful drones can be made in India. Student exchange programs can be a very effective tool. Our students will go to the best universities and defense research institutions in the world; learn the technology and come back to India. These great scientists and researchers and their families should be given all kinds of facilities at par with the U.S. and U.K. institutions. I want to see that by 2047, India shall supply its computers, laptops, mobile phones, ships, drones, tanks, and Rafale-like multi-role fighter aircraft to the world. Indian building materials, iron and steel, clothes, fish, meat, vegetables, flowers, and other goods have huge demand in the world market. I can see the day in my mind's eye when India will be a top supplier country of these weapons and other electronic goods and gadgets and earn billions of dollars. I dream of such an India that will be technologically a very advanced country by 2047.

25. India Must Attract More Foreign Direct Investment

Foreign direct investment is favored over other capital flows by emerging market countries such as India. FDI is not debt-creating; rather it is less volatile than portfolio flows, also, it is relatively resistant during any financial crisis. Foreign direct investment enhances export performance, increases Gross Domestic Product, and ensures growth of a country. Though after the economic reforms in the 1990s of the last century, foreign direct investment has increased, still it is not as much as China and other top four economies in the world. "In 2004 India received FDI inflows of around 0.5 percent of GDP, whereas China received FDI worth 3.2 percent of GDP. In dollar terms, China received 16 times the FDI than India in 2004 (Jain-Chandra, IMF eLibrary, p. 73). In an article, Sonali Jain-Chandra points out that, "At the same time, investor surveys point to a strong interest in India as a destination for FDI. Investor surveys by the United Nations Conference on Trade and Development (UNCTAD) and A.T. Kearney in 2004 and 2005 place India as the second most attractive destination for FDI" (Jain-Chandra, IMF eLibrary, p. 73). However, the consecutive governments have not been able to translate this into actual FDI inflow. As per the World Economic Forum, 2005, 'India's overall infrastructure quality ranks low " and, "The significant burden of bureaucratic red tape and regulation in India further worsens the investment climate. For instance, it takes 89 days to start a business in India, more than double the time required to start in China. The enforcement of contracts takes longer in India (425 days) than the average in the sample. Also, once in business, firms find it difficult to exit" (Jain-Chandra, IMF eLibrary, p. 78). In addition to these, the labor market is volatile, trade unionism is strong, and extortion by politically supported goons are some of the reasons that hinder FDI. Hence, all these issues must be dealt with sternly by the administration of the state and Union governments and political leaders.

26. Rural Youths Must be Encouraged to Participate in Nation Building

The young and educated people in rural areas should come forward to engage themselves in the development of their locality. They should also actively participate in economic, political, and social institutions. When the villages in India will develop, the country as a whole will be developed. Every village in India is a vital source of energy and entrepreneurship. Rural youths are pure at heart, energetic in the body, and spiritual in the psyche. All the Local Government Bodies including Municipalities must arrange for a skill development program for the youths; undertake the Make in India campaign through capacity building of the rural youths, and popularize eco-tourism and hospitality management. The PRIs can implement and execute identified circuits covering national parks, lakes, and historical sites. Agriculture, horticulture, floriculture, and animal husbandry should be encouraged and popularized among youths. Rural youths are always very good in games and sports; they can be motivated to win gold medals in the Olympics and other international events. Only our students and young people can transform the present status of India from all aspects. I have full faith in our youths. I believe that every young mind is inquisitive. They are full of vigor and vitality. Our job is to make them understand their inherent power. Once they realize their inner strengths, they will embark on creation and new discoveries. With their participation, India will become a great nation.

The philosophy of life should be to think good, do good, and be good to others. On the occasion of BAPS: International Karyakar Suvarna Mahotsav (Modi, Video Lecture, 7.12.2024) Prime Minister Narendra Modi delivered a virtual address to the one lakh young *karyakars* (selfless volunteers) to take an oath at the beginning of every year (starting from January 2025) to either raise the consciousness of people about environment pollution or serve the country by taking a *sankalp*. PM Modi emphasized the importance of selfless service, highlighting that in Indian culture, "*seva param dharma*" (service is the highest duty). He remarked, "We not only speak about it, but we also practice it," underscoring the deep-rooted values of service and compassion within Indian society"(India TV, 2024).

The Prime Minister called upon the BAPS volunteers to continue their service-oriented efforts, directing them to work towards the goal of transforming India into a developed nation by the time it celebrates 100 years of independence in 2047. His vision of a prosperous and developed India resonated with the attendees, urging them to play an active role in the nation's growth. He also told the *karyakars* to follow the *Ghar Sabha* popularized by Pramukh Swami, which is actually praising and respecting each other in a family. "Prime Minister Narendra Modi on Saturday (8 December 2024) urged citizens to become the force behind the country's march towards the target of "Viksit Bharat 2047" and announced that next month a "Viksit Bharat Young Leaders' Dialogue" would be held to give the youth a platform to exchange ideas" (The Tribune, 2024). Thus, we find that the present Prime Minister Sri Narendra Modi is very much open to receiving suggestions even from the youths of India to fulfill his vision.

27. Mitigate the Menace of Climate Change

Climate change is going to be a great menace to the people in the world. India is already the world's third-biggest polluter country after China and the United States. Indian government must adhere to the Central Electricity Authority's projection that seeks to have a solar energy installed capacity of 280 GW and a wind energy installed capacity of 140 GW. The rest of the energy needs will come from nuclear power. India's target of achieving net-zero carbon emission by 2070, must be respected by all including government, non-government, and individual stakeholders. India cannot bear the toll of climate change. Already dust storms, lightning, rise and fall of temperature, the rise of ocean level, melting of ice, frequent droughts, floods, storms, etc. have abruptly increased. In this situation, we as a whole need to come forward to mitigate climate change. Children from childhood days must be imparted education about the effects of climate change and they must be grown habits to protect and promote our mother environment. The developed nations must enhance climate finance for the 2021-2030 period. According to the CEA, India's total installed electricity capacity will be 1,100 GW by 2030. The CSE said that the target is achievable if India stops investing in coal. So, let us all stop the use of coal, wood, and other fossil fuels for cooking, production in iron, cement, thermal factories, and other related industries. With our combined efforts, India is capable of winning over the climate menace in the days to come.

28. Population Control is Indispensable

Excessive population always cannot be the strength of a country; though a quality population is constantly indispensable for the development and growth of a nation. And India is not an exception. Hence, the population must be regulated and unproductive labor should be suppressed. John Rae in his book *Contemporary Socialism* delineates that, "The necessity for regulating population comes, of course, from the limitation of the natural resources at society's command. In any community there is a certain normal limit of the population – the limit at which all the natural resources are distributed among all the inhabitants according to their powers – and the community will learn when this limit is reached from the number of workmen who are unable to obtain private employment and are obliged to seek work from the State....The obligation to labor and the curtailment of luxury would come into exercise before the restrictions on population, and be more and more rigorously enforced as the normal limit of the population was approximated" (Rae, 1891). The government and local people might check infiltration from other countries; it may increase the upper age of marriage for both boys and girls; it may initiate extensive consciousness-raising programs about the ill effects of more than two children; the government may prevent illegitimacy, and encourage emigration.

29. The State Should Play a Minumum Role

In the modern era, the art of governance is really a challenging task before the political masters. Gradually the gap between governance and government is widening. In contemporary India, actors other than the state have come to acquire a greater role in the exercise of control and authority in the allocation of resources. The locus of policymaking has moved from the state to other actors such as markets and civil society that have created greater space for themselves. At this crucial stage, the state has to play its role very wisely and carefully. The women's and children's rights and social security for all must be ensured by the State. These egalitarian ideas prompted some American historians and philologists to talk about reformism in the USA three centuries back. Similar egalitarian measures might be considered by the Government of India. The execution of the 'equality of opportunity' policy and promotion of 'scopes for flourishing' for all professionals, students, and researchers must be ensured. The State must not interfere in economic and social relations until it affects the interests of economic prosperity, social cohesion, and national integration. Let the State encourage free competition among the small and medium enterprises and producers. But the State must protect the property of every citizen as well as an institution including the State itself. Entrepreneurial consciousness must be grown holistically among the students from the early stage of education i.e. from schools. The State should play a limited role and encourage the private players to play openly for the socio-economic growth of the country. The black marketers, the tax evaders, and the looters of national wealth must be dealt with sternly. Not for retaliation or for taking political vendetta, in real terms, all black money must be recovered and deposited to the government's treasury. Digitization and Make in India programs are required to be popularized and spread universally. For this purpose, computer literacy needs to be more comprehensive. Let us all learn basic computer, Spoken English, and any other foreign language, and at least complete graduation by 2040.

The survival issue of all lowly educated and lowly paid people must be looked after; the booming middle class has to be encouraged and motivated more, while the rich industrialists must be protected through sound public policy. Encouraging meritocracy is always productive and profitable for a nation. Finally, the State must not interfere in any matter, maybe academic or policy-related, in the functioning of higher academic institutions such as universities and research centers until it hurts national goals, national interests, and national security. The State must induce the private actors and, in turn, the industries in India must donate or sponsor research funds, particularly in Science and Technology, artificial intelligence, space research, and infrastructure development. The government should also increase its annual budget for the academic development of schools, colleges, and universities with world-class research facilities.

In a recent international symposium (19 February, 2022) on Capacity Building for Effective Governance and Administration: Perspectives from South Asia, where this author was an attendee, almost all the speakers including Professor Mahendra P. Lama, a senior professor of Jawaharlal Nehru University; Prof. Lalitha S. Fernando, a senior Professor in Public Administration, University of Sri Jayewardenepura, Sri Lanka; Dr. Sabith Khan, California Lutheran University, USA and others unanimously advocated for the institutional capacity building. There is a lacuna in institutional capacity. Knowledge skills, attitude skills, and performance skills for public sector officials, young entrepreneurs, and the general public are highly required to achieve India's ambitious goal. More concrete planning – short-term, mid-term, and long-term - right from Parliament to Panchayat is necessary. Let all the states, districts, and local bodies make respective developmental plans in line with the national plan or vice versa, and work according to the plan. With planned work at all levels, India will surely achieve the goal before the deadline. A long-term strong Union government is conducive to reaching India at its zenith. Remember, when the poor and unprivileged people will rise, prosper, and smile, India as a whole will prosper and smile. Hence, the topmost priority has to be given to the upliftment of the poor and backward people.

30. Self-Development is Imperative

Many of us try to change our friends, children, and students. But very few of us try to change ourselves. Our great philosophers and saints have taught us to be moral and spiritual. If we, the educated and privileged few, are moral and disciplined, we need not instruct others to be moral and disciplined. The people who live in and around us will see us closely, follow us, and get influenced automatically, and with the change of individual citizens, the nation will be changed inherently. Again, I remember the words of Swami Vivekananda. He said, "It is easy to point out the defects of institutions, all beings are more or less imperfect, but he is the real benefactor of humanity who helps the individual to overcome his imperfections under whatever institutions he may live. The individuals being raised, the nation, and its institutions are bound to rise"(Vivekananda, 2013, p. 48) Hence, the rise of a nation depends upon the rise of a human being. Let us awaken ourselves from within first. India has ample philosophical and spiritual books. Any man can pick up a book of his choice to awaken himself. The world will, then, be awakened and enlightened spontaneously. Through our personal and spiritual development, not only our own, but our family, society, and ultimately the country's all-round development and growth will take place by the time when India observes its centenary celebration in 2047. India was a spiritual leader, and again it would be a world spiritual leader with your leadership. Therefore, we all have to change our perceptions of life by ourselves.

31. Learning the Art of Living is Cardinal

Let us keep in mind the maxim that, 'work is worship.' We must not stop working until we reach our goal and beyond. At the same time, it is also true that in the workshops, institutions, and even families; always there is tension and stress. The world is full of suffering for all of us. Hence, to get respite from all sufferings and pains, we need to abide by the lessons imparted by our ancient philosophers. Without keeping our bodies and minds healthy, happy, and peaceful, it would be difficult for us to work hard and compete with our stronger global counterparts. Hence, we have to keep our bodies, souls, and minds healthy and salubrious. Indian philosophy highlights some methods of permanent removal of suffering and the attainment of timeless bliss. It is said that no true freedom for man is possible without knowledge of the ultimate reality. The later Upanishads upheld the Yoga Sutras as the most efficacious method for achieving the direct perception of truth. Through the practical techniques of yoga, a man leaves behind forever the barren realms of speculations and is cognized in the experience of the veritable essence of life. The Yoga system as outlined by Patanjali, is almost similar to the Buddhist philosophy of Astangik Marg, which is also known as the Eightfold Path. The first two steps are (1) Yama, and (2) Niyama. These two systems require observance of negative and positive moralities, avoidance of injury to others, untruthfulness, or stealing, incontinence, or gift-receiving (which brings obligations); and purity of body and mind, contentment, self-discipline, study, and devotion to

God. The next six steps are (3) Asana (right posture); the spinal column must be held straight, and the body firm in a comfortable position for meditation; (4) Pranayam (control of prana, subtle life currents); and (5) Pratyahara (withdrawal of senses from external objects). The last steps are forms of yoga proper: (6) Dharana (concentration); holding the mind to one thought; (7) Dhyana (meditation), and (8) Samadhi (superconscious perception). This is the Eightfold Path of Yoga, which leads one to a final goal of Kaivalya (Absoluteness), a term which might be more comprehensively put as "realization of the Truth beyond all intellectual apprehension" (Yogananda, 1946, pp. 282-83).

32. Let Us Ensure Equality, and Promote Friendship and Love

Without equality and equal treatment between and among members in family, office, or in larger society there cannot be peace; without peace, there cannot be progress, without progress, there cannot be personal development; without personal development, there cannot be national development. Hence, it is our duty now to treat all equally. Subhas Chandra Bose said, "In order to ensure equality, we must get rid of the bondage of every kind, social, economic, and political and we must become fully and wholly free. But freedom does not imply the absence of law. It only means the substitution of our own law and our own discipline. Discipline imposed on us by ourselves is necessary, not only when we have attained freedom, but is more necessary when we are struggling to achieve freedom. Therefore, discipline whether for the individual or for society is necessary as the basis of life" (Saggi, 1954, p. 46).

33. Let us Live Together in Peace and Harmony

Peace and prosperity have a close relationship. Without mental peace, family peace, and societal peace, achieving prosperity in a country seems a distant dream. The United Nations considers that living together in peace is all about accepting differences and having the ability to listen, recognize, respect, and appreciate others, as well as living in a peaceful and united way. In this modern world, we have to uphold the desire to live together, to feel united in differences and diversity, and to build a world of peace, solidarity, and harmony. Let us renounce hate from our minds from today itself. Further, our political leaders, faith leaders, and other relevant actors must adopt a well-established approach to tackling conflict and political differences. Professor Amartya Sen in *Peace and Democratic Society* envisages that "In a world in which different people, despite sharing a common interest in peace, security, and justice, find themselves divided by mutual incomprehension and skepticism, and sometimes even suspicion, the affirmation of the importance of multilateralism, with mutual respect, can help to create a more positive climate for toleration, support, and collaboration." Professor Sen attached great importance to the use of a dialogue-based approach to dealing with issues of group-based conflict in the world today.

My understanding of establishing peace and living together with harmony is very simple i.e. to lead an ethical, spiritual, and disciplined life. Whatever works we may do, whatever gender and color we may have, and wherever we may live; if we work very hard ethically with sincerity for the benefit and profit of the institution, organization, or person for whom we work; if we look after our children and family members as per our capacity, and show love and affection for our children, respect our elders, parents, and teachers; if we meditate daily and practice yoga or do some physical exercise, or play some outdoor games; if we extend our helping hand towards our relatives, friends, colleagues and neighbors; if we refrain from illegal and unethical activities such as stealing, extortion, taking bribes and harming others for narrow personal gain, our country will turn into a Heaven on Earth.

This chapter winds up with the aspiration and expectation of whole-hearted participation of Indian citizens, especially the youths, women and girls, minority and tribal population, rural poor people, entrepreneurs, ministers, people's representatives, and different professionals. Both the Union and state governments must act proactively with all their knowledge, expertise, manpower, technical know-how, and financial capacity to make their respective states and the country as a whole become a developed country by the time it completes its 100th year of Independence. Necessary policy reforms, wherever necessary, must be done forthwith to actualize the vision of Viksit Bharat. It is a fact that there is diversity in the region, political faith, size, nature, and capacity of the state and Union Territories. Despite all the limitations, forgetting all personal and political differences all the stakeholders should come forward to make our beloved country brighter and stronger within the next quarter century. This author and you both of us are well aware that, the dream is not so easy to achieve. There are a lot of challenges standing in the way of the achievement of this goal. Therefore, the following chapter discusses a few root causes of growth and development with an urge to plug the problems by the concerned stakeholders.

References:

1. Citizens real force behind march towards 'Viksit Bharat 2047': PM. (2024, December 8). *The Tribune.*

2. Press Information Bureau. (2023, December 11). Government of India.

3. Semasinghe, W.M. (2020, January). Development, what does it mean? *Acta Politica Polonica*, p. 52.

4. UN Document: Development. (1997, October 15). Agenda for Development, *The United National General Assembly.*

5. Semasinghe, W.M. (2020, January). Development, what does it mean? *Acta Politica Polonica*, pp. 53-54.

6. Robbins, L. (1966). In Semasinghe, W.M. (2020, January). Development, what does it mean? *Acta Politica Polonica*, pp. 53-54.

7. Amartya Sen: A More Human Theory of Development. (2004, December 6). *Asia Society.*

8. Capacity Building, United Nations, https://www.un.org/en/academic-impact/capacity-building accessed on 11.12.2024.

9. Hicks, N. and Streeten, P. (1979). *Indicators of Development: The Search for a Basic Needs Yardshick.* World Bank Reprint Series: Number 104, p. 567.

10. Hicks, N. & Streeten, P. (1979). *Indicators of Development: The Search for a Basic Needs Yardshick.* World Bank Reprint Series: Number 104, p. 570.

11. The World Bank: IBRD-IDA, https://datatopics.worldbank.org/world-development-indicators/themes/ economy.html.

12. Sustainable Development Goals, the United Nations, https://www.un.org/ sustainabledevelopment/ blog/2023/08/what-is-sustainable-development/ accessed on 11.12.2024.

13. Explained | What is 'Viksit Bharat 2047' and what does it aim to achieve? (2024, March 4). *Deccan Herald.*

14. Mandal, K. (2024). How Can India Become a Superpower by 2047: A *Vision.* Ukiyoto Publishing, p. 51.

15. Singh, R. (2023, January 27). The Wonder that is India. *The Times of India.*

16. Beveridge, H. (1867). *A Comprehensive History of India, Civil, Military and Social from the First Landing of the English, to the Suppression of Sepoy Revolt; including An Outline of the Early History of Hindoostan* (Vol. 1). Blackie and Son.

17. Will Yakowicz, W. (2019, October 8). How America's Rich Get So Rich. *Forbes.*

18. Robert E. Wright, R.E. (2020, January 30). How America Became Rich, According to a Historian in 1802. *The Daily Economy.*

19. Takada, M. (1999, March 23). Japan's Economic Miracle: Underlying Factors and Strategies for the Growth, IR 163, Professor Wylie, p. 12.

20. Takada, M. (1999, March 23). Japan's Economic Miracle: Underlying Factors and Strategies for the Growth, IR 163, Professor Wylie, pp. 12-13.

21. Takada, M. (1999, March 23). Japan's Economic Miracle: Underlying Factors and Strategies for the Growth, IR 163, Professor Wylie, p. 13.

22. Md Zafar Alam Bhuniyan, MZA. (2019, June). The miracle of Japanese Economy after the Second World War (WW2), Researchgate, DOI: 10.13140/RG.2.2.10191.53925.

23. Takada, M. (1999, March 23). Japan's Economic Miracle: Underlying Factors and Strategies for the Growth, IR 163, Professor Wylie, p. 15.

24. Ministry of Micro, Small and Medium Enterprises. (2023, July 31). *Govt. of India.* https://www. dcmsme.gov.in/ssiindia/census/ch6.htm.

25. GDP of India: Current and historical growth rate, India's rank in the world. (2024, July 17). *Forbes India.*

26. Unicorns in India: List of startup companies with unicorn status in 2024. (2020, August 22). Forbes India.

27. Suzuki, Tessa Morris. Quoted in Takada, M. (1999, March 23). Japan's Economic Miracle: Underlying Factors and Strategies for the Growth, IR 163, Professor Wylie, p. 13.

28. Suzuki, Tessa Morris. Quoted in Takada, M. (1999, March 23). Japan's Economic Miracle: Underlying Factors and Strategies for the Growth, IR 163, Professor Wylie, p. 15.

29. Report on "Electronics: Powering India's Participation in Global Value Chains. (2024, July 18). *Press Information Bureau.*

30. Bocca, R. (1997, May 21). India facing record power shortfall for June, and other top energy stories this month. *World Economic Forum.*

31. Porecha, M. (2020, June 19). 11% of India's medical devices imports are from China. *Businessline.*

32.UN Document: Development. (1997, October 15). Agenda for Development.*The United National General Assembly,* A/RES/51/240.

33. India Skills Report 2023: Indian employable talent leaps from 46.2% to 50.3%. (2022, December 29). *The Economic Times.*

34. Cherian, J. (2021, April 11). India now a major defence partner for the USA as gangs up on China. *Frontline.*

35. Purfield, C & Schiff, J.A. (2006). How Can India Attract More Foreign Direct Investment? *IMF eLibrary.* https://www.elibrary.imf.org/

36. Modi, N. (2024, December 7). Video Lecture, Gujarat.

37. Bhattacharjee, S. (2024, December 7)). PM Modi praises BAPS volunteers, urges efforts to make India a developed nation by 2047. *India TV.*

38. Citizens real force behind march towards 'Viksit Bharat 2047': PM. (2024, December, 8). *The Tribune.*

39. Rae, J. (1891). *Contemporary Socialism.* Charls Scribner's Sons.

40. Vivekananda, S. (2013). Vivekananda: His Call to the Nation. *Kolkata: Advaita Ashrama.*

41. Yogananda, P. (1946). *Autobiography of a Yogi.* The Philosophical Library.

42. Saggi, P.D (ed.). (1954). *A Nation's Homage, Life and Work of Netaji Subhas Chandra Bose.* Overseas Publishing House.

VI
Challenges and
Solutions

"Only the fools think about problems; the wise ignore the same and go ahead
smilingly to achieve the goals."
– Keshabananda Bharati

I have elaborately discussed in the last three chapters about India's public policy, foreign policy, and how present India can be transformed into a Viksit Bharat. It seems to me that despite making tremendous progress in different fields, India is not completely free from problems. There are myriad challenges in achieving the goal of a Viksit Bharat. It is argued that India has attained a certain level of growth in the last seven and a half decades. But is that enough? Are we satisfied with our success story? You may be happy or satisfied, but I am not. Why am I not satisfied with the achievements of the government? Let me tell you in brief about the reasons behind my dissatisfaction with the present style of governance, and the growth story. When the majority of my friends, colleagues, and students are unhappy, how can I be happy? When I visit rural India for the purpose of the latest research on Sustainable Development Goals and interact with locally educated but unemployed youths, poor farmers, wretched rickshaw pullers, unemployed students, Panchayat members, and office-bearers, lowly paid workers of private and unorganized sectors, and daily laborers, I find a tune of frustration, pain, and impassivity in their words. Being a teacher the agony and dejection of the University pass-out unemployed youths are most visible to me. It is a fact that India suffered a lot of tyranny and oppression

• 202 •

at the hands of foreign invaders, overseas merchants, and non-native rulers. But when I ask myself "Have the foreign invaders or the English merchants and the British Monarch only made us ruined or we are responsible for our own degeneration?" Are not some corrupt politicians and mafias still looting our country? Can we ignore our responsibility for our own present situation? I remember the words of Swami Vivekananda in this regard. He said, "We are responsible for what we are; and whatever we wish ourselves to be, we have the power to make ourselves. If what we are now has been the result of our own past actions, it certainly follows that whatever we wish to be in the future can be produced by our present actions; so we have to know how to act" (Vivekananda, 2013, p. 47). Swamiji's above words are very appropriate and still relevant.

Many Indian scholars might think it an audacity if I write here about the hard reality of our shortcomings. Another section of people might start researching my life and works and try to find faults with my past and present actions, while others might trace out my caste, character, family background, education level, service, or many other things that are beyond my imagination. But I am sure that, most of my students who have attended my classes in the last two decades have heard my lectures in classes, seminars, and conferences, or have read my books and articles right from the beginning of the new millennium and have definitely tasted the flavor of my thoughts, actions, and works. That is why I dare to be a little audacious. Besides, I feel it a duty of mine to highlight the shortcomings of ourselves, so that we can rectify and go ahead with full energy and enthusiasm. However, my teachers as well as friends are my best adjudicators. Here my work is like a bus conductor, who always warns the driver to run the bus properly and make him cautious about the vehicles coming from behind and running parallel on either side. Let me clarify it. When a bus driver drives a bus on the high road he can see everything through the big front window glass, but the conductor standing on the footstep slaps the body of the bus loudly to tell the driver about the vehicles moving in front or either side or even behind. His duty is to warn the driver, though the driver sees everything on the road ahead of him and side through the window screen and mirror. Similarly I, like a bus conductor, am indicating the constraints that I found in the road-like country. I consider it my noble duty to point out some most important shortcomings and deficits that stand in the way of the attainment of our ambitious dream to be a Viksit Bharat or a developed country by 2047. In the following part, I will delineate the existing challenges in India. I know the problems are numerous, but still, as a teacher and a development author I must point out the same for rectification by different stakeholders.

The Roots of Various Problems

India has so many limitations that it will take hundreds of pages to write them in detail. But that is neither possible nor desirable here in this small concluding chapter. Moreover, it is not my aim merely to highlight the problems of our country; rather it is my sole aim as how to take our country ahead of our counterparts in the world. Nevertheless, I must point out a few of our deficiencies that might help us, our policymakers, and other stakeholders to plug the same. Let me enumerate a few most reasonable shortcomings that are indispensable to overcome without wasting our valuable time. I will start with education because education is the main pillar on which a society is built.

1. Absence of Good, Modern, and Scientific Education System

It seems to me that education is the panacea of all social evils. Also, education is the mother of all progress and the propeller of Sustainable Development Goals. Achievement of SDGs is the first step to attain the goal of Viksit Bharat. In India, many of our teachers and parents do not inspire students to become what they want to be. Further, no education policy in India has so far helped us to learn about healthy living, patriotism, discipline, punctuality, morality, etc. Also, we rarely learn in our schools about how and why to respect elders, parents, and teachers; and what are our duties and responsibilities as students, sons, daughters, and citizens in our country. Our education starts at home, where about one-third of children do not get an educated mother. Millions of children find uneducated and immature parents, and teenage mothers at home; who are living in unhealthy and unhygienic dwelling places with non-purified drinking water at home or in the locality. Many children grow up seeing illegal and immoral behavior and abusive language of elders at home, on-road, and locality; intoxicated fathers or parents at home, and such neighbors in the locality. Millions of children cannot have the opportunity to attend schools and complete primary education. The Right to Education Act of 2009 has accomplished 100 percent enrolment in primary schools; made millions of our children complete elementary education merely in black and white without learning simple mathematics, and reading textbooks, and how to write even their addresses in English. Millions of students do not attend schools due to family problems like parental disputes, the beating of mothers by their fathers, separation of parents, looking after the siblings and performing domestic work, lack of food, and lack of mental peace, stability, and happiness in the family. When students come to school, millions of them see their teachers come late to the school; avoid the classes on some pretexts; engage in non-academic activities in the school; engage in gossiping on nonsense issues; watch videos in the staff room; exchange videos and good-wish morning messages with their friends; and sometimes quarreling with the fellow teachers in the staff room. These are the common picture of government-sponsored or aided primary and high schools in India, particularly in the state of West Bengal.

In college also the problem is almost the same. The University and college teachers know better how many teachers are teaching in the classes after taking full preparation at home; and how many teachers can teach without the help of notes or laptops. Many of the teachers are engaged in politics, personal non-academic work, or personal academic work to earn extra money, while only a few are engaged in scientific research and serious studies. The serious and sincere teachers are often taunted by colleagues in the staff rooms. Only the Heads of the Institutions know where the shoe pinches.

If you are a member or a staunch supporter of the ruling party in the state, you are out of reach of the Head Master, Principal, Vice-Chancellor, or any other government officials. You may not attend your institution daily, you may not take your classes regularly, and you may not follow the instructions of your Head, no matter what. Nothing harm can be done to you by any authorities as long as you are in the good book of the ruling party – maybe in a state or the Centre. This is the situation everywhere in India. Whosoever may be the ruler, whatever party may rule the state, the character of political bosses or their representatives in educational administration are almost the same everywhere. The higher authorities are also, it seems, averse to taking administrative actions against the truant teachers and non-teaching staff in an educational institution. Can a country survive and thrive with this kind of education system? Why there is not a single Nobel Prize winner in Physics, Chemistry, Mathematics, Medicine, or Literature after Independence from Indian universities? Have you ever thought? Why Indian football team, hockey team, or basketball team cannot be ace teams and win in international tournaments? Why Indian students are not learning to be competitive and creative in the fields of the Nobel Prize? How many Universities in India are 'the institutions of excellence?' Why do they lag behind? Is the government not paying enough salary to the teachers? Are not the students attending classes properly? So, where does the gap remain? What is the problem in making our higher educational institutions "the institutions of excellence?" If this pathetic condition goes on in our educational institutions, how the Universities will produce Nobel Prize winners? The government, the teachers,, and students must think and find reasonable solutions to it. I have a clear idea of this problem and its solution. The best and mediocre students should be identified first. The teachers must give extra effort in remedial classes to the backward students to fill up the deficits in their knowledge and skills. On the other hand, "special classes" can be taken by the teachers for the serious and promising students.

Have you ever thought about why and how Indian students are doing better after leaving our country? They are performing better in a foreign land only because of their teachers and the high-quality academic environment they avail themselves of in foreign universities. But I am not saying that the majority of our teachers and students are not working hard, they are not sincere and they are not engaged in scientific research and serious studies. There are thousands of great teachers and students, researchers, and guides, who have been holding our education system high. Without them, India would have been collapsed. The only gap that I have found is a dearth of goodwill of the government, both state and Union and a lack of institutional freedom. It seems that there is a peculiar mismatch between government intention and the policy implementation process. The paucity of a sound education policy was a great hurdle. The heads of the educational institutions have been captivated in the hands of political Managing Committee and Governing Body Presidents. They are always politically inclined to the ruling political party in a state. So, the heads of the Institutions will perform, take action against the truant teachers and non-teaching staff, and implement the ongoing schemes without their help? Hence, the system itself is faulty. This is the root cause of all the socio-political problems of India.

2. Lack of Role Models in Society

Many of our students and fellow citizens tend to keep on the age-old practice of any ongoing method. There is a proverb, "Practice makes a man perfect." But who will assist our children to adopt and follow good practices such as leading an ethical life, and being punctual, honest, sincere, and honest in life? It is the primary duty of the mothers in childhood, teachers in schools and colleges, and colleagues and friends in later life. But how many of you received the same ideal persons as I mentioned above? So, how our little students and children will learn? This is another problem of society. They often do not find good, honest, sincere, hard-working, and ethical teachers, parents, and neighbors. So, they follow in the footsteps of their seniors, parents, relatives, and even teachers in learning a filthy language, cheating, beating, violence, and corruption.

It seems to me that, we should encourage our children, grandchildren, and young people to practice good habits, pursue good hobbies, and respect the elders in family, society, and schools. Never say any student or person is 'hopeless,' because he only represents a character, a bundle of habits, which can be checked by new and better ones. Character is nothing but repeated habits, and repeated habits alone can reform character. The country needs many more men of character today. If we can teach our younger generation, and especially our children and students to reform their character, India might shine like the brightest summer Sun in the global arena in the days to come. Any good and innovative research for achieving the goal of Viksit Bharat starts from patriotism, respect for the country, and love for work. We, the seniors, have a great role to play for our youths, who are the actual makers of a Developed India.

A teacher or a parent has the best chance to become a perfect role model, whom students and children watch closely, follow purely, and revere, respect, and rely on. Unfortunately, these role models are gradually waning in society. The responsibility of teachers is more now to become role models to the students. Regarding the lack of a role model in society, I would like to mention a survey report conducted by this author in 2007, in which only two questions were asked to students aged between 18-25 years. The questions were - (i) Do you find a role model in your family and society? (ii) Do you know an honest person who never told a lie in life? Interestingly, in both the questions the answer was "No". I, further, asked the students if their answer included their parents and other family members. They said, yes, even in the family they do not find an honest, and truthful person including parents. What an awesome situation prevailing in India! The spiritual leaders must come forward to purify the society. The Union and State governments must relook at the issue and introduce such policy as has been introduced by the West Bengal Government to read the book of Swami Vivekananda. Spiritual and moral lessons are rarely taught in our educational institution. Without learning value education and spiritual education, how can our students learn about it? Hence, when all the students study will study properly there will a pure society with pure mind. It would facilitate India to become a Viksit Bharat by 2047.

3. Value (Less) Education System

Many teachers are good, sincere, and honest, and doing excellent work in their institutions; and a substantial number of students are also good, obedient, and sincere, but the negative exceptions are increasing by leaps and bounds in society as well as in education institutions. We have a large number of great teachers and very meritorious and obedient students who are making history in academic institutions and creating records in different fields. But what I see and experience among the majority of students in India is that they have lack in respect or *sraddha* for their teachers and elders. Swami Vivekananda said, "What we want is this *sraddha* (respect). Unfortunately, it has nearly vanished from India, and this is why we are in our present shabby state. What makes the difference between man and man is the difference in this *sraddha* and nothing else. What makes one man great and another weak and low is this *sraddha*" (Vivekananda, 2013, p. 60). By imparting value education and discipline education we want to build the character of a student. Does the Indian school education system help our students to form good character; to respect our teachers and seniors, and to increase the strength of mind? There is enough scope for rethinking it. The government of India realized this truth and introduced the National Education Policy (NEP) 2020 to impart value education to the students. To impart the value of education, discipline education, sense of patriotism, and infuse soft feelings such as love, respect, and fellow feelings for friends, siblings, parents, teachers, and elders of society is the highest need of the hour. To save society and increase the inherent strengths of our students, value-based education, moral education, and spiritual education with yoga will surely make a better India in the future.

4. People are Superstitious

Average Indian people believe in luck or fate. Remember, strength is life and weakness is death. It is known to the people of the world. Mill & Wilson in their book *The History of British India Vol. 1* (1848, p. 436) wrote that "...every Hindoo considers all his action as the effect of his destiny." If something better happens, they claim it as their own credit or the result of their hard work. But if they cannot attain a target or fail in any attempt, they say that their luck is not supportive. Swami Vivekananda has rightly pointed out: "Where is fate, and who is fate? We reap what we sow?" My teacher

Dr. Parimal Kanti Sarkar in Class XI taught me while teaching the subject - English, "As you sow, so will you reap." Since then I have been a staunch believer in the theory of hard work. I never believe in luck or fate, rather I keep faith in my own strength, knowledge, education, and skill. I always believe in my own inner purity and honesty, because I know that faith in self is a sign of greatness. "Swamiji said, "We are the makers of our own fate. None else has the blame, none has the praise. The wind is blowing; those vessels whose sails are unfurled catch it and go forward on their way, but those which have their sails furled do not catch the wind. Is that the fault of the wind?" (Vivekananda, 2013, p. 49).

5. Fault-finding Mentality of People

I have seen many of my friends and relatives speak about the faults of others. They never see any fault of their own. It is not only my friends or relatives, but rather many common people; nay many educated elites in both rural and urban localities also find faults with others. The blame game is best visible and experienced during various political debates on television channels and even in Parliament House. My friends and fellow researchers, and even some of my teachers often advise me to be more critical in my writings. But, I do not find fault in others; rather I consider the failure of others as their deficiency of knowledge and dearth of good guidance and company. In India when a person fails in an examination, he often expresses his dissatisfaction with the question papers, teachers, or the government. But it is not true that nobody passed in that year by writing answers with the same question paper. Most of them do not accept their failure as their lack of preparation or skills. What is the use of blaming others? Instead of that, we should try continuously till the end to achieve our goals through harder work with skill development.

6. People are Timid

I have seen here in India and particularly in West Bengal that most people are afraid to speak the truth in front of senior officers, politicians, and other influential people. Do you know why? It is because if the words go against them, or if the boss is hurt somehow, the speaker will be judged as an opponent or anti-national. Always there is a nexus between police, politicians, media, and businessmen. Suppose a chief minister is making a wrong decision, and if due to such a faulty decision there is an adverse impact on society, the economy, and even the public mind; still, the bureaucrats and top advisors, being the wisest persons, often remain silent or nod with the chief minister. They rarely dare to tell in front of the chief minister. The same thing happens in the case of the Prime Minister too.

Likewise, the same policy of 'maintaining silence' is observed in the lower level of hierarchies too. In an institution, if the boss talks foul, or makes any wrong or unethical decision, he is always supported by some sycophants. If you, being a far-sighted and knowledgeable person, tell any unfavorable word or give any different opinion you will be marked as an anti-party, anti-government, or anti-national element. Indian researchers and authors mostly write and speak in favor of a government – either state or national. At the state level, the majority of authors, writers, and university professors speak in favor of the state government, despite knowing the high level of corruption and bad activities of top-level political leaders, ministers, and a section of bureaucrats. Similarly, at the national level also people worship the ruling party leaders. Do you know why? It is because they want (mostly) to have some government benefits in the future or are already the beneficiaries of the government and the ruling party. But we all should learn how to call a spade a spade. But all the discussions must be held in a sober and amiable manner without hurting others. For this reason, all such persons should learn the art of speaking, and know the skill of how to debate.

7. Self-centred Indians Mostly Seek Personal Happiness and Comfort

I see many of my colleagues, relatives, and friends remaining busy most of the time to attain personal happiness and comfort. Another few do not understand at all what they want but keep on working. I have seen many educated people in town areas talk rubbish and most of them are self-centered. However, this trend is spreading in semi-urban and rural areas too. You see, the demands of people change with the change of time. The demands of childhood change in adulthood; and the demands of both childhood and adulthood change in subsequent life with the increase of age and experience. If you are a student, your demand now is a decent job. If you are a newly employed unmarried man, you crave for a handsome income and a good-looking life partner, a four-wheeler, and a beautiful flat or home with modern furniture and decoration. If you are a middle-aged man, you will seek your children's welfare, a good education, and a peaceful settlement. If you are an old man, you will need mental peace and physical fitness to survive. If these are the eternal demands of people, why all people do not achieve so in life? Many people do not achieve mental peace and happiness because they do not know the art of living; the way of leading a fitful life, and mantras for self-development through doing good to others.

Only demanding comfort and happiness does not bring the desired fruits. It needs action – good and affirmative action for self and for others. Happiness lies in the service for others and fitness comes through physical and mental exercise.

Remember, our future depends on our present work. So, let's do good work from today itself. Doing well to others and making others happy only makes you eternally happy with good health. "The self-seeking man who is looking after his personal comforts and leading a lazy life – there is no room for him even in hell," said Swami Vivekananda. Further, in the *Autobiography of a Yogi*, Paramhansa Yogananda wrote, "Gross man seldom or never realizes that his body is a kingdom, governed by Emperor Soul on the throne of the cranium, with subsidiary regents in the six spinal centers or spheres of consciousness. This theocracy extends over a throng of obedient subjects: twenty-seven thousand billion cells endowed with a sure if automatic intelligence by which they perform all duties of bodily growths, transformations, and dissolutions – and fifty million substrata thoughts, emotions, and variations of alternative phases in man's consciousness in average life of sixty years" (Yogananda, 1946).

8. Low Patriotism

India needs patriotic people. Many of us, I have seen, are not patriots. How will you understand that you are a patriot? Patriotism means loving one's country. As you love your mother, in the same way you should love your motherland and its people. When I see that someone is talking illegally and to malign or disgrace our Constitution, national flag, parliament, and the country as a whole, I put a humble protest, and try to make him understand the right path which is both ethical and legal. If I see that the man is not aware of the basic structure of the Indian Constitution, I try to make him understand the Constitution and its provisions according to my knowledge of the Constitution and the laws of the land. When someone attacks India, its territory, or its border, and intends to harm its economy, social fabric, national integration, unity, or communal harmony, I intervene straightforwardly. In a word, I live with my mother (land) and I die for my motherland. This living and dying for our motherland is patriotism, according to me. We have learned about the deplorable condition of India and its people under the subjugation of foreign invaders, particularly during British Rule. So, let us all love and respect our country most, work hard for the development and growth of our income, health, social, and political life, and even get ready to sacrifice life to safeguard our country and its men. See the contribution of our defense personnel – how they are working day and night, in heat and cold, in storm and rain to save us. Let us extend our love and respect to them and give a salute to millions of our national security and border security personnel. At the same time, we must abjure any work and words that may cause any damage to our image and growth process.

9. Government Fails to Increase Knowledge of Fundamental Duties

Our Constitution has included a total of 11 Fundamental Duties which, if we follow and abide by, India will become a golden country. The duties of every citizen are, to me, the best guide to all of us for making this country the most powerful, the best, and a very developed one. What are the Fundamental Duties enshrined in our Constitution? Our first duty is to abide by the Constitution and respect its ideals and institutions, and National Flag, and the National anthem. It is written in the Constitution. But how the people, who never attended any school, about millions in numbers, and who have never read the Constitution can abide by it? The people who come to India from other countries mostly do not know the Indian Constitution and its ideals. Secondly, to cherish and follow the noble ideals that inspired our national struggle for freedom should be our fundamental duty. How many Indians know about the ideals that inspired our freedom fighters? Did the government ever spread the ideals among the general masses? Without the knowledge, is it possible to abide by any duty? Is it not an absurd idea? Thirdly, it is our Fundamental Duty to uphold and protect the sovereignty, unity, and integrity of India. It can be done by respecting our country, and dedicating our life to its protection; loving and respecting all communities and their customs and practices. The fifth duty is to defend the country and render national service when called upon to do so. Yes, we have to be ready always to defend our country, particularly in times of foreign aggression or any national crisis. The sixth duty is to promote harmony and the spirit of common brotherhood amongst all the people of India transcending religious, linguistic, and regional or sectional diversities; to renounce practices derogatory to the dignity of women. Average Indian people are generally good-natured. They love to live with people of all religions. But the thing is that we have to make them aware of these duties. Every student in India must learn by heart the Fundamental Duties and they must follow the same in life from the day one of their learning. In West Bengal, all the Duties are printed on the inside cover page of the textbooks, but rarely any of them are read and memorized. If they are unaware of the Fundamental Duties, how can they follow the same?

Further, the majority of Indian citizens respect women as their mothers and sisters. But it is a lamentable fact that the rate of crime against women, domestic violence, bride beating, rape, and eve-teasing is on the rise in India. Hence, the derogatory practices against the dignity of women must be stopped together at any cost. To value and preserve the rich heritage of our composite culture is also our Fundamental Duty. The other five fundamental duties are as follows: to protect and improve the national environment including forests, lakes, rivers, and wildlife, and to have compassion for living creatures; to develop scientific temper, humanism, and the spirit of inquiry and reform; to safeguard public property and to abjure violence; to strive towards excellence in all spheres of individual and collective activity so that the nation constantly rises to higher levels of endeavor and achievement; and lastly who is a parent or guardian, to provide opportunities for education to his child, or as the case may be, ward between the age of six to fourteen years. India, being a large country with millions of uneducated or lowly educated people, requires awareness campaigning through special camps by local governments in both rural and urban areas to spread and propagate the noble duties of Indian citizens. Along with these, our Fundamental Rights should also be informed to our citizens, particularly young students through textbooks, and verbally by parents, teachers, and other educators. All people should also know the reasonable restrictions mentioned against the Rights. All State Boards must include the Fundamental Duties and Rights with reasonable restrictions enshrined in the Constitution in their school syllabus. It should be compulsory.

10. No Educational Qualification Bar for the MLAs, MPs and Ministers

Indian leaders do not need any educational qualification to be an MLA, MP, Minister, or President. The irony is that, to become a Group – 'D' staff or peon, an Indian citizen needs at least a Class VIII Pass certificate. To be an IAS or IPS, you need to go through the rigorous process of Preliminary, Main, and Interview tests. However, for the Ministers who control the bureaucrats, no academic qualification is required for them. Should the Indian Constitution be changed ever to correct this big defect? Political administrators should also be highly qualified and skilled enough to take tests and pass through a rigorous three-tier examination just like the Central bureaucrats. There must be certain criteria such as age, minimum education qualification, and non-criminal background to enroll as a political aspirant. An educated country cannot and must not be ruled by uneducated and unqualified or lowly qualified political masters. This change in the system has to be brought about by the existing [educated] elected Members of Parliament only. The Election Commission of India has a major role in this regard, and it must show its grit to implement the criteria for the elected members, who are governing us as ministers and policymakers. Can the Prime Minister and his cabinet take an affirmative decision in this regard? Can the Government of India expect support from the Opposition parties in this effort? I appeal to all the MPs and MLAs to think about it and make our democracy the best in the world full of educationists, lawyers, technocrats, and scientists. Not a single criminal should be allowed to sit in the holy place of India's highest decision-making body.

11. Political Interference in Educational Institutions

In every major education decision, instead of only academicians political leaders get involved in finalizing the same. It is the scenario of every state and every institution in India. All political parties want to enter and capture the educational institutions first. The funny fact is that the non-academic persons, mostly local politicians in the name of MLA or Social Worker, sit at the top of the Vice-Chancellors, Principals, and Head Masters. They often have lesser or very low academic qualifications and experience than the heads of Institutions. When they start dictating the matters related to examination, study, expenditure, recruitment, promotion, and other development of the institution, the executive heads are instantly depreciated and disrespected. Without being more qualified, more experienced, and more aged, how can a younger, lowly qualified and lesser experienced person dictate the head of an academic or research institution? This is the root cause of India's failure to perform fully and comprehensively. I extend a bit of advice to all the State Governments and the Union Government to reform the existing educational management policy by giving a whole responsibility to the head of the institution. At best, the Administrative Officers like the District Magistrates, Sub Divisional Magistrates, and Block Development Officers can be appendaged with the governing bodies and managing committees of Schools, Colleges, and Universities. You see the result within a decade only. This one decision of the government(s) shall play the catalytic role in transforming India from a developing country to a developed country by 2047.

12. Unbridled Corruption Prevailing in India

When corruption is well established in any state, it not only undermines the state institutions and their authority but also creates widespread anguish and anger among the general masses. When left unaddressed the serious problems of corruption for decades together, create an unstable environment that is susceptible to disturbance triggered by internal as well as external factors. The state institutions lose the trust of their citizens. Almost every conscious Indian is well aware of the rampant corruption and nepotism in India. You may visit any government office, you will rarely find discipline, ethics, and punctuality among the majority of its employees, but one common thing you must find i.e. corruption – from a local municipality office to a state general hospital. Even it is found from an electricity office to the office of the District Inspector of Schools. An example of West Bengal can be given here. What happened in West Bengal in recent times (August-September, 2022) is really shocking. The ex-Education Minister and his girlfriend have looted almost 100 crores of people's money. Both of them are in ED custody (12.11.2023). People found heaps of cash, land deeds, thick gold ornaments, hundreds of bank accounts, foreign currency, life insurance policies, and others broadcast on television channels. Even the School Education Board President, Primary Board President, their advisors, and other accomplices are now either in jail or under the custody of central investigating agencies. They are undergoing trial. If the highest level office bearers take bribes and accumulate crores of money, how can they check the corrupt practices of their subordinates? It seems corruption starts from the top and it comes down to the grassroots level.

In a recent report, India has been ranked at the 80th position in the Corruption Perception Index (CPI) prepared by Transparency International. The CPI was released by the World Economic Forum (WEF) 2022 which ranked 180 countries and territories by their perceived levels of public sector corruption, according to experts and business people. The best and corruption-free countries in the world are Denmark, New Zealand, Finland, Singapore, Sweden, and Switzerland. Denmark is the world's least corrupt country in the world with a score of 90. The second and third positions are occupied by Finland (score 87) and New Zealand (score 87). The USA ranked 24 position with a 69 score, Germany ranked 9 with a 79 score, and Japan held 18 position with a 73 score. But India, with a score of 40, ranked at the 85th spot (Eriksson, Transparency International, 2022). In India big black money is being flowing into election campaigns and the government only listens to the voices of the wealthy or politically well-connected individuals. In most government offices, the dealing clerk to any higher level of officers mostly asks for money for doing any work – small or big, though they earn a good amount of salary every month. For distributing a government benefit while selecting a beneficiary, and after the distribution of government benefit or relief, a section of political leaders and even administrative officers ask for money from the beneficiaries contractors, or middlemen either directly or through agents.

13. Constant Security Threats from Within and Outside the Borders

India's strategic location is a natural challenge to its security. "India faces a diverse array of security challenges both on and within its borders. Pakistan, with whom India fought three wars, poses a complex hybrid challenge and certainly preoccupies Indian military officials. The provinces of Jammu and Kashmir are the principal areas of contention...Pakistan's large and well-equipped conventional forces cannot be ignored. To the northeast, Indian officials view China's rapid military modernization with some trepidation, although relations between the two countries are relatively close and cordial. India must also remain concerned about instability in such neighboring countries such as Nepal, Bhutan, Bangladesh, Afghanistan, and Sri Lanka. In the maritime domain, India is situated in the middle of the world's busiest and most constricted trade routes, including the Straits of Hormus to the west and the Straits of Malacca to the east" (Johnson, Moroney, Cliff et. al., 2009, p. 179). Moreover, "India's strategic context and imperatives contrast sharply with those of the United States. India faces significant conventional challenges on its borders, whereas the United States' borders with Canada and Mexico are not militarized. India faces considerable international instability, whereas the United States has not experienced violent internal conflict for over a century. The United States is the sole remaining superpower, whereas India struggles to attain regional hegemony" (Johnson, Moroney, Cliff et. al., 2009, p. 182).

India has both internal and external security threats. China and Pakistan are the two countries that have posed the most security threat to India. "New Delhi's biggest challenge in the maritime domain is undoubtedly China. Since 2008, when Beijing first sent its warships to the Gulf of Aden for anti-piracy duties, China's military presence in the eastern Indian Ocean has significantly expanded. Beijing has sought to exert influence over the Bay of Bengal states through investments and infrastructure development projects. Bangladesh, Myanmar, Sri Lanka, and Thailand have all benefited from China's Belt and Road Initiative (BRI), as has Pakistan, China's all-weather friend in South Asia. Some countries have even allowed Chinese-built commercial facilities on their territories to be used for quasi-military purposes" (Singh, Observer Researcher Foundation, 14 Aug. 2023). After the downfall of Sheikh Hasina in Bangladesh, security in border areas has become a serious challenge for India. Our other neighbor is constantly instigating and fuelling Bangladeshi terrorists and fundamentalists to attack the Indian state of West Bengal. This has become a major challenge for the Indian Government, which needs deep and continuous dialogue at the diplomatic level.

14. India's GDP and Per Capita Income is Shamefully Low

The Focus-economics report published in November 2024 highlights that in 2025 the United States of America's size of Gross Domestic Product will be US$ 30.4 trillion making it the world's largest and strongest economy. The tech industry, anchored by Silicon Valley, driving innovation in AI, biotech, and software are the strengths of the US economy in addition to healthcare and pharmaceuticals. China has strengthened its economy to $19.6 trillion consisting of 20% of global GDP in nominal USD. Their economy is grown based on the production of electronics, machinery, and textiles and it is powered by investment and export-led manufacturing. By overtaking Japan, Germany has become the world's third largest economy with US$5.00 trillion. "The Mittelstand - a dense web of medium-sized industrial enterprises - forms the backbone of this. The country benefits from a skilled workforce, prudent fiscal management and a favorable geographical position at the heart of Europe" (FocusEconomies, 2024). Japan is the world's fourth largest economy now with a GDP of US$4.4 trillion. "Like Germany, Japan has a large manufacturing sector worth close to 20% of GDP, with strengths in electronics, motor vehicles, and robotics; Japanese companies like Mitsubishi, Sony, and Toyota play leading roles globally. Japan also has a significant banking and financial services sector. The economy is export-oriented and has persistently registered trade and current account surpluses in recent years" (FocusEconomies, 2024). India has substantially hiked its GDP size and at present it is US$4.3 trillion. However, India's GDP per capita is very low in comparison with the top four economies in the world.

India is still an agro-based economy, "which employs a large portion of the population and still accounts for around a fifth of the economy, remains less productive and vulnerable to climate risks" (FocusEconomies, 2024). At present, India's GDP per capita income is merely US$2.7 thousand, while it is US$86.6 thousand in the USA and US$12.94 in China. Luxembourg holds the topmost position with a US$ 151,150 GDP-PPP per capita. Singapore

(US\$ 148,190) and Macao SAR (US\$ 130,420) hold second and third positions respectively. It is a fact that India's large population is a hindrance in calculating the GDP per capita income. Despite that, India needs to further reform its industrial policy, incentivize foreign direct investment, emphasize on information and communication technology, AI, robotics, space research and exports, manufacturing of electronics, drones, computer software, airplanes, missiles, sophisticated weapons, tanks, missiles and export the same to earn profit.

15. India is a Land of Millions of Illiterate and Unskilled Workers

India's literacy rate is also much lower than the developed countries. In 2023, the total literacy rate in India is only 77.7%. This means there are approximately 30 crore illiterate people living in India, which is almost similar to the total population of the USA. Moreover, the gap in literacy between men and women is also wide i.e. 14.4% (Men's literacy rate is 84.7% and female's literacy rate is only 70.0%). Further, the latest World Economic Forum (WEF 2023) report shows that "...out of the 13 million people who join the workforce per year, only one-fourth of the management professionals, one-fifth of engineers, and one-tenth of graduates are employable. In addition, the Global Skills Gaps Measurement and Monitoring Report of ILO 2023 indicates that 47% of Indian workers, especially 62 of females are underqualified for their jobs" (India Today, 2024, November 1).

In the 21st century, Indian students must be empowered with digital learning. The world is now digitized. Ankit Chourasiya in a recent article (2023, April) highlights the challenges of skill development in India: "Skills development is a significant challenge in India. While there is a vast pool of talent, the employability of the workforce remains low due to a lack of skills relevant to the job market. The skills gap is particularly evident in industries such as manufacturing, healthcare, and engineering, where the demand for skilled workers is high. Skills development is critical for the economic development of a country. It enables individuals to acquire the necessary skills and knowledge to succeed in the job market and contribute to the growth of the economy."

Though the Union Government has initiated a policy through National Education Policy 2020 to impart vocational training from Class VI, in government schools. But where are the teachers to train the students? Further, the National Policy on Skill Development and Entrepreneurship is inadequate to meet the demands of the market. Besides, some state governments have not taken any concrete steps in this regard. Also, I must mention that the skill development programs such as Pradhan Mantri Kaushal Vikas Yojana and Jan Shikshan Sansthan are, similarly, not very effective equitably throughout the country.

Apart from the above shortcomings, India's mean years of schooling is also poor; teacher-student ratio is abnormal; and women's labor force participation rate is lower than the developed countries. Women's participation in Parliament and State Legislatures is also discouraging. India's military strength and defense budget are comparatively lower than that of the USA, China, Japan, and, Germany. Over-population is also a great challenge before India. India's natural resources are not properly discovered and utilized. India's infrastructure needs more improvement. Space research, the use of AI, and STEM to be encouraged and funded more. There is lack of freedom in academic institutions and research institutions. There is also a dearth of both public and private funding in the research and education sectors. Little collaboration between the academy and industry is found. Foreign Direct Investment in the education sector is comparatively lower in India than in China, the USA, and some other countries. Truants and malingerers are too many in academia, workplace, and social sectors. Government vigilance and restriction measures are loose. Skill development training and management training are the two most common drawbacks for India's entrepreneurship development. Unavailability of funds, extortion, and 'cut money' are also serious obstacles for India's business startups. Infiltration through vulnerable borders in India from our neighboring countries is also a big challenge. Finally, I would say that political culture is detrimental and trashy nowadays.

Recommendations For Policy Makers and Other Stakeholders

It seems to me that, students are the brain and backbone of a country. If our students are transformed into strong, hardworking and disciplined workforce, the country also becomes strong and developed. Hence, emphasis should be given to students' discipline and strength-increasing mechanisms. I am not advocating for the Indian military to be an innovation incubator. But military training for all High School students can be made feasible, who could learn at least discipline, punctuality, and hard-working mentality like the Israeli youths. Indian youths can be taught science and know-how of cyber warfare including app development from their school life training period. It might be only a two-year program, but it will make our youths disciplined, patriotic, and inquisitive. Our youths can be trained to be problem-solvers. The National Education Policy 2020 has the potential to make this program successful. Some Indian states are averse to abiding by the educational program formulated by the national government of India. The training of startups can be initiated from school days.

1. Students Should Be Trained to Think Out of the Box

Only the formulation of policy will not be sufficient. Our students should be imparted an "Out-of-the-box" thinking spirit which is considered as the most important entrepreneurial skill. It should not be only optional and left on the goodwill of the state governments; rather it must be compulsory. Can a nation grow on the goodwill of some people? I don't think so; rather it depends on the goodwill, patriotism, and love of millions of people for the country. And the developmental works cannot be let on the whimsical regional political bosses; rather it should be strictly and mandatorily implemented by the Union Government. This training should be given from the Schools. There must be recruited management trainees or students to impart the training the students to think in a different way, a better way to be entrepreneurs and learn various skills for personal development. The mantra would be to "National development through self development."

2. A Target-oriented Development Plan is Highly Necessary

Why our country cannot make at least 10,000 companies by engineering college or university pass-out students like the Waze and Check Point of Israel? Government colleges and universities should be given a target of not giving inflated marks to their students. In place, they should be mandatorily given targets to produce entrepreneurs. India produces one million engineering graduates annually. Indian technical infrastructure includes 3500 engineering colleges, 3400 polytechnics, and about 200 schools of planning and architecture, where lakhs of students are passing out every year. Can India not produce only 10,000 companies in a year with these vast engineering background students? Yes, I believe it can be possible. How it can be possible? Let me tell you my plan. At present (2024) India is divided into 785 districts and a total of 7129 sub-districts or tehsils (https://wiki.openstreetmap.org/wiki/Subdistricts_in_India accessed on 17.12.2024) are existing in India. If only two factories and startups are established in every sub-district continuously for the coming 20 years; there could be 2,85160 factories and startups, where at least 28.5 lakh new jobs can be created, if only 10 people are employed in one factory or startup.

Every District Magistrate should be given a fixed target (according to the size and potentiality) to set up at least 10 factories or Micro Small and

Medium Scale Enterprises in every sub-district. In turn, the Sub Divisional Magistrates (SDM) will take up the issue with the young pass-out students, NGOs, and financial institutions. It would take a maximum of one year to fulfill the target by each SDM. It needs a positive attitude, cooperation from both ruling and opposition party leaders, and a good policy with strict target fixing by both the Union and State governments. This is called proper planning. Indian NITI Aayog can take the guiding role. I am sure; they can take up this initiative by 2025. The Indian government has prepared the ground most fertile for skill development and financial help. Now what needed is "goal fixing, and working towards the achievement of goals."

3. More Funds to be Allocated for Research & Development

At present, India has almost 1,140 centers that are dedicated to Research and Development where about nine lakh professionals are working. Indian Gross Expenditure in R&D (GERD) has been nearly tripled from 2007-08 ($10 billion) to 1,13,825 crore ($17.5 billion) in 2017-18. Despite that, currently, it is only 0.7 percent of the Gross Domestic Product which is definitely much lower than that of developed countries (1.5-3%), and lower than the target of 2 percent. Indian private sector spends 42 percent of R&D, while Defence (DRDO) and space account for half of the remaining 58 percent of public spending. The Business Line (January 21, 2021) highlights that the Indian Departments of Science and Technology (DST), biotechnology (DBT), and Scientific and Industrial Research (DSIR) under the Ministry of Science and Technology must demand more allocation for research and development. And, the government of India should assist the scientists through the allocation of required funds. Medical research and space travel should be prioritized too. Agriculture and Industry also have to bring forward innovative ideas and schemes so that they can run their show after initial support from the government – maybe for the first ten years. They should plan for earning more revenue from their inventions, and exports.

Indian companies should plan for setting up multinational R&D centers as was established by companies like Google, Amazon, Microsoft, Apple, etc. in Israel. India should either build or collaborate with hi-tech companies to fully realize the "Make in India" program. In Israel, there are approximately 300 multinational R&D centers. Can India not do so by 2025 or latest by 2030? Moreover, to support the start-ups Israel has a strong venture capital ecosystem. The start-ups in that country have easy access to financing. Indian students from colleges and universities must be encouraged to get easy loans and other facilities to begin world-class start-ups on Indian soil.

India is the land of the world's renowned entrepreneurs such as Dhirubhai Ambani, Jehangir Ratanji Dadabohy Tata, Nagavara Ramarao Narayan Murthy, Shiv Nadar, Laxmi Niwas Mittal, Ghanshyam Das Birla, Dilip Shanghvi, Azim Premji, etc. India has the potential to produce more than one hundred such billionaire entrepreneurs by 2030, maybe by 2040, and two lakh entrepreneurs by the time India celebrates its one hundred years of Independence. Even more entrepreneurs may come out from our poor, middle-class, and so-far "Unknown villagers" in the coming quarter-century. I have full faith in our youths and their recently infused "out-of-the-box" thought process. One thing has to be kept in mind, "Success means going global." If Tel Aviv can do it; then why not New Delhi can do the same? I must caution the Government of India about a hard reality, i.e. to keep a balancing behavior towards the global powers particularly with the US to avoid major security threats.

4. Clues For India to become a Hotspot of Investment

If Israel can be ranked one of the eight most favorite and most powerful countries to investors ahead of Saudi Arabia and the United Arab Emirates, why India not be the more favorable destination to investors? What does India not have? India has everything - from sufficient electricity, developed infrastructure, millions of English-speaking educated youths, and very skilled adults to a positive and welcoming attitude of the government, and entrepreneurship encouragements - that can transform our country into "one of the best and most attractive countries" in investment ranking. India has the beauty of Switzerland and the technical know-how of Japan, still, the country is lagging! Why India will remain behind the top ten most technologically and economically powerful countries such as the United States, Russia, China, Germany, the United Kingdom, France, and Japan? From a recent survey (2020) on the issue of FDI - 'How can India step up its game?' conducted by the Confederation of Indian Industry (CII) and Ernst & Young (EY) it came to light that, "About 50% of respondents see India amongst the top three economies or leading manufacturing destinations of the world by 2025. The respondents have pinned down market potential, skilled workforce, and political stability as the top three reasons to make India their favored destination. Other key factors that contribute to the attractiveness of India as an investment destination include cheap labor availability, policy reforms, and availability of raw materials" (The Times of India, 14 October, 2020).

The power ranking is based on five attributions such as a country's top leader, its economic influence, its political influence, strong international alliance, and a strong military. India has all these five attributes, and still, it cannot stand in the competition. My question is why? Is its large population a hindrance? Israel is a small country, having landmarks of significance to several religious and strained relationships with many of its Arab neighbors. India is also having a good relationship with its neighboring countries, except Pakistan, and keeps good international relations with big economies of the world. Recently the UAE, Singapore, and China have come as the three highest-ranked nations in the power ranking. What needs to be done more for India? Based on the international criteria of interest, I may dare to recommend these things: stronger skill development and entrepreneurship training from the school level; military training from the school level; preserving its culture and heritage; teaching risk-taking methods, attitudes, and benefits to our youths; give liberty to all the citizens irrespective of any religion, caste or creed; improve the quality of life of people; openness in business and control of corrupt practices.

5. Strong Competition to be Introduced Among the Indian Industries

India is a very big country. There are a thousand types of work for each category of people such as highly-skilled, skilled, semi-skilled, and non-skilled personnel. India can overcome China by just producing low-cost fancy and durable tools, toys, cars, sanitary materials, and others. "India has the capability to become a lower-cost country than China if the industry and the government work together" (Business World, 10 November, 2020), Maruti Suzuki India Chairman R.C. Bhargava also considers so. For this purpose, the only objective of government policies has to be modified a little to increase the competitiveness among Indian industries so that they can make things at the lowest cost, and the best quality in the world. It is to be kept in mind that, "The more the industry can sell, the more jobs will be created in the economy." For example, I can point out here that, Maruti Suzuki produces more cars each year without adding to its workforce, but the increased sales of cars each year create more jobs in the service economy.

6. Various Innovative Ideas to be Introduced among Different Stakeholders

So far China is called the "manufacturing hub" of the world. Indian population has already surpassed China. When I think about why our country cannot become the manufacturing hub of the world, it seems to me that it is because of the policy poverty of our political and administrative Gurus. There were neither strong policies nor effective encouragement to young entrepreneurs on the part of the government as well as family members. The deficiency of these two major factors has kept us confined merely within thoughts of clerical jobs in a government organization, where there will be all facilities of social security with less working pressure, and low or nil accountability and responsibility. Only recently the government of India has put substantial emphasis on start-ups and micro small and medium scale industries (MSMEs). Moreover, the recent measures for the protection of the MSME sector will bring about a positive outcome in the days to come. It seems to me that the MSMEs should be nourished in such a way so that they can be globally competitive with the quality and price of the large companies in the world. They require business management, financial management, and entrepreneurial training from time to time. Better labor relations and owner and worker relations are very important in continuous and comprehensive production. The laborers need a fair share of the profit they make for the owners. The owners must be respected for the opportunity they are providing to the laborers and their families through salary, incentives, and social security. Career growth for the employees is another vital factor for the increase of production without much wastage. The career growth of the children of employees must be taken care of by the employers in terms of higher education and professional courses. This will strengthen the relationship between employer and employee. The orientation programs, meditation programs, and cultural programs jointly with family members during the holidays and local festivals can be effective tools for improving the employer-employee relationship. Various prizes for workers' meritorious children and any outstanding performance of the kids of the locality will improve the neighborhood and factory relations. All these will bring forth growth and development of production as well as human relations. This exercise will bridge the misunderstanding and remove the distrustful environment between local people and industry, which is considered a major constraint on policymakers in India. I ask people to shun all trade unionism. Avoid all violence and destructive political activities, and save public property.

7. Dadagiri (hooliganism) of Local Leaders with Industrialists Must be Dealt with Sternness

Indian political leaders, being responsible for the local area's development and answerable to the electorate before the elections, often interfere in the functioning of the company management. Many of the political masters even try to influence recruiting the familiar and lowly qualified personnel in the factory, which often clashes with the interest of management. The companies express dissatisfaction with those political interventions. They express that the leaders should interfere only in times of crisis or when are called for to solve certain problems. If the management does not seek any assistance or request any help, it is better that the political leaders should refrain from interference in the factory management. It is not the responsibility of the political leaders to see if the companies are working in tandem with the government's norms and if they are working and trading in fair and legal ways. There are various government institutions and officers to look after all these thing. In India, the financial and business institutions generally play their role fairly from setting up a new enterprise to enhancing production and sale or exports of their goods so that they can earn more revenues and in turn help the government in earning taxes and revenues.

8. Skill Development Training Should be Introduced from Schools

India has a deficiency of skilled workers. Skill development of our younger generation students is very important. The New Education Policy 2020 envisages enhancing skilled personnel right from the school level. Some states have not yet accepted and implemented the Policy yet, but it will only satisfy the ego of a section of political masters at the cost of general citizens and particularly the students. Imparting skill education from Class VI in government schools has such potential that it could transform India as a Viksit Bharat even before 2047 by supplying skilled employees and manpower required by various government, non-government, or private organizations and institutions. Vocational training introduced in Japan and China has helped them to supply constantly the needs of factories, manufacturers, and general households. Indian manufacturing policy needs to be more competitive and encouraging on the part of both government and non-government players. Finally, it can be said that "India can beat China in low-cost manufacturing if policies allow."

9. Smart Plan Required for both Big and Small Car Manufacturers

Indian carmakers are facing problems with each buyer. Car buyers are now mostly opting for smaller and cheaper cars. Families are getting smaller day by day, so also the choice for cars getting smaller. But the most important thing is that the outlook of average people has changed. In rural and backward areas people are buying two-wheelers and four-wheelers for easy transportation from home to the workplace. The average road condition has improved a lot in the last decade, and the salary or income of general citizens has increased a lot. Moreover, the COVID-19 lockdown has compelled many emergency service providers including women to attend office either regularly or on a rotational basis. To maintain a safe distance, and for maintaining personal safety even moderate-income people are purchasing cars. Hence, Indian car makers should concentrate on low-cost cars for average-income Indian buyers. At the same time some traditional societies such as Haryana, Punjab, Himachal Pradesh, Uttar Pradesh, and even the southern states, carmakers need to plan for big cars for big families.

Not only that more authorized service centers should be set up to provide better service to the customers. More spare parts shops in both urban and rural localities should be established. The need for trained mechanics is too much. Training centers should emphasize the motor mechanical courses for the youths including girls and women. It is noted that "...buyers are now changing their cars less frequently, compared to the past. Consequently, revenues from spare parts and vehicle servicing are growing at a faster clip than revenue from vehicle sales in the domestic market" (Business Standard, 12 October, 2020). Thus, separate cars for rural and urban areas, and for big and small families to be manufactured by the car makers.

10. India Can Beat China in Manufacturing with Policy Reforms

Jeff Sinclair, leader of McKinsey's global manufacturing practice considers that not too long ago, China was declared the world's factory and India its back office. But it is not really so. The government of India realized the deficits and took many affirmative steps to break the myth. India has huge potential for manufacturing. India has started encouraging start-ups and as a result, a lot of aggressive, smart, and young entrepreneurs have grown up. Indian entrepreneurs are very skilled and highly educated with an excellent knowledge base. The government's assistance in setting up thriving industries has helped entrepreneurs to produce and market their products. India has a huge domestic market. China has a problem of high labor costs, high inflation, and talent constraints. On the other hand, India's lower labor cost, availability of raw materials, entrepreneurial spirit, smart strategies, and engineering skills are capable of global champions. "India will see a sweet spot of skill-intensive, medium-volume complex manufacturing" (Goyal, The Economic Times, 23 Nov., 2010).

India is already a global leader in medicine and vaccine manufacturing. Now India should emphasize generic pharma, specialty chemicals, auto components, and electrical machinery. Unlike China's contract manufacturing status of the world, India should stand as the direct manufacturing hub of the world. India's English-speaking urban cultured, engineering, and specialized students are capable of taking up any challenging job from research to innovation and from manufacturing to service. India's infrastructure is developing world-class. Every day approx. 30-kilometer roads are being built in this country. "The center plans to build 12,500 km of roads in the current fiscal year ending March 31, 2024" (Bhutani, Business Today, 26 June, 2023). The Union government is trying hard to construct 40 km of roads per day. Roads are now all-weather friendly. Trade and commerce are growing tremendously large for good physical infrastructure. Indian IT sector, defense sector, spacecraft manufacturing, bullet train manufacturing, drone manufacturing, and airplane and ship manufacturing industries should be encouraged more to compete with global leaders in their respective fields. India's engineers and technocrats are highly qualified and talented; they have ample excellent potential to bring about revolution. The government of India needs to provide them with world-class facilities and laboratories for research and work. Experts feel that "To top its manufacturing potential, India must do the following things: One, very quickly figure out land acquisition and environment clearance – anything we could do to expedite it will be good. Two, up-skilling millions of people to meet the skill-intensive agenda will be important. And to figure this out, the government and the industry must come together...."

I want to see industry after industry in every district of our country. I have personally seen many empty land in different states in India. There must be small and medium-scale industries in every block and below. Those will at first fulfill the needs of the local people, and after that export the excess to those countries and regions where they are lacking. Indian steel industries and their allied industries can be very profitable businesses. Manufacturing mobile phones, tablets, and laptops and their spare parts can be a very lucrative trade in India in the days to come. Servicing and repairing these electronic goods will require a huge skilled workforce. There should be innovation in every product, and scientists and researchers should focus on this matter. Indian clothes, shirts, toys, and vests have great demand in the world market. Rural artificial jewelry, handicrafts, bags, and other things are liked by people across the globe. So the production and export of these goods should be explored by the entrepreneurs.

11. India Needs Acquiring Self-Sufficiency to Overtake China in the Pharmaceutical and Other Industry

Indian pharmaceutical industry is already holding a strong position. It "is the third-largest in the world, in terms of volume, behind China and Italy, and 14th largest in terms of value.' If India could double its share in world pharmaceutical exports within just ten years from 1.4 percent in 2010 to 2.6 percent in 2019. India has the capability to increase at least ten times in the next 23 years. But one thing that should be kept in mind is that the ratio of increase must be more in comparison with other pharma export countries such as Italy, Germany, Switzerland, and the USA. What can hold us back? Is there anything? Yes, the main issue is that "India's $42 billion pharmaceutical sector is heavily dependent on China for key active pharmaceutical ingredients or API - chemicals that are responsible for the therapeutic effect of drugs" still "India imports about 68% of its APIs from China as it's a cheaper option than manufacturing then domestically" (Bhddhavarapu, CNBC, 26 May, 2022). Indian start-up entrepreneurs and already existing giants in the pharmaceutical industry are great innovators. I am sure that they will now make a very effective plan, and conduct extensive research on how to manufacture API in India with lower costs than China. We cannot afford to pay more money to China for importing API. Many years ago while I studied Business Management I learned that at first "Make your plan, and work according to your plan." So, what is most important is making a plan – a realistic plan, doing research, and getting better Active Pharmaceutical Ingredients (APIs).

However, small business entrepreneurs can produce many items like phenyl, sanitary napkins, masks, gloves, hand wash, and sanitizer at low prices. Even India's young students of Engineering and Science can produce all these things at home or they may jointly do so with the help of some like-minded and similarly qualified friends in a local setup. Let the maximum number of entrepreneurs come out from our poor and rural huts. Let the extraordinary and meritorious students and pass-outs come forward to set up MSMEs and Start-Ups. They are millions in number, I know. Now what is needed is that these great sons of India should plough a lonely furrow and put their hands to the plough. I look forward to welcoming them to the noble mission of strong nation-building.

The Indian chemical industry is also growing a lot. According to the Federation of Indian Chambers of Commerce and Industry, the Indian chemical industry "is estimated to grow at about 9 percent per annum to reach US$ 304 billion by the financial year 2025." The production and growth history of the chemical and petrochemical sector in India is encouraging. If the growth rate was 5.57 percent in the past decade, India can improve it in the next quarter-century by about 20 percent growth. More exploration and research are required.

We require more funding from Indian and foreign investors. With more production in the chemical and petrochemical industries, India will move up to a higher spot globally, and India's domestic industry and economic growth will get an impetus.

India can beat China only with the active and smart participation of another ten percent students of our excellent Engineering, Medical, and Pharmaceutical students. Our students are very bright and energetic and stupefying with creative ideas. They are a few most important people who can transform our country in the coming days. With an affirmation in mind, if my beloved brothers and sisters put in some extra effort, say just 2 hours each day to increase production in the fields of pharmaceuticals, textiles, engineering goods, and chemicals, India could hit China and other competitors hard. Why my students, brothers, and sisters will fall behind any country in skill development? Why will they be kept in the darkness of ignorance and backwardness? Why will they carry the stigma of non-competence or laziness? I completely disagree with this claim of a section of people. I am a strong advocate and protagonist for my students and youths. I believe that my brothers and sisters are stronger than lions; they are more cunning than foxes; more hard-working than bulls; and more intelligent than Chimpanzees and elephants. There is not a single work in the world that our students cannot do. Our students are so intelligent and inquisitive that they can outperform students of any other country on this earth. Despite that, should we be living behind and with lesser dignity than our smaller European and American fellow citizens? Is it not a shame on us? Do you like to live a despicable and inornate life? I know that you don't like it. Let us change our lot by ourselves. So, we must stop laziness from today, nay from now itself. Let us believe in ourselves and test our strengths. Remember, every person has enough potential and special skills. Our work would be only to find out and awaken our inner wisdom, and then use the divine power to transform our own lives, and with the transformed and dignified life, we can bring about change in the status, dignity, and position of our family, society, and finally the country.

Let us not go to purchase our luxurious goods from Europe or America, let us produce them here. Let us not go to buy laptops and mobile phones from South Korea, China, or others; rather let us make it here in our state. Let us not buy software from America, we will make it here. Can we not have the ability to produce rockets, submarines, missiles, ships, and aircraft? Are not our students working in NASA and ESA? Can you name places where our students have not put their footprint? Then why did my mother hear the epithets like "poor," "developing," 'middle human development" et cetera? When Mother India's children are so rich and excellent in knowledge, wisdom, wealth, and capital and have ample ability to lift the economy, business, and trade of other countries; why our own motherland shall be so unsavory and disrespectful? Is it not our shame? What response shall we give to the Lord after our death? Therefore, let us pledge that instead of going abroad to purchase their goods, let others come to India to buy our goods. Let us make our country neat and clean, let us make our country computer-literate, and let us make it an all-purpose destination for other countries. How is the idea to make our country a hive land? Let all the bees from across the borders come to collect honey from our hives.

12. We have to Increase the Use of Robots and Drones in Production, Trade, and Industry

Stephen Hawking (2018) considers that "By 2025, there will be about thirty mega-cities, each with more than ten million inhabitants, with all those people clamoring for goods and services to be delivered when they want them, can technology help us keep pace with our craving for instant commerce. Robots will speed up the online retail process." You see change is inevitable. Human intelligence will expedite our progress. Hawking (2018), further, considers that "Intelligence is characterized as the ability to adapt to changes. Human Intelligence is the result of generations of natural selection of those with the ability to adapt to changed circumstances. We must not fear change. We need to make it work to our advantage."

The countries that have proven themselves as developed and earned the reputation of "rich" or "technology-savvy," and "very high human development" countries have attained such attributions mainly because of their technology, and the brains working behind it. See how Israel, a small country, is doing well. Recently it came up in the news headlines for its creation of Pegasus, a spyware developed by Israeli cyber arms firm NSO (Niv, Shalev, and Omri, the names of the company's founders) Group that can be covertly installed on mobile phones running most versions of iOS (mobile operating system) and Android. India, though late, has started to explore the manufacture and use of technologies in various sectors. India already used its i-Drones for transporting medicines and medical equipment in hilly and troublesome areas quickly and effectively on an experiment basis. Also, the use of drones in agriculture and other surveillance purposes has begun producing very good results. But, India's use of modern technologies in robotics is limited till now. But I want to see its use in different difficult fields. Presently, robotics are being used in manufacturing industries only, and industrial robots are playing a vital role in material handling, welding, and painting too. In the manufacturing of aircraft, missiles, ships, supersonic airplanes, bullet trains, and defense manufacturing sectors robots can be used. Service and security sectors can also benefit from robotic engineering. In the infrastructure building works, and the risky and vulnerable areas, robots are very helpful. A day will come when robots might be man's good friend at home or workplace. They can be used in maintaining law and order, and also border security in India.

13. India Should Provide Better Facilities to Robot Makers

On the other hand, when we look at China we find that China is progressing very rapidly. Chinese Government is also giving all kinds of facilities to industrialists and especially robot makers, who are manufacturing and modernizing its vast factory sector and advancing technological progress. Following the Chinese model, Indian engineering and heavy industries need to focus on automated vehicles to move bulky items around industrial spaces and in other fields. China gives tax breaks and government-guaranteed loans to the makers of robots intending to shift the country's manufacturing up the value chain. The attention being paid by the Chinese government is boosting the manufacturing sector and increasing the country's real economy. China is also backing the research and development efforts of its high-tech manufacturers to reduce reliance on imported technology and reinforce its dominant role as a global factory power. The great goal of making their economy the best and even excelling the US economy is making them run faster than almost all other global powers. China is playing dual roles – the first one is to expand its economy, and the second one is to crack down on the economies of its competitors. This obnoxious politico-economic policy, though is helping them grow faster than many of their global counterparts, might act as a boomerang in the near future. China has almost lost global trust. Despite having so many criticisms against China it is globally recognized as a major challenge to the US economy. Hence, India should also run faster than China to increase its manufacturing industry to pose a real challenge to both the existing economic giants – the USA and China. But it should always be done by ethical means.

14. More Big Manufacturing Industries to be Set Up

However, Beijing's boldness lies in its focus on advanced manufacturing. It relies less on the service sector than on manufacturing for steering its goal of the world's largest economy. One significant mantra of growth pursued by China as well as most of the developed nations is "pressure," which is the driving force, and without pressure, it is difficult for companies to develop and fulfill targets. Do, we, the Indians, love to work under pressure? Most of us know well that average Indian people don't like to perform under any kind of pressure. But it is a valuable and proven mantra for attaining excellence.

15. Public Private Partnership is Sine Qua Non

Let India make a long-term industrial plan to receive investment either from public or private agencies or foreign direct investment in the PPP (Public-private partnership) model in the manufacturing industry. Not only on the MSMEs, but India should also refocus on big manufacturing industries such as Tata's various projects, Maruti Company, Ambani's Reliance Industries, etc. It is high time that India must give priority to manufacturing and exporting cars, ships, airplanes, fertilizer, rockets, missiles, textiles, laptops, smartphones, robots, vaccines, iron and steel, garments, and others. India's plan to set up a total of four thousand oxygen plants to meet the requirements of Indian plants and industries as well as private use and medical purposes is a welcome step. The government must put some pressure on industrialists to manufacture highly powerful robots and other heavy manufacturing industries. India's infrastructure is rapidly growing, and in the future, the demand for iron, steel, cement, etc. will be greater in quantity. The next five years (2022-2027) may be taken for finding locations for setting up industries, getting approvals, infrastructure building, and beginning of production. Afterward from 2027-32, the industries should search for markets and make contracts for selling their products. Thus within a decade, India's revenues from exports, and domestic markets will be billions of US dollars, which will add to our national income. Research and development should be given more impetus by both industrialists as well as every department of the Union government. Indian corporate houses must do market research, product research, quality research, and price research. Investments by both corporate houses – from India and foreign – and various state governments in India of US$1 trillion in manufacturing industries in the coming five years will automatically help transform India's manufacturing map, and it will have the potential to give employment to at least 10 lakh young people in our country and generate revenue of billions of dollars every year. India's GDP will grow and per capita income will also increase proportionately.

16. More Automated Guided Vehicles to be Manufactured

Automated guided vehicles (AGVs) are to be explored more and more in the coming days. What is this? Automated guided vehicles are those vehicles controlled by computers and which are wheel-based. The vehicles are used to carry loads that travel along the floor or a facility without an onboard operator or driver. The movement of AGVs is directed by a combination of software and sensor-based guidance systems. These vehicles provide safe movement of loads without loss, theft, or damage of loads. Typical AGV applications include transportation of raw materials, finished goods, etc. in support of manufacturing production lines and storage/retrieval of other movements in support of picking in warehousing and distribution applications. Investment in automated guided vehicles will help to manufacture at least 25-30 percent of the Indian economy. It might be challenging initially, but in the long run, this will give many dividends to India as a whole.

17. Control of Carbon Emissions is Necessary for Making a Healthy India

It is learned that total carbon emission from China is the highest in the world at 30.34%, while the United States holds second place with less than half (13.43%) of China, and India stands in third place with 6.83% of the global carbon emission. Carbon emissions are rebounding strongly and are rising across the world's richest countries. It is reported in the Climate Transparency Report that CO2 will go up by 4% across the G-20 countries in 2021, which dropped by 6% in 2020 due to worldwide pandemics. The rich countries are mostly responsible for around 75% of global emissions. The rebound of emissions is powered by fossil fuels, especially coal. According to the report, coal use across the G20 was projected to rise by 5% in 2021, and China is responsible for around 60% of the rise because of the increase in the use of coal. China's increasing demand for energy to recover the global economy requires coal-fired electricity plants to generate electricity. In terms of the use of gas, the Climate Transparency Report found that its use was up by 12% across the G20 in the 2015-2020 periods. As a result, the world is currently around 1.1C warmer than pre-industrial times. The report highlighted that between 1999 and 2018 there have been nearly 500,000 fatalities and close to $3.5 trillion of economic costs due to climate impacts worldwide, with China, India, Japan, Germany, and the US being hit particularly hard in 2018.

Hence, what we need now is to have a green focus. We need a strong national emission reduction target by 2030. Emphasis on the production and use of renewable energy such as solar power, and wind power is in demand. Renewables are now supplied around 12% of power compared to 10% in 2020. India needs more use of battery-run vehicles. E. Fantin Irudaya Raj and others have pointed out that, "Electric and Hybrid Electrical vehicles are now popular products in the market and are accepted internationally. However, their full potential for penetrating the automobile market is not yet fulfilled, even with the ever-expanding awareness of the global warming problem due to fossil fuel use" (Raj, Appadurai, and Thiyaharajan, 2020, preface). The development of internal combustion engines in automobiles is one of the greatest achievements of modern technology. The highly developed automotive industry and the increasingly large number of automobiles in use around the world are causing severe problems for the environment and hydrocarbon resources. The deteriorating air quality and global warming issues are becoming serious threats to modern life. Progressively more rigorous emission and fuel efficiency standards are stimulating the development of safe, cleaner, and more efficient vehicles. It is now well recognized that electric, hybrid electric, and fuel cell-powered drive train technologies are the most promising vehicles solution for the foreseeable future.

There are many reasons why people are moving to Electric Vehicles (EVs). These include: "(a) EVs are fun to drive because they are fast and smooth. (b) Many studies show that emissions from burning fossil fuels such as gasoline produce harmful greenhouse gases. EVs produce no smelly fumes or harmful greenhouse gases. (c) EVs are innovative and cool, (d) EVs only cost approximately Rs. 25,000/- a year to operate compared to Rs. 200000/- for a gasoline vehicle, and (e) EVs are a smart and convenient choice" (Raj, Appadurai, and Thiyaharajan, 2020).

India must increase its non-fossil energy capacity to 500 gigawatts (GW) and achieve its target to meet 50 percent of its energy requirements from renewable energy by 2030. India's projects to generate non-fossil energy for electricity generation such as solar, wind, hydel, and nuclear must be supported and augmented by all the States and Union Territories. India's budgetary allocation for climate change should be increased. However, we find the total budgetary allocation for India's Ministry of Environment, Forest, and Climate Change has been decreased to US$400 million from US$ 420 million in 2020-21. India must keep its promise of a climate-responsive budget. The Prime Minister of India in December 2020 pledged at the UN Climate Ambition Summit that, "Centennial India will not only meet its own targets but will also exceed your expectations." India must honor its climate-responsive budgeting. Climate-responsive budgeting involves a range of tools and approaches, such as climate tagging of budget lines, environmental cost-benefit analysis, carbon pricing, etc. More advanced approaches involve a legislative review of public expenditure contributions towards national climate goals, assessing tax revenue effects of climate-oriented policies, and induced economic transition on fiscal sustainability.

18. Artificial Intelligence Must be Popularized among the Students

The term artificial intelligence (AI) was coined in 1956, and after seven decades of performance, AI is a very popular term today as we find its application in diverse sectors such as medical diagnosis, computer search engines, and voice or handwriting recognition. Most AI examples that we hear about today are from chess-playing computers to self-driving cars – which rely heavily on deep learning and natural language processing. Using these technologies, computers can be trained to accomplish specific tasks by processing large amounts of data and recognizing patterns in the data. Artificial Intelligence or AI is a field of Data Science that trains machines to learn from inputs, adjust to inputted fields and criteria, and perform tasks of computational logic that match certain human cognitive levels. Over the last few years, AI has emerged as a primary data science function – by utilizing advanced algorithms and ever-increasing computing power. AI is transforming business domains and organizations as AI algorithms are now designed to make real-time decisions and interpret various types of data and media.

According to the Britannica English dictionary, artificial intelligence (AI) is the ability of a digital computer or computer-controlled robot to perform tasks commonly associated with intelligent beings. The term is frequently applied to the project of developing systems endowed with intellectual processes characteristic of humans, such as the ability to reason, discover meaning, generalize, or learn from experience. Since the development of the digital computer in the 1940s, it has been demonstrated that computers can be programmed to carry out very complex tasks – as, for example, discovering proofs for mathematical theorems or playing chess – with great proficiency.

The Artificial Intelligence technology function is no longer an emerging technology segment – AI as a function has pervaded almost all industries and functions – from e-commerce to BFSI (Banking, Financial Services, and Insurance) and from Manufacturing to Agriculture – Data Science and Deep Learning are increasingly utilized to solve complex business challenges. AI is increasingly adopted across Contact Centre Customer Services (RPA-driven Chat-Bots), Media Delivery (ML and AI-driven Social Media, Streaming content, and e-commerce recommendations), and Intelligent Networks/Telecom Services, to name a few. Machine Learning and AI technologies are central to the functioning of Smartphones, Smart TVs, Household Appliances, and Automobiles.

Balendu Sharma Dadhich writes in an article published in Yojana (April, 2022, p. 31) that "AI plays a vital role in the technologies that monitor and analyze customer behavior and activities. If it is analyzed properly, it can be used to get the best results in economic, political, defense, and other such areas. It also applies to the financial sector, where banks can grow their business and reach good and safe customers by analyzing such data....It can be predicted who may need a loan, who will want to transfer the loan taken from another location, and will face this kind of need in the coming years." These technologies can also be used for the prevention of fraud. AI can recognize similar patterns, and it can indicate what methods can prove effective in solving this. If a criminal ever repeats a fraudulent pattern, this technology can alert security systems, and block payment systems. "The Indian Artificial Intelligence market is valued at $7.8 billion as of July-August 2021. This represents a 22% increase in the size of the market over 2020. The AI market share and size with the Types of Companies are the highest across the broad MNC IT, Technology, and Electronic category, which includes High-end Software and Hardware Technology, IT Services, Semiconductors, and Electronics firms. The combined market share was 32% in 2020 and came down to 32 in 2021. More interestingly, there are close to 109000 Artificial Intelligence personnel working in India across enterprises and sectors – this represents a 20% jump in personnel in 2021 from the year 2020 (91000 Artificial Intelligence personnel) – the median salary of the AI personnel is INR14.3 lakhs" (Analytics India, 18 Oct, 2021).

According to Stephen Hawking (2018), "If the computer continues to obey Moore's Law, doubling their speed and memory capacity every eighteen months, the result is then computers are likely to overtake humans in intelligence at some point in the next hundred years. When an Artificial Intelligence becomes better than humans at AI design so that it can recursively improve itself without human help, we may face an intelligence explosion that ultimately results in machines whose intelligence exceeds ours by more than ours exceed that of snails." He further pointed out that, "AI may automate our jobs, to bring both great prosperity and equality. The real risk with AI is not malice but competence. A super-intelligent AI will be extremely good at accomplishing its goals, and if those goals are not aligned with ours we're in trouble" (Hawking, 2018). India's future lies in the maximization of the use of artificial intelligence in the next quarter-century.

19. India's Future Lies in the Use of High-tech Knowhow

India must concentrate on increasing its indigenous high-tech know-how to harden its strength in the global manufacturing sector. We must stop depending on other's technology. We have to develop our indigenous technology. India's best brains are leaving the country daily. Hence, Indian engineering students must be given all world-class facilities so that they do not leave the country. I have seen only patriotism is not sufficient; money is also a great determining factor. With monetary benefits, the government's encouragement, and provisions of all top tech laboratories and research facilities for the students and researchers, India will stand on its own legs within a decade only. The wealth and assets that will be created by our engineers and technocrats will strengthen the Indian economy, and infrastructure, and help India to rise as a superpower when we mark our centenary celebration of Independence in 1947.

20. India Needs to Balance Between Manufacturing and Service Industry

India has the potential to be the global manufacturing hub of medicine and vaccines. Not only that India has the potential to produce modern and sophisticated medical equipment and other materials. India has proven it to the world during the COVID-19 epidemic. Indian industries, educational institutions, and corporate houses must allocate more funds for research and development. Students can be selected through necessary tests for research and development. Further, India should not and cannot afford to neglect its service sector. India's service sector employs many youths every year. The service sector has a large share of India's GDP. It might be less productive than manufacturing, but it has all probability to contribute to long-term growth and strengthen cultural bonds between states and inter continents.

It is learned that "Beijing does not want manufacturing to dip below 25% of GDP, roughly in line with South Korea's economic profile." Similarly, India should also make a balance between the service industry and the manufacturing industry. Indian policymakers should keep in mind the requirements of both the creation of employment opportunities for educated youths and the need for the attainment of the national goal of economic growth. Like China, India also needs to boost its research and development by over 7% annually focusing on "frontier" technologies such as artificial intelligence, quantum computing, and semiconductors. India's 'Make in India' initiative must target the emerging industries of new-generation information technology, biotech, new energy, new materials, high-end equipment, new-energy vehicles, environmental protection, aerospace, and marine equipment.

21. Students Must Prepare Themselves to Cope with Future Challenges

Indian students must explore new ways of employment and engagement. In the coming decades, many of the existing jobs will vanish from the Indian market. There is nothing to be worried about because a lot of new job opportunities will emerge in India. In a recent article in *The Times of India* (30 July 2021), Chandrima Banerjee wrote that coal and petroleum are big employers now. India has about 8.6 lakh energy jobs at present. But a new study has found that phasing out fossil fuels would add 80 lakh jobs in the energy sector across the world by 2050 of which over 5.4 lakh would be in India. Now it is being said that climate action results in more jobs. Recent data show that, if the Paris Agreement target of temperature rises staying well below 2 degrees Celsius were met, the number of jobs in India's energy sector would go up from 8.6 lakh to 14 lakh by 2050. At the same time, the Chinese job market will add more than 27 lakh jobs. The reason behind this job argument is low-carbon technologies. During the expansion of renewable energy capacity, more job opportunities will be created in India.

Further, the report of the United Nations Development Program (UNDP, 2016) indicates that between 1991 and 2013, the size of the working-age population increased to 300 million. Of these, the Indian economy could employ only 140 million due to its limited capacity in the job market. The report estimated that by 2050 at least 280 million people will be entering the job market. "According to labor ministry data, about 1 million people enter the workforce every month in India" (Mishra, Livemint, 28 April, 2016). At any given point in time, about 30 million students are studying in higher educational institutions in India. Considering the small capacity of employment opportunities (only 11%) in the manufacturing sector, the government of India has introduced the 'Make in India' project.

The world is moving faster towards automation and machines. Human emotions and values are being replaced by machines and robots. The coming days will be based on more technology and science. The advancement of science and technology will open many job opportunities in the world, especially in India. Do you find nowadays peons to ring their bells at your doorsteps with letters from your relatives and friends? The postal letters have been replaced with electronic mail, and messages. Hence, learning computers, at least MS Word, Excel, PowerPoint, and the Internet will help students to get jobs. People are getting rich day by day in India. They are earning a lot and saving a lot too. For this purpose, they need more tax consultants. The students of Commerce will find many jobs in emerging markets, and new enterprises being constructed across the country. Banking is always a lucrative job for commerce students. The job market in the banking sector will gradually increase. The Indian banking system is the world's third-largest, and the establishment of new PSU banks will open job opportunities for our students. Actuarial Science helps people to decide what would be the insurance premium for what they purchase. Students who are studying Maths and Science of Insurance to assess risk, worth, and liabilities would find better job opportunities. Financial companies, insurance companies, and banks would require their expertise to design their investment instruments. Financial planners are in huge demand now, and they will grow day by day. Earlier, fixed deposits were the only preferred way of investment, but now the investment instruments in the market have been increased many-fold. Everyone needs expert financial advice to earn more profits from their investments, create long-term financial goals, and invest in better and safer places for their hard-earned money. Financial planners are the people who keep our money at work to pay us more profit. Hence, the job of financial planners will increase by thousands every month in India, and it might add to one million by the next two and a half decades.

For designing a website and mobile application, it needs a 'back-end developer.' The back-end developer is the core computational logic behind the software or the website. Back-end developers majorly work in C++, C#, or Java. Every IT company needs Back-end developers and this can be considered as an evergreen job. We have not heard about career counselors in our student life. But nowadays we see career counselors. Expertise in career counseling will give dividends to the students in getting employment or earning a livelihood by setting up their consultancy farms. The rapid change in the job industry increases the need for Career counselors. The US has 2.6 million counselors per 1.8 million candidates, while India has only 500 counselors per 1.5 million candidates for their future job growth. It was found out that, there is 12 times growth globally in data security jobs. It is estimated that there will be around two million cybersecurity professionals by 2047. Data scientists are the upcoming and very lucrative professions in the world. In India, there is ample scope for very high-paid jobs in this sector.

Companies are required to collect, dissect, and analyze various data to interpret and find all information to garner the businesses. Digital marketing specialists are highly in demand. Almost all small and mid-size businesses are now venturing into the online space, and it will cover almost 70-80 percent in the next two decades. Thus the need for digital marketers will continue to rise making it a sphere of great job opportunity. India is a very highly IT-driven sector; digital marketing will be the fastest-growing career in India.

Another completely new sector has been created in the Indian market. The drone has emerged as a new device in the world. India has witnessed the use of drones in agriculture, health, infrastructure management, disaster management, aerial photography, and maintaining law and order. Every year thousands of students are getting employed as drone makers and repairers. Drones are unmanned aerial vehicles mainly used for surveillance. Though drone is now confined within the defense sector, the local drone market is believed to grow by the end of 2021. Further, it is reported by the Businesswire (May 25, 2022) that, "The Global Commercial Drone Market size was estimated at US\$ 14.95 billion in 2021, US\$ 18.92 billion in 2022 and is projected to grow at a Compound Annual Growth Rate (CAGR) of 26.73% to reach US\$ 61.95 billion by 2027."

Environment management is another sector where there will be great job opportunities. India is planning to use clean energy. In the coming years, scientists in solar power, wind power, and hydel power, will find many job opportunities. In the solar power and wind power sectors, every year there will be millions of jobs. Robotic engineering is a very lucrative field. It is believed by a section of scientists that by 2030 human thoughts will be a hybrid – the combination of both biological and artificial. Robotics will be one of the top future jobs in India. Industrial robotic markets will grow about $100 billion in the next two and a half decades. It has been found that machines have started replacing humans in hazardous jobs like defense, space, nuclear plants, etc.

With the growth of economic capacity, people in India are getting obese, which has made a negative health impact. For making a perfect diet plan, better lifestyle, and awareness of health and hygiene, you personally need a dietician. The hospitals, nursing homes, and private clinics are hiring dietitians, and this opportunity will continue to increase in the days to come. The financial growth of people leads them towards a luxurious lifestyle that follows very pompous events at the time of their birthday celebration, marriage ceremony, anniversary, or corporate events. Everybody wants to make it a grand and memorable one. Who will plan and execute the plans? The event managers are doing this these days. Thousands of events are happening every day. At least two million jobs will be created in the sector. Event managers use their ability in creativity, management, communication, negotiation, and budgeting skills to craft meaningful solutions for clients. They take care of the end-to-end events, take the entire load on themselves, and thus make a good amount of money in doing so. Interior design is a growing industry. Though it was earlier a call of the rich, now it has become a need of both rich and middle-class people. Both couples being workers find little time to decorate and design the homes. Hence, they put it on the shoulders of an expert interior designer. It is a new business now. With the rise of the real estate industry, the job opportunity for interior designers has been increased. Marriage counselors are also being employed by people. The job of marriage counselors has increased, and it will increase much more in the days to come. Marriages are getting lost within a short period. The incidents of divorce are now happening a lot. Many people want to live alone out of marriage bonding. A time will come when people will sleep with artificial men and spouses. Hence, artificial rubber-made good-looking toys for young boys and girls will be in huge demand. The rubber industries and other doll-making industries will be required to produce bigger and more human-like attractive dolls.

Teaching in the traditional method will be drastically changed. The coming teachers must learn how to teach efficiently electronically. The teachers' room will be converted into a virtual classroom with a mere computer or laptop and headphones. Millions of new laptops and mobile phones will be required only in India. Hence, the manufacturers of electronic gadgets must focus on manufacturing cheap, easy-use, and light laptops, tablets, and computers for personal use as well as official use. Many more beauticians will be required in the coming days. People are being health-conscious as well as beauty-conscious. Both men and women are taking care of their skin, hair, figure, and overall beauty. More beauty parlors will be required in semi-urban and even rural areas in India. Hence, the course of beauticians will be effective and demanding in the days to come.

Further, there are sunrise opportunities for Artificial Intelligence (AI), Geospatial Systems and drones, Semiconductor and their ecosystems, space economy, genomics, and pharmaceuticals, green energy, and clean mobility systems, which hold immense potential for assisting sustainable development at a large scale and modernize the country. Hence, studying these subjects will provide ample scope for jobs. Another area of blockchain technologies is opening up, which has the potential for new possibilities. Parents and students both should keep the above things in mind before selecting a subject for higher studies in India.

22. Indian People Especially the Youths Must Realize their Power of Mind

Do you know how powerful and capable are you? You have the power of 10 elephants, 5 tigers, and 2 horses. I think you are the wisest person on this planet. You have got all the organs and senses. You are getting 3-time square meals; you have shelter over your head and have gotten a pure heart. With these divine gifts holy thoughts, and favorable circumstances you alone can take the country much ahead. So, let us pledge today. Without taking a pledge, it might not be possible to attain our goals. It is said that, plan your work and work according to your plan. Hence, come, take a pledge with me. Say, "I shall be honest. I shall be healthy. I shall be hard-working. I shall be a patriot. I shall respect my family, elders, and teachers. I shall give priority to my motherland above all things and persons. I shall think for my country first, work for my country first, and devote all my time and energy to make my country the best in the world."

With these pledges in mind, if I, you, my other friends, your friends, my children, your children, and everyone directs all our thought, spunk, time, and energy; rise early in the morning, study hard for 16-18 yours, develop our skills and engage in production and creation of public-necessary goods and instruments for comfort of people within a reasonable price, the day will not be far from achieving our goals. Every person has some specific work and duties to family, society, and nation. Students will study the whole book with sincerity to secure 100 per cent marks; teachers will teach in the class room with full preparation and due respect for his profession; farmers will cultivate their land with scientific fertilizer technological support, and developed seeds; mothers will bring up children with love and affection; fathers will take care of children, and other family members; technocrats will engage in research and innovation works; scientists and technologist will give their full to make the national dream successful; doctors and nurses will treat the patients politely and carefully, and general people must have respect for the doctors, nurses, technical staff, ambulance drivers, cleaners etc; administrators and bureaucrats will prepare innovative and full proof plans, executives will carry out the same without fear and biasness; politicians must stand by the wretched and poor people to extend their help in availing of government benefits, and cooperate with the administrators and government officers; ministers will look after the interests of the country first; ensure the professional and personal safety and security of all the employees and workers; and always work in tandem with the bureaucrats in an atmosphere of mutual respect and cooperation. In this ideal situation, when all people will work with noble thoughts and high aims, I am sure our country in no time will be a heavenly place on earth. Actually, in a country, people are the real wealth. Serving people means serving the Gods and Goddesses.

The rich urbanites and educated people are already empowered; here I am not talking about them, rather I am giving particular thrust on the needy and underprivileged people of society. Unless and until the unprivileged and poor people's development takes place, no holistic development and growth can be possible. Our country is already not less than a paradise; still, the deficits that exist in our society and environment need to be compensated with hard work, honesty, and sincerity by all the people with elevated spirits. Ethics will be the basis of our every thought process. Morality will be the principle of our work, and integrity will be the cornerstone of our actions. Hence, with a competitive attitude and innovative mind, when we start working to rebuild our country as the best place in the world and determined to take it ahead of all the contemporary advanced countries, India is sure to be reckoned as a place of best talents, the adobe of best scientists, doctors, researchers, philosophers, and of course the most attractive destination of the world pilgrims. Apart from all these values, ethics, and integrity on the physical front, India needs to be more practical and sensible in the formulation of policies, and implementation of the same for making it a center of manufacture in the globe.

23. Let Us Breed Confidence and Build National Unity

National unity is invisible, but it can be felt and realized in times of national emergency. Herbert Hoover, the 31st president of the United States, and Heinrich Bruning, the last chancellor of democratic prewar Germany, saw the common interest of all groups as the catalyst of genuine national unity. National unity cannot be formed by excluding certain groups or community people. It must be inclusive. Therefore, with the unity lessons, we must try to be united with our rivals and opponents to bring about peace and prosperity. But the task is not so easy; it is the most difficult one. Building unity amongst diverse religious and social groups is a challenging task indeed. Still, it is achievable with the good gesture and well-formulated policies by the top executive. A philosopher king with modern administrative management skills can be successful in creating a feeling of unity among all the citizens in a state. With the 'voice of love' for all, and in exceptional cases treating the miscreants and anti-nationals with an iron hand might bear desired fruit in building national unity. But the philosophy of the state will be respect and tolerance toward all communities, castes, and creeds. The adoption of the stick and the carrot policy is always helpful in building national unity and integration.

24. Duties of Indian People

Different people have different jurisdictions of work. We, the parents, students, teachers, and workmen must do our best i.e. we must perform our duties assigned by the concerned departments and for which we have been employed or engaged. There are many voluntary nature of works. All should worship the work they perform. The laborers and farmers will produce their goods sincerely and honestly; the tradesmen and businessmen will do business honestly (it is expected) and others will do their duties sincerely, honestly, and perfectly. The common people cannot amend the Constitution and bring about policy changes. It is the primary duty of the Members of Parliament, who make or amend laws for us in Parliament. Hence, they should take the initiative to bring affirmative changes in the lives and works of people in India through the formulation of sound policies. Only the ruling political masters can extend the tenure of an elected government. They must act fast. Time is limited. Another great issue is electoral reforms. The more full-proof voting system through the introduction of biometrics in EVM, and connecting Aadhar and Epic might remove proxy votes in the elections. The Election Commission of India must introduce biometrics in Electronic Voting Machines (EVMs) and check electronically the greatest electoral corruption of proxy voting and multi-voting by a single person. Online voting arrangements can be devised by the government.

In addition to all these, what we require now is to making India the world's largest trading nation of goods. But poverty is a great challenge in India; hence, the government must act to eliminate poverty to a zero level. Poverty is a curse. We must come out of this curse. We all have to take the initiative to remove the evil of poverty from the soil of India. Poverty has different dimensions. Despite that, to understand poverty, we may remember the ideas of the World Bank. According to the World Bank, poverty is pronounced as deprivation in well-being and comprises many dimensions. It includes low income and the inability to acquire basic goods and services necessary for survival with dignity. Poverty also encompasses low levels of health and education, poor access to clean water and sanitation, inadequate physical security, lack of voice, and insufficient capacity and opportunity to better one's life. Through the implementation of existing schemes poverty in India can be removed. What China did in this regard was give educational empowerment to the students. In China, around 27 percent of its workforce has a university education, which is almost the same as in Germany. India also requires spreading its university education compulsorily among workers of all categories. Without skill development, discipline education, and value education, it would not be possible to infuse a sense of patriotism, the mentality of hard work, and respect for self, family, and the country as a whole. With our combined efforts, we can increase our GDP, and our per capita income will also become at par with the other top 4 economies in the world.

India can do all these, I am sure. Indian youths are very enthusiastic, hard-working, inquisitive, and meritorious; they are the greatest wealth of this country. They can outperform any others anywhere in the world and in any field – from education to agriculture, and from industry to space research. China has been carving out a new front in global economic development and the country's next chapter in nation-building being unfolded through a wave of funding in the massive global infrastructure project, the Belt and Road Initiative. The so-called new Silk Road aims to connect almost half the world's population and one-fifth of global GDP, setting up trade and investment links that stretch across the world. If China, our neighbor, and an old friend, can perform it perfectly, why should India be left behind? India is very adaptive and enthusiastic to learn from anywhere in the world. With the above lessons, India will move fast towards the attainment of its national goal of Viksit Bharat.

Concluding Remarks

In conclusion, I would like to indicate that without more advanced technological innovation and its implementation, skill development, digital knowledge, export quality production of goods, foreign direct investment, popular acceptance of STEM subjects, proper and scientific utilization of both man-power and natural resources, Indian Prime Minister's vision of a Viksit Bharat would be difficult to materialize. The Government of India and the majority of state governments have already realized this fact and taken a few good measures through policy reform and implementation in their respective states, but the measures and momentum are not satisfactory. I like to ask a simple question to my student brothers and sisters: if American, Chinese, Israeli, or Japanese students learn technical know-how why don't you learn the same and excel them? If the USA, China, Japan, and Israel can do fundamental research, invent and sell the world's best technology, develop infrastructure, and adopt "competition" as the secret of success in life, we too have to do the same. As soon as you complete reading this book, immediately take an oath to "Do or Die" for the growth and development of the nation. If the schools do not teach, I call every young person to start learning and developing skills from Class VI with individual initiative. Parents and teachers should encourage and help as per their capacity. It seems to me that, political parties and ministers can do little to transform the lot of a country; it is the general people particularly the youths and poor villagers are the main force behind the development of a nation. The duty of political leaders is to formulate policy, make aware the citizens about the availability of the services and motivate the people through their personal lives, words, and actions. But the real work - the hard work - will have to be performed by the young citizens of this country.

Therefore, I call upon my fellow young people particularly the students, rural boys and girls, and disadvantaged people, who are full of vigor and vitality. I also urge the parents and senior members of society to come forward with a liberal heart and open mind to extend all your energy, experience, money, and wealth for the welfare and betterment of the people especially the unprivileged people. They are the real future of India. They are the future-makers of India. Remember, your children's development means your own welfare, your family's welfare, and ultimately the country's welfare and development. Along with general school education, a student must carry on technical education or skill development training. Those who are very meritorious will continue specialized education, may it be in medical science, engineering, technology, management, administration, or any other professional field. But those who are less meritorious and have more interest in any technical work should undertake training and start work from the age of 19 to 23 even before that age with the attainment of vocational training. The traditional job market is getting squeezed day by day, so non-traditional sectors must be explored from school days, and don't sit idle. Complete your study first, then join in the economic activity and then start earning money without wasting time. Or you may engage in economic activity along with your studies to help yourself, your family, your society, and ultimately the country. Many students study and work together. Without hard work, sincerity and honesty, we could not stand in life. Remember there is no alternative to hard work. The people in the USA spend more money on education and investment. They spend more time studying, learning, and exploring. So let's work hard, learn specialized skills, and become economically stronger. When we are economically stronger, then our country is also economically stronger. Understand this truth: you are the most precious jewel of our country. Always remember this word – "I am the most precious jewel of my family, society, and ultimately the country." After getting up from bed and before going to bed regularly say this sentence. This thought will make you a great person. And with the greatness and development of yourself; the development, well being, and growth of our society, locality, and the country as a whole will be accomplished. I see in my mind's eyes that the day is not far when India will achieve the goal of a Viksit Bharat and celebrate the day with great pomp and glory. *Jai Hind. Vande Mataram.*

References:

1. Vivekananda, S. (2013). Vivekananda: His Call to the Nation. *Kolkata: Advaita Ashrama.*

2. Vivekananda, S. (2013). Vivekananda: His Call to the Nation. *Kolkata: Advaita Ashrama. p. 60.*

3. Mill, J. & Hayman, W. (1848). *The History of British India* (Vol. 1). Library of the Leland Stanford Jr. University.

4. Vivekananda, S. (2013). Vivekananda: His Call to the Nation. *Kolkata: Advaita Ashrama. p. 49.*

5. Yogananda, P. (1946). *Autobiography of a Yogi.* The Philosophical Library.

6. Eriksson, Daniel, Corruption Perceptions Index, *Transparency International*, 2022.

7. Johnson, D. E., Jennifer, D.P., Moroney, R. C., Markel, M. W., Smallman, L. and Spirtas, M. Preparing and Training for the Full Spectrum of Military Challenges: Insights from the Experiences of China, France, the United Kingdom, India, and Israel', Rand Corporation. (2009). In *Preparing and Training for the Full Spectrum of Military Challenges* (1st ed.).

8. Singh, A. (2023, August 14). India's maritime power is growing, but challenges loom. *Observer Research Foundation.*

9. The Top 10 Largest Economies in the World in 2025.(2024, November 20). *FocusEconomies.*

10. India's skill gap is stealing futures: How right education cackle the job crisis. (2024, November 1). *India Today.*

11. Chourasiya, A. (2023, April). Education and Skills Development: The Role of Education and Skills Development in Enhancing Employability in India. *Researchgate.*

12. BusinessLine. (2021, January 21).

13. Nandini, S.G. (2020, October 14). India will be a global investment hotspot, survey finds. *The Times of India.*

14. India Can Be A Lower Cost Producer Than China If Policies Allow: Maruti Suzuki Chairman. (2020, November 10). *Business World.*

15. Smaller, cheaper vehicles take centre stage amid economic slowdown. (2020, October 12). *Business Standard.*

16. Goyal, M. (2010, November 23). India can beat China in Manufacturing: Jeff Sinclair. *The Economic Times.*

17. Bhutani, C. (2023, June 26). Government plans to ramp up highway construction to 40km/day. *Business Today,* 26 June, 2023.

18. Bhddhavarapu, R. (2022, May 26). India wants to be the 'pharmacy of the world.' But first, it must wean itself from China. *CNBC.*

19. Hawking, S. (2018). Brief Answers to the Big Questions. *John Murray.*

20. Irudaya, R.E.F., Appadurai, M. and Thiyaharajan, D. (2020). *Hybrid Electric Vehicle.* Shanlax Publications.

21. Dadhich, B.S. (2022, April). Artificial Intelligence in Finance Sector. Yojana, *66*(4), p. 31.

22. Report: State Of Artificial Intelligence in India 2021 - By AIM & TAMPI. (2021, October 18). *Analytics India Magazine.*

23. Hawking, S. (2018). *Brief Answers to the Big Questions.* John Murray.

24. Banerjee, C. (2021, July 30). Switching to renewable energy will add 5 lakh jobs in India by 2050,' finds study. *The Times of India.*

25. Mishra, A.R. (2016, April 28). India to see severe shortage of jobs in the next 35 years. *Livemint.* https://www.livemint.com/Politics

26. businesswire. (2022, May 25).

BIBLIOGRAPHY

Abou-Jaoude, A.L. (2016, November). A Pure Invention: Japan, Impression, and the West, 1853-1906. *The History Teacher*, 50(1). https://www.jstor.org/stable/44504454.

About 82 per cent decline in triple talaq cases since law enacted by Modi govt: Mukhtar Abbas Naqvi. (2020, July 22). *The Economic Times.*

Act East Policy 2015. (2015, December 23). Press Information Bureau.

Adrian, B. (2020). How Israel Became A Technology Start Up Nation. *Forbes..*

Amartya Sen: A More Human Theory of Development. (2004, December 6). *Asia Society.*

A. Appadorai quoted in Batria, P. (n.d.). *India's Foreign Policy.* Nath Publishing House.

Bakshi, G.D. (2016). *Bose An Indian Samurai: Netaji and the INA - A Military Assessment.* K.W. Publishers Pvt. Ltd.

Banerjee, C. (2021, July 30). Switching to renewable energy will add 5 lakh jobs in India by 2050,' finds study. *The Times of India.*

Barnett, B. & Duvall, R. (2005). Power in International Politics. International Organization, 59(1),

Basak, S. (2022, October 31). Modi Madness Among Indian Diaspora In The West Puts Spotlight On India Too. *Outlook.*

Becker, S. O., Mergele, L., and Woessmann, L. (2020, Spring). The Separation and Reunification of Germany. *Journal of Economic Perspectives,* 34(2).

Benjamin, G.R. (1997). *Education in Japanese Society. in Japanese Lessons: A Year in a Japanese School Through the Eyes of An American Anthropologist and Her Children.* NYU Press.

"Better Policies" Series Germany Keeping the Edge: Competitiveness for Inclusive Growth. (2014, February). *OECD Report.*

Beveridge, H. (1867). *A Comprehensive History of India, Civil, Military and Social from the First Landing of the English, to the Suppression of Sepoy Revolt; including An Outline of the Early History of Hindoostan* (Vol. 1). Blackie and Son.

Bhattacharya, N. (2023, August 23). Chandrayaan – 3: what to know about India's moon landing mission. *Reuters.*

Bhattacharjee, S. (2024, December 7)). PM Modi praises BAPS volunteers, urges efforts to make India a developed nation by 2047. *India TV.*

Bhutani, C. (2023, June 26). Government plans to ramp up highway construction to 40km/day. *Business Today.*

Birkland, Thomas A. (2011). *An Introduction to the Policy Process: Theories, Concepts and Methods of Public Policy Making. Third Edition*, Routledge.

Blass, N. (2018). The Israeli Education System: An Overview, Taub Center: For Social Policy Studies in Israel.

Bocca, R. (1997, May 21). India facing record power shortfall for June, and other top energy stories this month. *World Economic Forum.*

Bombing of Hiroshima and Nagasaki. (2023, April 18). *History.com editors.*

BrahMos. (2023, October 24). *Aerospace.*

British Prime Minister David Cameron's Top Quotes at Wembley Stadium. (2015, November 13). *The Times of India.*

Brooks, D. (2002, June 9). Why the US Will Always be Rich. *The New York Times Magazine.*

Buddhavarapu, R. (2022, May 26). India wants to be the 'pharmacy of the world.' But first, it must wean itself from China. *CNBC.*

BusinessLine. (2021, January 21).

Businesswire. (2022, May 25).

Cabinet approves foreign investment of up to Rs. 9589 crore in M/S Suven Pharmaceuticals Limited. (2023, September 13). *PIB.*

Carlisle, M. (2021, August 8). Here's How Many Medals Every Country Won at the Tokyo Summer Olympics. *Time.*

Celebrating GST Day: A Milestone in Economic Reform. (2024, June 28). Press Information Bureau, Government of India.

Chakraborty, A. (2024, October 22). "Even Without A Translator": Putin On How Well PM Modi Understands Him. *NDTV World News*, Kazan, Russia.

Chari, P.R. (1976). Non-Alignment and International Security. *India International Centre Quarterly, 3*(3).

Chitravanshi, R. (2023, July 5). FDI inflows into India rise 10%, outflows shrink 16% in 2022: Unctad. *Business Standard.*

Chaturvedi, A. (2021, August 5). 2 years of abrogation of Article 370: 5 big changes in Jammu and Kashmir. *The Hindustan Times.*

Cherian, J. (2021, April 11). India now a major defence partner for the USA as gangs up on China. *Frontline.*

Chourasiya, A. (2023, April). Education and Skills Development: The Role of Education and Skills Development in Enhancing Employability in India. *Researchgate.*

Chengappa R. (1991, September, 30). PM in Germany: Striking the right note. *India Today.*

Chikermane, G. (2018, July 27). Policies that Shaped India, 1947-2017: Independence to $2.5 Trillion. Observer Research Foundation.

Citizens real force behind march towards 'Viksit Bharat 2047': PM. (2024, December 8). *The Tribune.*

Clapson, M. (2019). *The Blitz Companion: Aerial Warfare, Civilians and the City since 1911.* University of Westminster Press.

Cochran, et al. (1999). *American Public Policy: An Introduction.* 6th ed. St. Martin's Press.

Collins, M. (2023). Red carpets and yellow yoga mats: Five moments from Indian PM Modi's state visit. *USA Today.*

Dadhich, B.S. (2022, April). Artificial Intelligence in Finance Sector. Yojana, *66*(4).

Dadhich, B.S. (2023, May). AI Chatbots: Future and Challenges. Yojana, *Yojana, 67*(5).

Das, K. (2023, March 6). India's per capita income doubles, but does not mean you are richer. *India Today.*

Deka, K. (2019, December 23). Everything you wanted to know about the CAA and NRC. *India Today.*

Demands from Grants. (2021-22 to 2022-23). *Ministry of Rural Development.*

Department of Commerce. (2023, April 13). *India's Foreign Trade.* Ministry of Commerce and Industry, Government of India.

Department of Financial Services. (N/D). Government of India, Pradhan Mantri Jan-Dhan Yojana.

Dixit, P. (2023, July 9). Ram temple work in full swing, completion nears. *The Hindustan Times.*

Dobbins, J., Poole, M.A., Long, A. and Runkle, B. (n.d.). After the War: Nation-Building from FDR to George W. Bush. In *Post-World War II Nation-Building: Germany and Japan,* RAND corporation.

Drucker, P. F. (1981, January). Behind Japan's Success. *Harvard Business Review.*

Dwivedi, Y.K. & Kar, A.K. (2023, May). Transforming Technology. *Yojana, 67*(5).

Dye, Thomas R. (1992). *Understanding Public Policy.* 7th ed. Prentice-Hall.

Ease of doing business: Govt. working on to reduce compliance issues. (2022, July 6). *The Economic Times.*

Embree, T.E. (1964). *1857 in India: Mutiny or War of Independence?* Columbia University.

Eriksson, Daniel, Corruption Perceptions Index, *Transparency International*, 2022.

Evelyn, C. & Nee, L.Y. (2021, January 31). New chart shows China could overtake the US as the world's largest economy earlier than expected. *CNBC.*

Explained | What is 'Viksit Bharat 2047' and what does it aim to achieve? (2024, March 4). *Deccan Herald.*

Factsheets: How much crude oil does the EU still import from Russia? (2022, September 20). *Reuters.*

Feldstein, M.S. (2017, April 20). Why the US is Still Richer Than Every Other Large Country. *Harvard Business School.*

Fetscherin, M. (2010, July). The determinants and measurement of a country brand: the country brand strength index. *International Marketing Review.*

Frayer, L. (2023, February 23). A year into the Ukraine war, the world's biggest democracy still won't condemn Russia. *NPR.*

From Local to Global: How India's Digital Payment Revolution is Inspiring the World. (2023, March 19). *Press Information Bureau*, Ministry of Information & Broadcasting, Government of India.

Fukui, & Lakatos. (2012). cited by Casella, B., Borga, M., and Wacker. (2023, June). K. M. Measuring Multinational Production with Foreign Direct Investment Statistics: Recent Trends, Challenges, and Developments. *International Monetary Fund, Working Papers.*

Gandhi, M. (1942). *Non-Violence in Peace and War.* Navajivan Publishing House.

Garg, S. (2022, April). Digital Identity. *Yojana*, 66(4).

Gaurav, K. (2022, November 3). No matter how powerful...' PM Modi's firm message on corruption. *The Hindustan Times.*

GDP of India: Current and historical growth rate, India's rank in the world. (2024, July 17). *Forbes India.*

"GDP (Current US$) - Japan", World Bank. Quoted by Gerstel, Dylan, and Goodman, Matthew P. (2020). In *Japan: Industrial Policy and the Economic Miracle.* Center for Strategic and International Studies (CSIS).

Gershon, L. (2016, November 2). The Social Responsibility of American Industrialists. *Jstor Daily.*

Ghosh, D. (2022, April). Fintech Revolution. *Yojana*, 66(4).

Gilboy, G.J. & Heginbotham, E. (Summer 2013). Quoted by Bronson Pervical (2013). *China, India and the United States: Tempered Rivalries in Asia.* S. Rajaram School of International Studies.

Goldberg, P. (2020). Countless Americans have been influenced by Swami Vivekananda, even if many don't know who he is. *Hindu American Foundation.*

Golden devotion: Tirumala gets record 130 kg yellow metal in July. (2019, September 1). *The Times of India.*

Goyel, A. (2022). An Insight into India's Foreign Policy. *Indian Journal of Law and Legal Research*, 4(2).

Grosier, A. (translator). (1788). *A General Description of China, Containing the Topography of the Fifteen Provinces Which Compose This Vast Empire, That of Tartary, the Isles, and Other Tributary Countries* (Vol. II). J. Robinson.

Gupta, A. (2006). India's Soft Power. *Indian Foreign Affairs Journal*, 1(1).

Gupta, R. & Shah, S. (2023, May). Potential of India's EdTech Sector. *Yojana.* 67(5).

Guzzine, S. (2009). On the measure of power and the power of measure in International Relations. Danish Institute for International Studies, DIIS. Working Paper January.

Hart, J. (1976). Three approaches to the measurement of power in international relations. *International Organization, 30*(2).

Hawking, S. (2018). *Brief Answers to the Big Questions.* John Murray.

Hemmings, J. (2020, September 1). The Evolution of the U.S. Alliance System in The Indo-Pacific Since the Cold War's End. In *Hindsight, Insight, Foresight: Thinking About Security in the Indo-Pacific.*

Hicks, N. and Streeten, P. (1979). *Indicators of Development: The Search for a Basic Needs Yardshick.* World Bank Reprint Series: Number 104.

Holsti, K.J. (1964). The Concept of Power in the Study of International Relations. *Background, 7*(4).

Imperial Gazetteer of India, The Indian Empire VOL. IV, Administrative, Oxford: At the Clarendon Press, 1909.

"INDIAN FOREIGN POLICY." (1983). *Pakistan Horizon*, vol. 36, no. 2, JSTOR,

India at 75: all Villages Electrified. (2022, August 13). *The Times of India.*

India's Foreign Trade. (2023, April 13). Department of Commerce. Ministry of Commerce and Industry, Government of India.

India's GDP sees sharp growth trajectory; a look at the progress from 1947 to 2023. (2024, August 18). *The Financial Express.*

India's skill gap is stealing futures: How right education cackle the job crisis. (2024, November 1). *India Today.*

India Skills Report 2023: Indian employable talent leaps from 46.2% to 50.3%. (2022, December 29). *The Economic Times.*

International Monetary Fund. (2023, October 16). https://www.imf.org/external/datamapper/

Irudaya, R.E.F., Appadurai, M. and Thiyaharajan, D. (2020). *Hybrid Electric Vehicle.* Shanlax Publications.

Jacob, Happymon. (2323, April 4). Why India downplays China's Border Threat. *FP.*

Jaffe, E. & Nebenzahl, D. (2001). National Image and Competitive Advantage: The Theory and Practice of Country-of-Origin Effect, Copenhagen Business School Press, Copenhagen. Quoted by Fetscherin, M. (2010, July). The determinants and measurement of a country brand: the country brand strength index. *International Marketing Review.*

Jain, D.K. (2014). India's Foreign Policy, Ministry of External Affairs (GOI). In Goyal, A. (2022). *An Insight into India's Foreign Policy. Indian Journal of Law and Legal Research,* 4(2), pp. 219-235. https://mea.gov.in/indian-foreign-policy.htm.

Jain, J. (2022, May 26). 8 years of Modi government: How PM Modi radically transformed India's foreign policy. *OpIndia.*

Jain, S. (2023, June 12). *Forbes India.*

Jana, P. & Franke, U.E. 2020). *The Big Engine That Might: How France and Germany Can Build a Geopolitical Europe.* European Council of Foreign Relations.

Jayakumar, PB, & Vinaykumar, Ravi. (2021, April 14). How much vaccines can India make? *India Today.*

Jha, G. (1993, July-December). Seventy Fourth Constitutional Amendment and the Empowerment of Municipal Government: A Critique in Urban India. *A journal of the National Institute of Urban Affairs,* XIII(2).

Johnson, D. E. et al. (2009). In *Preparing and Training for the Full Spectrum of Military Challenges* (1st. ed.). (n.d.). Preparing and Training for the Full Spectrum of Military Challenges: Insights from the Experiences of China, France, the United Kingdom, India, and Israel. Rand Corporation.

Joseph, S.V. & Mucheli. (2024, March 2). R.D. *Economic and Political Weekly*. Vol. 59, Issue No. 9.

Kapur, D. & Mehta, B.P. (2006, January). *The Indian Parliament as an Institution of Accountability.* United Nations Research Institute for Social Development.

Kato, T. (1953). *India Through Japanese Eyes.* The Indo-Japanese Association.

Kitchen, N. (2012). India: Next Superpower? *LSE IDEAS SPECIAL REPORT.*

Kosambi, D.D. (1956). *An Introduction to the Study of Indian History.* Popular Prakashan.

193. Kumar, K. P. (2012). *The Teachings of Kapila* (2nd ed.). Dhanishta.

Kumar, M. (1969). Theoretical Aspects of International Politics. *JSTOR*, 25(4).

Lakshman, S. (2024, October 10). Donald Trump praises PM Modi, says he is the 'nicest human being' but can also be a 'total killer.' *The Hindu.*

Lal, D. (1967). Indian Foreign Policy, 1947-64. *Economic and Political Weekly*, 2(19).

Landes, D.S. (1990, May 2). Why are We So Rich and They So Poor? *The American Economic Review, 80(2).*

List of ISRO's space missions: From Aryabhatta to Chandrayan. (2024, August 23). *The Times of India.*

Literacy Rate in India 2023. (n.d.). *The Global Statistics.*

Lyon, P. (1963). *Neutralism.* Oxford University Press.

Md Zafar Alam Bhuniyan, MZA. (2019, June). The miracle of Japanese Economy after the Second World War (WW2), *Researchgate.*

M. Prothero, M., and Vidyabhusana, S.M. (1915). *History of India down the end of the reign of*

Queen Victoria. Macmillan.

Madhukalya, A. (2023, April 18). India has 3rd-highest number of unicorns, gazelles: Hurun's Global Unicorn Index 2023. *bt Upstart.*

Malone, D.M. (2011). Soft Power in Indian Foreign Policy. *Economic and Political Weekly, 46(36).*

Mandal, K.C. (2010). *Empowerment of Women and Panchayati Raj: Experiences from West Bengal.* Levant Books.

Mandal, K. (2024). How Can India Become a Superpower by 2047: A *Vision.* Ukiyoto Publishing.

Mandelbaum, M. (2014, May 21). The two things India can learn from China. World Economic Forum.

Mannathukkaren, N. (2024, November 6). On India-Canada diplomatic relations Explained. *The Hindu*.

Manoj, C.G. (2023, September 19). Handing fire for 27 years: How Women Reservation Bill kept lapsing through its tumultuous journey. *The Indian Express*.

Measures to combat corruption. (2021, February 10). Ministry of Personnel, Public Grievances and Pensions, Government of India posted, *PIB*.

Mehta, D. (2015). The Ayodhya dispute: The absent mosque, state of emergency and the jural deity. *Journal of Material Culture*.

Merchant, Minhaz. (2013, November 9). Congress: Why 2004 was a false dawn. *The Economic Times*.

Meyer, J.M (2016, December 19). The Royal Indian Navy Mutiny of 1946: Nationalist Competition and Civil-Military Relations in Postwar India. *The Journal of Imperial and Commonwealth History*.

Mihik, T. (2020). *Japan after Fukushima in Re-imagining Japan after Jukushima*. ANU Press.

Mill, J.S. (1859). *On Liberty* (3rd ed.). Longman, Green, Longman, Roberts & Green.

Mill, J. & Hayman, W. (1848). *The History of British India* (Vol. 1). Library of the Leland Stanford.

Ministry of Agriculture and Farmers Welfare. (2023, March 21). *Government of India*.

Ministry of Commerce and Industry. (2022, September 22). *Make in India completes 8 years: annual FDI doubles to USD 83 billion*. Government of India.

Ministry of Ayush. (N/D). Government of India.

Ministry of Commerce and Industry. (2024, February 7). Government of India.

Ministry of Commerce and Industry (2024, December 16). Department of Commerce, Government of India, Press Information Bureau.

Ministry of External Affairs, Government of India. (2024, November, 18). Rio de Janeiro.

Ministry of Labor and Employment. (2023, February 13). Government of India, Press Information Bureau.

Ministry of Petroleum and Natural Gas. (N/D) Government of India.

Ministry of Health and Family Welfare, Govt. of India. (2023, October 30).

Ministry of Foreign Affairs. (2021). MOFA.

Ministry of Micro, Small and Medium Enterprises. (2023, July 31). *Govt. of India.*

Mishra, A.R. (2016, April 28). India to see severe shortage of jobs in the next 35 years. *Livemint.* https://www.livemint.com/Politics

Mishra, V. (2023, January 13). India's Foreign Policy in 2022: A Year in Review. *South Asian Voices.*

Modi, N. (2024, December 7). Video Lecture, Gujarat.

260. Mohammad Ali; from the Presidential Address, I.N.C. Session. (1923). [Status update].

Morgenthau, H. J. (1948). *Politics among Nations: the Struggle for Power and Peace.* Alfred A. Knopf.

Murty, R. N. (2023, August 15). India's R&D needs a boost. *The Hindu Businessline.*

Mustafa, F. (2019, August 6). Explained: What are Articles 370 and 35A? *The Indian Express.*

My Gov. (2022). *PM's 3 Day Visit to Europe – Part I.*

Nandini, S.G. (2020, October 14). India will be a global investment hotspot, survey finds. *The Times of India.*

Narendra Modi Calls Himself Pradhan Sevak in his Maiden Independence Day Speech. (2014, August 15). *The Indian Express.*

National Education Policy 2020. (2020).Government of India.

National Family Health Survey (NFHS - 5) 2019-21, Compendium of Fact Sheets. (n.d.). *Ministry of Health & Family Welfare, Government of India.*

National Quantum Mission. (2023, May). *Yojana.* 67(5).

Nayyar, A. & Singh, I. (2018). A Comprehensive Analysis of Goods and Services Tax (GST) in India. *Indian Journal of Finance*, Vol. 2.

'Non-alignment' was coined by Nehru in 1954. (2006, September, 18). *The Times of India.*

Nye, J. (1990). cited by David M. Malone. (2011). Soft Power in Indian Foreign Policy, 46(36), p. 35. *Economic and Political Weekly.*

Okuno-Fujiwara, M. (1991). Quoted by Gerstel, Dylan, and Goodman, Matthew P. In *Japan: Industrial Policy and the Economic Miracle.* Center for Strategic and International Studies (CSIS), 2020.

"Pass Impasse," *The Economist*, February 4, 2010. Quoted in Lyod, R. (2010, May 20). The India-China Relationship: A Tempered Rivalry? Policy

Analysis 61. *Australian Strategic Policy Institute*.

Pattanayak, B. (2019, May 20). In gold we trust: India's household gold reserves valued at over 40% of GDP. *Financial Express*.

Pawar, A. (2023, August 23). India creates new research funding agency, but doubts linger. *Science*.

Pervical, B. (2013). *China, India and the United States: Tempered Rivalries in Asia*. S. Rajaram School of International Studies.

Peters, B. Guy (1999). *American Public Policy: Promise and Performance*. Chappaqua.

PM Modi and his British counterpart Rishi Sunak agreed on 'enduring importance' of UK-India relationship. (2022, November 16). *The Economic Times*.

Population of India. (2023, October 18). *Worldometer*.

Porecha, M. (2020, June 19). 11% of India's medical devices imports are from China. *Businessline*.

Pouchpadass, E. *My Truth: Indira Gandhi*. New Delhi: Vision Books, 1981.

Powell, B. (n.d). *Japan, The Library of Economics and Liberty*.

Power Sector at a Glance. (N/D). Ministry of Power, Government of India.

Pradhan, R.G., (1930). *India's Struggle for Swaraj* (1st ed.). *G.A. Natesan & Co., Publishers*.

Pradhan, S.D. (2022, January 9). Key features of Indian Foreign policy under PM Modi. *Times of India*.

Precedence Research Report. (2022, May). https://www.precedenceresearch.com/medical-devices-market

Press Information Bureau. (2021, November 30). Government of India, Ministry of Agriculture and Farmers Welfare.

Press Information Bureau. (2022, July 20). *Year End Review-2022: Ministry of Road Transport and Highways*. Government of India.

Press Information Bureau. (2023, December 11). Government of India.

Prime Minister Internship Scheme 2024: Who is eligible, last date to register, how to enrol for PM Internship Scheme (PMIS) online. (2024, November 8). *The Economic Times*.

PRS Legislative Research. (n.d.). *Ministry of Law and Justice, Government of India*.

Purfield, C & Schiff, J.A. (2006). How Can India Attract More Foreign Direct Investment? *IMF eLibrary*.

Rae, J. (1891). *Contemporary Socialism*. Charls Scribner's Sons.

Rajagopal, K. (2023, August 28). Article 35A took away fundamental rights while giving special rights to permanent residents of J&K, says CJI. *The Hindu.*

Rasheed, M. F. (1995). The Concept of Power in International Relations. *Pakistan Horizon, 48(1).*

Rapson, E.J. (1914). *Ancient India: From the Earliest Times to the First Century A.D.* Cambridge: at the University Press.

Rathore, M. (2023, July 10). Gender ratio in India 2018-2020, by region. *Statista.*

Reddy, N. D. (2017, November 8). Demonetization, corruption and black money. *The Front Line.*

Report: State Of Artificial Intelligence in India 2021 - By AIM & TAMPI. (2021, October 18). *Analytics India Magazine.*

Report on "Electronics: Powering India's Participation in Global Value Chains. (2024, July 18). *Press Information Bureau.*

Research and Development. (2023, March 13). *White House.*

Robbins, L. (1966). In Semasinghe, W.M. (2020, January). Development, what does it mean? *Acta Politica Polonica*, pp. 53-54.

Robert E. Wright, R.E. (2020, January 30). How America Became Rich, According to a Historian in 1802. *The Daily Economy.*

Roy Chaudhury, D. (2014, February, 23). India's foreign policy: With landmark deals, Manmohan Singh government promised much, delivered little. *The Economic Times.*

Roy Choudhury, S., Thankachan, S., and Bakshi, P. (eds). *Indio-Japan Relations@ 70: Building Beyond Bilateral.* K.W. Publishers Pvt. Lte.

Russian arms supplies to India amounts to $13 bln in past 5 years. (2023, February 13). *The Economic Times.*

Saggi, P.D. (ed.). (1954). *A Nation's Homage, Life and Work of Netaji Subhas Chandra Bose.* Overseas Publishing House.

Samanta, D. (2020, March 22). Infrastructure Development. *Kurukshetra.*

Sarkar, B. (2013, December). India's Foreign Policy Under the Prime Minister of Dr. Manmohan Singh. *International Journal of Scientific Research,* Vol. 2, Issue 12.

Sarkar, P. (2024, December 5). Bangladesh mission in India attacked: Why are ties in freefall? *Al Jazeera.*

Saxena, S. (2014). *Edicts of Ashoka - Rock Edict VI,* Puratattva.

Science, Technology, and Innovation Policy (STIP). (2020, December). Government of India, Ministry of Science & Technology, Department of

Science and Technology.

Semasinghe, W.M. (2020, January). Development, what does it mean? *Acta Politica Polonica*.

Sengupta, S., Munjal, T., Dhuria, A., and Vaish, A. (2020, May). A Study of Goods and Services Tax (GST) [Conference Paper].

Sharma, AK, and Kumar, J. (2015 Dec.). Shashi Tharoor's Reasons of State: A Study of Indira Gandhi's Foreign Policy." *The Literary Herald*, Vol. 1, Issue 3.

Sharma, K. (2017, June 30). India's traders protest in the hours before GST. *Nikkei Asia*.

Sharma, R., (2023, August 5). Arjun Tank: India Pitches Its 'Hunter-Killer' Arjun MBT To African Countries As Indian Army Places Its Last Order. *The Eurasian Times*.

Sharma, S.R. (1947). *Ancient Indian History and Culture*. Hind Kitabs Limited.

Sealy, C. (2023, September 2003). Healthy competition. *materialstoday*, Elsevier Ltd.

Sharma, Ashutosh. (2023, February 10). Electrification still a challenge in rural India, *Frontline*.

Sharma, H.L. (2022, March). Strengthening Rural Economy. *Kurukshetra*, 70(5).

Shaw, K.M. (2023, January 18). Budget 2023 can boost India's march to global leadership in research & innovation. *The Times of India*.

Singh, A. (2023, August 14). India's maritime power is growing, but challenges loom. *Observer Research Foundation*.

Singh, M.K. (2020). From Civilizational to Strategic Partnership: Waling the Road. In Roy Choudhury, S., Thankachan, S., & Bakshi, P. (eds). *Indio-Japan Relations@ 70: Building Beyond Bilateral*. (p. 26). K.W. Publishers Pvt. Lte.

Singh, R. (2023, January 27). The Wonder that is India. *The Times of India*.

Smaller, cheaper vehicles take centre stage amid economic slowdown. (2020, October 12). *Business Standard*.

Smriti Sawkar was quoted. (2022). "Champion of the Third World: Indira Gandhi and the Spectacle of the 1983 NAM Summit." In Commonwealth and Comparative Politics, Vol. 60, Issue 4, 23 Nov.

Solomon, S. (2018, April 18). From 1950s rationing to modern high-tech boom: Israel's economic success story, *The Times of Israel*.

Srinivas, I. (2022, April). Fintech Beyond Boundaries. *Yojana*, 66(4).

Stevenson, H.W. (1991, September). *Japanese Elementary School Education, in The Elementary School Journal.* The University of Chicago Press.

Stopdan, P. (2020). *India and Central Asia: The Strategic Dimension.* K.W. Publishers Private Limited.

Suneja, K. (2021, September 18). No irregularities found in World Bank's 'Doing Business' data on India. *The Economic Times.*

Sustainable Development Goals, the United Nations.

Suzuki, Tessa Morris. Quoted in Takada, M. (1999, March 23). Japan's Economic Miracle: Underlying Factors and Strategies for the Growth, IR 163, Professor Wylie.

399. Swami, T. (2022, August 22). *Ramanujacharya - the Vashishtadvaita Philosophy, DNA of Hinduism.* Sri Ramakrishna Math.

Takada, M. (1999, March 23). Japan's Economic Miracle: Underlying Factors and Strategies for the Growth, IR 163, Professor Wylie.

10 Years of Make in India. (2024, September 25). Ministry of Commerce & Industry, Press Information Bureau.

Tharoor, S. (2012). India as a Soft Power. India International Centre Quarterly, *38*(3/4), p. 330.

The Economic Survey 2022-23. (2023). Ministry of Finance. Government of India.

The Factories (Amendment) Act, 2016.

The Formulation And Development of Public Policies in India. (2023, March 28). Indian School of Public Policy.

The Muslim Women (Protection of Rights on Marriage) Act, 2019, cited by Prime Minister during Independence Day Speech. (2019, August 15). *Ministry of Information and Broadcasting, Government of India.*

The World Bank data (GDP growth (annual % - India, China). (n.d.). https://data.worldbank.org/

The World Bank. (2023, April 4). *Indian Economy Continues to Show Resilience Amid Global Uncertainties.*

Top 10 largest economies in the world. (2022, April 13). *Business Insider India.*

Tourangbam, M. (2022, March 14).The New Geometry of India's Foreign Policy. *The Diplomat.*

Transforming India into a Global Manufacturing Powerhouse. (2024, September 10). Press Information Bureau, Ministry of Commerce and Industry, Government of India.

Tripathi, S. (2020, June 11). PM Modi to steer India's space dreams: What lies ahead in Modi 3.0? *India Today*.

Ullekh, N.P. (2012, September 24). $10 bn business: How Israel became India's most important partner in arms bazaar. *The Economic Times*.

UN Document: Development. (1997, October 15). Agenda for Development, *The United National General Assembly*.

Unicorns in India: List of startup companies with unicorn status in 2024. (2020, August 22). Forbes India.

US has world's most powerful military, Pak in 7th place, Bhutan weakest. Is India in top 10? LIST. (2023, July 10). *The Hindustan Times*.

U.S. Relations with India. (2022, July 18). U.S. Department of State.

Verma, D.P. (1989). Jawaharlal Nehru: Panchsheel and India's Constitutional Vision of International Order. *India Quarterly*, 45(4), 304.

Vivekananda, S. (2013). *Vivekananda: His Call to the Nation* (a compilation). Advaita Ashram.

Vivekananda, S. (1908). *A Study of Religion*. The Ramkrishna Mission.

What is Article 35A? (2023, October 8). *Business Standard*.

What is a soft landing, why did India send Chandrayaan – 3 to the Moon's south pole and what happened after the landing was accomplished? We explain. (2023, August 29). *The Indian Express*.

Why the United States dominates the Nobels. (2021, October 12). *The Deccan Herald*.

Will Yakowicz, W. (2019, October 8). How America's Rich Get So Rich. *Forbes*.

World Economic Outlook: Navigating Global Divergences, International Monetary Fund. (2023, October). *Washington DC*.

8 World Leaders who got Narendra Modi's invitation in swearing-in. (2014, May 23). *The Times of India*.

Year Ender 2020: From Boycotting Brands to Apps: India's Response to China Post Galwan Valley Attack. (2020, December 25). *ABP News Bureau*.

Yogananda, P. (1946). *Autobiography of a Yogi*. The Philosophical Library.

Zhou, W. (2014, Winter). Comparing the Economic Growth of China and India: Current Situation, Problems, and Prospects. *World Review of Political Economy*, 5(4).

Glossary

Atithi Devo Bhavo - Guests are equivalent to God
Atmanirbhar Bharat Abhiyan - Self-reliant India Campaign
Azadi Ki Amrit Mahotsab - 75th Anniversary festival of India's Independence
Beti Bachao Beti Padhao - Save girls and educate girls
Bharat - India
Bharat ko Janiye - Know India
Dharma - Duty
Ghar Sabha - Home meeting
Karma yogis - Workaholics
Karsevaks - Religious workers
Karyakars - Volunteers
Mantra - Secret of success
Matsanaya - Laissez-faire
Panchayati Raj - Rural local government system
Pradhan Sevak - Principal Servant
Rajya Sabha - The Upper House of the Indian Parliament
Sankalp - Oath
Sanstha - Organization
Sraddha - Respect
Triple Talaq - Divorce system in Muslim faith
Viksit Bharat - Developed India

INDEX

Other Books By This Author

1. A Panorama of Ghatal (2006)
2. West Bengal: Problems and Prospects (2008)
3. Poetry: The Mirror of Society (2009)
4. West Bengal Government: The Issues and Constraints of Development (2010)
5. Empowerment of Women and Panchayati Raj: Experiences from West Bengal (2010)
6. Gender and Empowerment: A Comparative Analysis of India and USA (2012)
7. Barack Obama: The Harbinger of Peace and Prosperity (2013)
8. Ghatal Pourasabha: Unnayan O Kichu Bhabna (in Bengali, 2014)
9. The Thoughts of an Uknown Indian (2014)
10. Mamata Banerjee: The Maker of New Bengal (2018)
11. Gender Empowerment in Local Governments: Prospects and Debates of Sustainable Development in India (2019)
12. Sustainable Development in India: A Comparison with the G-20 (2020)
13. Why BJP was Defeated and CPI(M) and Congress were Evanesced: A Study of 2021 West Bengal Assembly Elections (2021)
14. National Education Policy 2020: A Key to Development in India (2022)
15. Indian Philosophy and Ethics (2023)
16. How Can India Become a Superpower by 2047: A Vision (2024)